Local Government
Third edition

'The emphasis . . . is towards enabling the reader to appreciate those dynamic elements of local authorities which involve politicians, professionals and the public, and to understand how decisions are made and services are administered. . . . This is more lively than more general textbooks on local government: it is a book to be read, not just referred to.

British Book News

Since first publication in 1982, Howard Elcock's *Local Government* has established a reputation as a comprehensive, unbiased account of how British local government really works. This respected textbook has been completely revised and rewritten for its third edition, to take account of the changes in local government and the circumstances in which it operates. The author examines the new management structures and accountabilities under which UK local government works following the policy initiatives of the central Conservative administration. He appraises the impact of the three-pronged reform of the Thatcher years: on local authorities' financial resources, the structure of local government and the new pressure to contract services out to the private and voluntary sectors.

Howard Elcock is professor of Government at Northumbria University at Newcastle.

Local government

Third edition

Policy and management in local authorities

Howard Elcock

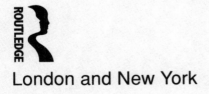

London and New York

First published 1994
by Routledge
11 New Fetter Lane, London EC4P 4EE

Simultaneously published in the USA and Canada
by Routledge
29 West 35th Street, New York, NY 10001

Typeset in Palatino by
Ponting–Green Publishing Services, Chesham, Bucks
Printed in Great Britain by
Clays Ltd, St Ives plc

Printed on acid-free paper

British Library Cataloguing in Publication Data
A catalogue record for this book is available from the
British Library.

*Library of Congress Cataloging-in-Publication Data has been
applied for.*

ISBN 0–415–10167–0

Contents

    local governments   290

11 Concluding speculations   308

    References   330
    Index   344

Figures and tables

FIGURES

TABLES

Preface

Now that it is into its third edition, this book has come to resemble my grandfather's axe, of which my father replaced the blade and I replaced the handle. The years since *Local Government* was first published in 1982 have been a period of tremendous instability for local government. On the one hand, it has been under sustained attack by the successive Conservative administrations which have held power since 1979. On the other hand, the 'new urban Left' brought a period of stimulating development of new policies, especially in economic development and equal opportunities, during the 1980s.

The increased variation and experimentation with local authority management processes and structures which developed after reorganisation in 1974–1975 in Scotland – has continued to develop apace, with the result that it is now even more difficult to generalise about local authorities' policy-making and management structures and processes than it was a decade ago. The internal decentralisation initiatives of the 1970s and 1980s; the imposition first of compulsory competitive tendering on a widening range of services and then of the community care scheme, have presented local authorities with a new range of management challenges, to which they have responded in varying ways. Financial pressure has forced local authorities to review their budgetary processes and has produced major conflicts between the Government and individual local authorities, notably Liverpool City Council and Lambeth Borough council.

The result of all this is that this book has been totally re-written for its third edition. Some of the old material is still there: there is continuity even in times of radical change. Members and officers have not changed their working practices completely, hence judgements and information contained in the first edition still have their relevance. Above all, the history of local government still needs rehearsing and still provides pointers to the future. However, there is now much greater stress on management in its various guises than there was in the earlier editions. Management is a very slippery concept and can only be adequately defined within the context in which it is exercised: there is no such thing as purely generic management, even within the world of local government, let alone the wider public sector. It could be argued that the word should be used only when prefaced by an adjective that identifies the field within which managers are working, as this must in part determine their approaches to their task. The very varied management arenas that local authorities and the services they provide are discussed here, with an attempt to identify the issues of policy and management with which councillors and officers must deal, both in the context of specific services and in that of the local authority *tout entier.*

In this process of revision and re-revision, I have incurred even more debts of gratitude than had to be acknowledged in the first two editions. My indebtedness to the members and officers of Humberside Council, on which I served in the 1980s, still remains, as does my debt to Judith Phillips who did much to inform my mind about social work, as well as to make the first edition easy to read. The debts previously acknowledged to Stephen Adamek, John Morris and others remain. Ken Harrop has again supplied a valuable section on Leisure Services. In preparing this edition, I must acknowledge further debts to Barbara Badger, Eileen Gill, Jill Dixon, Ruth Lingard, David Graham, the late Robert Baxter and Ken Harrop, among many others.

I thank my colleagues and students of local government at the University of Hull, Newcastle upon Tyne Polytechnic and the University of Northumbria at Newcastle, for the stimuli, ideas and information they have imparted to me over the years. I am particularly grateful to have been part of the lively team of academics working in the Local Authority Management Unit and Northern Network for Public Policy at Northumbria University. Lastly, I acknowledge a great debt to the members of the Public Administration Committee of the Joint University Council and the participants at the Committee's conferences, for the many insights they have offered me over the years. In this context, I must especially thank the participants in the Public Administration

Committee's study of local authority budgeting, in particular Grant Jordan and Arthur Midwinter, who oversaw the project with me.

For the blemishes that remain and for the idiosyncratic vision of local government and its services that is presented in these pages, I am alone responsible.

HOWARD ELCOCK
Hull and Newcastle upon Tyne

Abbreviations

ACC	Association of County Councils
ACPO	Association of Chief Police Officers
ADC	Association of District Councils
AMA	Association of Metropolitan Authorities
BASW	British Association of Social Workers
CCETSW	Central Council for Education and Training in Social Work
CCT	compulsory competitive tendering
CDP	community development project
CIPFA	Chartered Institute of Public Finance and Accountancy
COHSE	Confederation of Health Service Employees
COSLA	Conference of Scottish Local Authorities
DHA	district health authority
DSO	direct service organisation
DSS	Department of Social Security
GREA	grant related spending assessment
GLC	Greater London Council
HRM	human resource management
ICSA	Institute of Chartered Secretaries and Administrators
INLOGOV	Institute of Local Government Studies
IPM	Institute of Personnel Management
LACSAB	Local Authorities' Conditions of Service Advisory Board
LAMSAC	Local Authorities' Management Services Advisory Committee
LCC	London County Council
LEA	local education authority

LGMB	Local Government Management Board
LGTB	Local Government Training Board
NALGO	National Association of Local Government Officers
NUPE	National Union of Public Employees
OFSTED	Office for Standards in Education
PACE	Police and Criminal Evidence (Act)
RHA	regional health authority
RTPI	Royal Town and Country Planning Institute
SSA	standard spending assessment
SSD	social services department
TCPA	Town and Country Planning Association
UDC	urban development corporation
ZZB	zero-based budgeting

Part I

The world of local government

Chapter 1

Local government in the British political system

The place of local government in the British Constitution is both ambiguous and ambivalent. Britain is a small, densely populated island with a powerful central government. Little recognition is given to regional or national variations in culture, language or economic structure, yet systems of local government have existed since the Norman Conquest. They have long been regarded as bulwarks protecting us from centralised tyranny. The local control of the police, for example, has traditionally been valued as protecting us from the control of the state's entire machinery of coercion by a single minister. Again, local autonomy has ensured that educational structures and methods can be developed in a wide variety of different ways, in terms of the school curriculum, patterns of school organisation and teaching methods. Above all, local government provides a means whereby citizens can exercise control over their local affairs and express their will, through their votes as well as by lobbying their local authority, especially when they are disaffected from the policies of the central government (Stewart, 1983).

To develop these arguments in a little more detail, first, the varied political composition of local authorities reflects the differences in the party balance in the different nations and regions of Britain. Second, local authorities also provide the only fora in which public officials can be held accountable to elected representatives, apart from the House of Commons. Third, their varied policies and management practices permit experimentation, hence allowing local authorities and others to learn from their varied practices and experiences. The Audit Commission, established in 1982, encourages such learning processes by publishing reports which give examples of innovations or good management practice from individual authorities, both in general and in the context of particular services. Fourth, the Town or County Hall is closer to members of the public than Whitehall, hence service providers and officers can be more aware of local problems and desires and be more responsive to them. Last, the over-concentration of power at the centre is inhibited by the existence of local authorities with significant functions and responsibilities.

However, the power of the centre is formally absolute. Parliament is sovereign and hence has complete command over local government. It can grant or withhold powers from local authorities. It can create or abolish local authorities as it thinks fit. The doctrine of *ultra vires* reinforces that control because it states that a local authority can only do those things for which it is specifically granted power by legislation; local authorities are given no general competence as their French counterparts have. If local authorities exceed the powers vested in them by statute, thus acting *ultra vires*, the councillors who supported the illegal expenditure can be surcharged with its costs. If, as is almost inevitable, they cannot afford to pay the surcharge, they will be declared bankrupt and hence disqualified from holding public office as councillors. This power has resulted in several *causes celebres* in central–local conflict, including the surcharging of councillors in Clay Cross in the early 1970s for refusing to raise council house rents as required by the Housing Finance Act of 1972. It happened again to the majority Labour councillors in Liverpool and Lambeth when in 1985 they set their budgets late in an attempt to resist central government spending restraints. They were surcharged with the consequent lost revenue.

The relationship between central and local government is chronically tense because the central government constantly seeks to intervene in local affairs, for three main reasons. The first is to implement its main policy commitments, often by legislation. The second is to prevent local authorities from pursuing financial and expenditure policies that are contrary to those of the Chancellor of the Exchequer. Finally, the central government needs to ensure, especially as the population becomes increasingly mobile, that local services are provided to at least a minimum acceptable level throughout the country (see Widdicombe, 1986; Elcock, 1987). It is not always realised that local authority expenditures vary considerably: the highest-spending local authority will often spend between half and twice as much again as the lowest spender, so the central government needs to secure the provision of an acceptable level of service. This is frequently done through the deployment of central government inspectorates, such as Her Majesty's Inspectors of Constabulary and until recently the Inspectors of Schools and Colleges. An unsatisfactory inspector's report may result in financial penalties being imposed on a local authority.

In sum, as Beloff and Peele have put it:

> the prominence of the *ultra vires* doctrine has been combined with a fierce concern for local values and a belief that local self-government was an ideal at least as important as either economic administration or equality of provision.
>
> (Beloff and Peele, 1980, p. 246)

In consequence, local government has long been regarded by ministers, civil servants and MPs with a mixture of enthusiasm and suspicion. In the nineteenth century, John Stuart Mill and James Stephens argued for local government as an essential part of representative democracy but, in contrast, such social reformers as Edwin Chadwick saw local authorities as corrupt vestries whose dilatory and venal failures needed to be countered by central government intervention (Chandler, 1991; Kingdom, 1991). Today, local authorities are seen both as defenders of local opinions and values against the remote dictatorship of Whitehall and as incompetent, arrogant temples of bumbledom – extravagant, tyrannical and inefficient. In recent years local government has become highly controversial, from the House of Commons to the local saloon bar. We need to tease out some of these controversies to see what the major issues are and examine the major points of view that have emerged on each of them. In this initial survey, we shall consider central–local government relations, the efficacy or otherwise of structural reform, attempts to improve local authority management and changing the relationship between local authorities and their citizens.

CENTRAL–LOCAL RELATIONS

The proper role of local government in a unitary (as opposed to a federal) state has exercised both academics and practitioners in public administration for many years. Since 1979, it has been at the centre of some of the most bitter political confrontations of what we must still call the Thatcher era (Savage and Robins (eds),

1990). Tension between central and local government is endemic because, as we saw earlier, the values of local government conflict with the central government's need to ensure that its policies are carried out throughout the land. Above all, it is assumed that local government must entail significant local choice: that local electors should be able to perceive real differences between the various candidates and parties who offer themselves for election to the local council. Without such local choice, the democratic structures of elections and council meetings have no point (Stewart, 1983; Jones and Stewart, 1984). However, local choice is nowhere enshrined in a written constitution, whereas Parliament is sovereign: the Queen in Parliament can do anything. In consequence, central–local relations are nowhere defined and are hence a perennial subject of controversy. Hence, the balance between the centre and localities varies from time to time, either generally or in relation to particular policies or services.

Traditionally, the debate about central–local relations has been conducted between two poles. On the one hand, there are those who argue that local authorities are the agents of the central government, responsible for carrying out the instructions of ministers and Parliament. Thus highway authorities often act as agents for the Department of Transport in the construction and maintenance of motorways and other trunk roads. The Department determines that a new road is needed; the local highway authority (usually a county council) lets the contracts for the work and supervises the road's construction. Again, it is often said that education is a national service locally administered. Efficient schooling must be provided by the local education authority (LEA) for all children of between 5 and 16 years of age residing in its area. Only administrative details were left to LEAs to work out but these included the school curriculum and the organisational structure of the local schooling system, including methods of selection and the ages at which pupils transfer from primary to secondary schools. Hence, LEAs had real discretion over major aspects of school education. (see Jennings, 1977; Kogan and van der Eycken, 1973).

However, under the 1988 Education Reform Act, the Government has assumed increasing control over the school curriculum through the development of the national curriculum and the introduction of national attainment tests for pupils of various ages. Schools are also being encouraged to 'opt out' of LEA control altogether, in favour of central government funding, from 1993 through a schools funding council financed and appointed by the Secretary of State for Education. Thus LEAs are arguably both increasingly becoming agents of the central government and losing large parts of their functions as schools 'opt out' and as other institutions, such as further education colleges and previously the former polytechnics, have been removed from their control. LEAs are thus both increasingly being forced into the agent role and seeing their role diminished. In J.A.G Griffith's (1966) terms, the Department of Education's role is increasingly a promotional one, in which it seeks to secure the implementation of government policies and leaves the local authorities relatively little room for manoeuvre. The same can be said of highways policy, at least where trunk roads and motorways are concerned (Griffith, 1966, pp. 521–522).

The second suggested role for local authorities is that of partnership with the central government in providing services for the public. J.A. Chandler (1991) offers a modification of this analysis. He argues that local authorities act as stewards of the central government, who are left to discharge their responsibilities, with the central government intervening only if the steward's conduct is found to have been unsatisfactory. The broad outlines of policy are determined nationally; local authorities play a substantial part in interpreting those policies and mobilising the resources needed to bring them to fruition. Here, central government departments should restrict themselves to Griffith's regulatory or *laissez-faire* relationships with local authorities. In the first, central governments ensure that adequate standards of services are maintained, often through the deployment of departmental inspectorates. They also enforce national policies on local authorities from time to time. However, local authorities for their part have formed representative associations to present the case for local authorities to the central government and argue against the imposition of unwelcome central policies upon them. In England there are three main local authority associations: the Association of Metropolitan Authorities (AMA), the Association of County Councils (ACC) and the Association of District Councils (ADC.) In Scotland there is only one representative organisation: the Confederation of Scottish Local Authorities (COSLA), although tensions between the regional and district councils develop within it. Moves are afoot to unite the English local government associations into a single body. The example of Scotland is cited as an argument that if local authorities can speak to the central government with a single voice, this will strengthen their negotiating position. These associations negotiate with the major Government departments responsible for local government in a 'centre–centre' dialogue conducted largely in London between departmental civil servants and the local authority associations (Isaac-Henry, 1980; Rhodes, 1987).

Sometimes such interference has led to major confrontations between central and local government. For example, when Labour Governments in the 1960s and 1970s tried to compel all LEAs to abolish selection for secondary education (Jennings, 1977) and when the Heath Conservative Government tried to compel all local housing authorities to increase their council house rents to market levels in the early 1970s, local government services moved to the centre of national as well as local political controversy.

Both these policies resulted in major conflicts with individual local authorities. The Labour councillors of Clay Cross Urban District Council in Derbyshire were surcharged and disqualified from office for refusing to increase their council house rents in 1972. Here, the central government in the end enforced its policy successfully. However, in 1976, Tameside Metropolitan District Council successfully defended itself in court from an instruction by the Labour Secretary of State for Education and Science, Fred Mulley, not to retain selection for its grammar schools (Griffith, 1977).

In the *laissez-faire* case, the central department interferes as little as possible with local authorities in the belief that they are best left to learn from their own mistakes. In 1966 Griffith instanced the Ministry of Health's relationship with local authority health services as an example, but the *laissez-faire* approach is probably almost extinct now, especially in the light of the way central–local relations have developed since 1979. Since that year, the place of local government in the British Constitution has been challenged more fundamentally than at any time since the mid-nineteenth century. In consequence, the debate about whether local government is needed at all has resurfaced in a way reminiscent of the debates of that earlier period. (Chandler, 1988; Elcock, 1987; Jones and Stewart, 1984; Kingdom, 1991).

The Thatcher assault

This challenge to local government's usefulness and sometimes its very existence has been mounted on three fronts, the development of each of which can be very roughly correlated with the beginning of Margaret Thatcher's three successive terms of office. The details will be discussed later; here we will briefly summarise them and note their significance for the constitutional place of local government.

The first front was to compel local authorities to conform to the Government's stated intention from the beginning of its term of office, to reduce the proportion of the gross national product (GNP) which is absorbed by public spending. In addition, Mrs Thatcher and her colleagues took the view that people who lived in local authorities whose heavy, in their view excessive, spending caused them to levy high rates, needed to be protected from the activities of extravagent, 'overspending' councillors. This imposed an undue burden on householders who were responsible for paying rates, as well as on businesses which had to pay high commercial rates on their premises. These ratepayers, so the argument went, were being unfairly treated and should be protected from high-spending councils.

In consequence, whereas previous Administrations had relied on their ability to control the national totals of local authority spending – with a high degree of success because the outcome of each spending round almost invariably fell within 2 per cent of the Government's expectations (Jones and Stewart, 1984), the Thatcher Administrations sought to control the spending decisions of individual councils. This new approach to controlling individual councils' spending was begun with the 1980 Local Government, Planning and Land Act, which introduced a new system for the distribution of the Rate Support Grant. Instead of allocating grant on the basis of an authority's past spending by regression analysis, it was henceforth allocated on the basis of a calculation of what each council needed to spend in order to provide a standard level of services. Financial penalties are imposed on local authorities which exceed this level of spending by more than a given amount, which is itself determined by the Secretary of State for the Environment.

This assessment, known initially as the grant related spending assessment (GREA) and now the standard spending assessment

(SSA) has also been used as the main basis for further measures of control. Thus, in 1982 in Scotland and in 1984 in England and Wales, the Government took to itself the power to limit or 'cap' the expenditure of individual local authorities. This was seen as the removal of a discretion to set their own rate levels which local authorities had enjoyed for centuries and was widely attacked as an unwarranted restriction of local authorities' autonomy, but to no avail. The Secretary of State for the Environment is also empowered to restrict the spending of all local authorities but only after a further resolution has been passed by Parliament. This 'capping' power has been retained through the introduction of the Community Charge and its replacement by the Council Tax.

The second front was opened after the Conservative General Election victory in 1983. The Conservative Party included in its manifesto for that election a commitment to abolish the Greater London Council (GLC) and the six metropolitan county councils. This commitment, which was by all accounts adopted only at the last minute, was implemented against a flood of opposition mobilised by the seven threatened local authorities and almost everyone else concerned with local government. The Government's White Paper, *Streamlining the Cities*, (DoE, 1983) was published within a few months of the election. It argued that the councils whose abolition was proposed had few substantive functions (they were responsible for some 20 per cent of local government spending in their areas) and that they were creatures of 'a fashion for strategic planning, whose time has passed' (DoE, 1983). No-one was in any doubt that the real reason for their abolition was that the GLC in particular had become a major focus of opposition to Government policy, which was symbolised by the daily appearance of a banner on the riverside facade of County Hall (which faces the Palace of Westminster across the Thames) which announced London's increasing total of unemployed workers (Forrester, Lansley and Pauley, 1985). The seven councils ceased to exist on 1 April 1986 and were replaced by a messy structure of joint boards composed of members of the district councils in each metropolitan county area (Leach and Game, 1991).

Since then, further structural change has occurred in the form of the establishment of urban development corporations (UDCs) with missions to bring about the redevelopment of decaying inner-city areas. They took over many planning functions and powers

from local authorities. They were empowered to undertake redevelopment with a view to attracting private investment into their
areas. The first two of these bodies, for the London Docklands and
part of central Liverpool, were established in 1981. Further UDCs
have since been established in other areas, including Tyne and
Wear, Manchester and Sheffield (Butcher *et al.*, 1990). Some,
notably the London Docklands Development Corporation, have
come into frequent conflict with the local authorities in their areas
because the Corporation's vision of the future of the area conflicted with those of the local authorities there (Batley, 1989). Other
UDCs, such as Tyne and Wear, have by contrast been anxious to
develop co-operation and collaboration with their local authorities. Nonetheless, all the UDCs have been given functions
which were formerly enjoyed by local authorities and have power
to override local authority decisions, especially in town planning
(Thornley, 1990).

Further structural change is now in the wind. In 1992 the
Government established a Commission for Local Government to
review the local government structure in each county. There is a
presumption that its recommendations will lead to the replacement of the existing two-tier structures with unitary local authorities based either on the existing county or district councils. It is
widely anticipated that some unloved county councils, such as
Avon, Humberside and Teesside, all of which were created as
part of the 1972 local government reorganisation and have never
achieved popular legitimacy, will disappear, but other more
venerable counties may survive. The expectation is that the
structure of local government will again be changed, for the
third time in around twenty years, by Parliamentary (and hence
Government) *fiat*.

Third has come an onslaught on the ways in which local
authorities provide their services. This began in 1980 but gathered
pace rapidly after Mrs Thatcher's third victory in the 1987 General
Election. Before 1979, it was accepted more or less without
challenge that local authorities provide the services for which they
are responsible by their own directly employed staff. The 1980
Local Government, Planning and Land Act empowered local
authorities who so wished to submit services to competitive
tender, so that if a private firm submitted a tender lower than that
submitted by the appropriate council department, the private firm
would then provide the service. Only a few local authorities

initially availed themselves of this opportunity. Southend Borough Council let its refuse collection service out to a private contractor and Wandsworth London Borough Council contracted out a wide range of services but other examples were few and far between.

An indication of the shape of things to come came in 1982, when regional and district health authorities were required to put their manual and catering services out to private tender. In 1988 this compulsion was extended to local authorities, in the form of legislation which introduced a timetable for submitting an increasing range of their services to compulsory competitive tendering (CCT). The initial group of services to which CCT applied were mainly manual and catering services, including refuse collection, civic catering and building maintenance, but it is being applied progressively to such 'white collar' functions as architecture, legal services and accounting (Flynn, 1990; Ollive, 1990; Pyper, 1990; Painter, 1991; Fenwick, Shaw and Foreman, 1993). Despite periodic complaints about substandard performance by private contractors in both local government and the NHS, there will be a continuing drive to remove services from direct provision by local authorities and transfer them to provision by private contractors under local authority supervision – a change described by the Government as the development of the 'enabling' local authority.

This trend will be accelerated by the development of the community care provisions of the 1990 NHS and Community Care Act, because it is based on a presumption that as many as possible of the community care services to be provided by local authorities should be supplied by the private or voluntary sectors, acting under contract to the local authority. The latter is expected to dispose of such assets as residential homes and day-care centres to private companies or voluntary associations, then take out contracts with them for the delivery of services. The Government expects that local authorities will provide 85 per cent of their community services through contracts with private companies and voluntary organisations. The local authority is also to be responsible for inspecting private or voluntary homes in order to ensure that adequate standards of care are being provided.

This new 'enabling' role is intended to reduce to a minimum the direct provision of local authorities' services by their own departments and employees. Some of its advocates suggest that the ideal council would meet only once a year to let contracts, then leaving all other activities to the private and voluntary service providers. However, in practice the need to ensure that contractors fulfil the terms of their contracts, as well as the audit, inspection and regulatory functions relating to service providers that local authorities will still need to exercise, indicate that there will still be plenty of work for administrators, accountants and lawyers as well as a good deal of policy-making and grievance-chasing for councillors to do. Furthermore, the experience of CCT up to the early 1990s showed that relatively few contracts were in the event awarded by private sector bidders. On the one hand, there were many fields where private sector interest in contracts was limited, in particular because many local authority operations are so large that only a few large companies had the resources to make credible bids. One example of this has been the local authority catering services, where very few private companies have felt able to tender for very large operations which are beyond their scope to deliver. On the other hand, local authority departments and workforces were able to improve their efficiency to the point at which they were able to win contracts against the private sector. By August 1989 local authority direct service organisations (DSOs) or other 'in-house' tenderers had won almost three-quarters of the contracts offered by local authorities (Painter, 1991, p. 198). In 1993 a study of CCT in the North of England found that between August 1989 and April 1992, private contractors had won only fifteen (13 per cent) of the 115 contracts that the local authorities who took part in the study had put out to tender (Fenwick, Shaw and Foreman 1993, p. 21). Despite the repeated attempts by ministers to tighten the rules so as to improve private firms' chance of winning contracts (Painter, 1991; Fenwick, Shaw and Foreman 1993), the chief impact of CCT was in practice on internal local authority and particularly DSO management, rather than in terms of services being transferred from local authority control to the private sector. The impact of 'enabling' on local authority employment and the conduct of local authorities' business is likely therefore to be much less radical than its more fervent advocates have predicted.

The balance between central and local government

The changes of the last fourteen years have greatly increased the number and vigour of warnings that the central government is in danger of extinguishing local choice altogether and hence reducing local authorities to ciphers, responsible only for administering functions and services whose control is vested entirely in Whitehall. Such warnings are not new, however. In 1961, J.A.G Griffith warned the Association of Municipal Corporations that 'in the last resort a real choice has to be made between reforms which will give real responsibility to local authorities to determine major issues of policy and leaving local government to die slowly of anaemia' (Griffith, 1961, p. 818). In 1976 the Layfield Committee on Local Government Finance urged that Britain had to make a choice between a centralised system of government and one where local authorities have real freedom of choice. If local authorities' autonomy was to be protected, the proportion of their income which comes from central government grants needed to be reduced to not more than 40 per cent, from around 60 per cent (Layfield, 1976). In 1983, John Stewart published an eloquent defence of local choice.

However, there are real reasons for arguing that local authorities will continue to retain freedom of manoeuvre as long as they are allowed to exist. Jeffrey Stanyer (1976) reminded us that local authorities lie at the centre of local political systems which develop their own distinctive policies and approaches to local issues. Royston Greenwood and his colleagues (1978) applied contingency theory to local authorities to demonstrate that their policies, management structures and working methods vary in relation to their size, mixture of urban and rural areas, political complexion and a number of other factors. Most significantly of all, in an analysis originally prepared for the Social Science Research Council, R.A.W Rhodes (1981; 1987) has provided us with an analytical framework which enables us to understand much more fully the robustness of local authorities' autonomy.

The core of Rhodes's highly sophisticated analysis argues that both local authorities and the central government possess resources which enable them to defend their action space against encroachment by the other party and extend it where opportunities offer. The resources available to local authorities and the central government alike are of four kinds:

1 *Political resources*: Members of Parliament and councillors alike can claim the legitimacy conferred by popular election. Ministers and MPs can criticise the alleged inefficiencies and injustices

of local authorities but councillors equally can campaign against central decisions, organise lobbies of Parliament and influence the Government through the political parties, especially where councillors are themselves members of the party holding office nationally. They also exert pressure on the Government through the local authority associations.

2 *Financial resources:* although around 60 per cent of local authorities' income now comes from the central government and local authorities control only about one quarter of it, councillors can still vote for expenditures of which the Government disapproves. They can increase local taxation or revenue charges. They can also exercise powers of virement, transferring funds between budget heads in order to provide services or carry out projects which could not be included in the initial budget. Equally, the central government can reduce grants or impose spending restrictions in order to procure compliance with its wishes. It will be the more likely to do so if (as is usually the case) Government unpopularity causes an increasing number of local authorities to fall under the control of the party which is in opposition at Westminster.

3 *Information resources:* again, these are possessed by both central and local government and can be withheld as a sanction by either side against the other. Thus, the GLC and metropolitan county councils attempted to withhold information from the Government which it needed to bring about the continuance of their functions after their impending abolition. More generally, the local authority associations command a great deal of information about the provision of local services, which enables them to argue against central policies with considerable conviction because their members know much about local services and circumstances of which the central government is usually ignorant (Isaac-Henry, 1980; Rhodes, 1987).

4 *Legal-constitutional resources:* although all local authority powers stem ultimately from legislation, a grant of powers once made by Parliament can become a weapon to be deployed against the centre, since the local authority has been granted those powers to use and administer as it thinks fit. Local authorities' attempts to preserve their freedom of action when ministers have attempted to restrict it have provided many judicial *causes célèbres* from which ministers have by no means always emerged victorious (Griffith, 1977; Loughlin, Gelfand and Young 1985).

However, the centre alone possesses a fifth set of resources, *hierarchical resources*, which stem ultimately from the sovereignty of Parliament. The central government alone has the power to legislate to change, create or abolish local authorities, grant them powers or withdraw them and provide new sources of finance or take away existing ones. Some writers have argued that the existence of these hierarchical resources invalidates Rhodes's analysis because potentially the central government can always make its will prevail but often, the political and other costs involved in doing so are unacceptable. In any case, the courts will often defend local autonomy and the availability of Parliamentary time to legislate against local government is limited.

Hence, in practice, Rhodes's analysis remains valid. He regards central–local relations as a process of exchange in which the balance of power will be determined by the extent of the resources available to the participants in the relationship. It will also be affected by the parties' skill or otherwise in deploying their resources and countering the other side's use of them, as well as their understanding of and skill in using the rules of the game. His framework:

> suggests that variations in the discretion of the interactive organisations are a function of their resources, goals and relative power potential. Their relative power potential is a product of their resources, the rules of the game and the process of exchange. Finally, the process of exchange is influenced by the resources of the participants, strategies, personalities and the number of units. (Rhodes, 1981, p. 34)

The value of Rhodes's analysis is that it demonstrates that the central government and local authorities both enjoy a considerable amount of independent power and face each other on a more equal footing than other writers have assumed. His argument also implies that the frequent warnings we are given of the imminent destruction of meaningful local democracy at the hands of an overweening central government have been premature.

The extent of local autonomy can be illustrated by an examination of the surprisingly large extent by which the amount local authorities spend on the provision of services varies from one authority to another, even after many years of Government-imposed financial constraint. Table 1.1 illustrates this in the case of the 'shire' county councils.

The table shows that the expenditure per head of the lowest-

Table 1.1 Expenditure of non-metropolitan county councils on selected services, 1991–1992, (£ per head of their population)

Service	Lowest	Mean	Highest
Education: schools	Devon 210.30	252.60	Cleveland 318.04
Social services	Surrey 54.55	70.21	Cleveland 92.28
Libraries	Durham 7.17	8.95	Cleveland 11.15
Police	Hertfordshire 62.75	72.40	Cleveland 98.40
Fire service	Wiltshire 13.74	16.73	Cleveland 26.29

Source: Chartered Institute of Public Finance and Accountancy: *Finance and General Statistics 1991–1992.*

spending council is often 50 per cent or more below that of the highest spender. The consistent appearance of Labour-controlled Cleveland County Council as the highest spender indicates in part the making of political choices to spend more on higher levels of service provision than the Conservative or Independent-controlled county councils which dominate the lowest spenders. However, this is not the complete story. For instance, Cleveland's high expenditure on the fire service results in part at least from the presence of several very large and dangerous oil, steel and chemical plants in its area. Cleveland's inhabitants are in much greater potential danger from fires, explosions and noxious leaks than Wiltshire's. Equally, County Durham's low level of spending on libraries demonstrates that Labour-controlled councils are not always high spenders on their services.

However, local autonomy has been seriously reduced during the 1980s (Savage and Robins (eds), 1990; Lansley, Goss and Wolman, 1989). Furthermore, both the strength of the centre's hierarchical resources and the ability of local authorities to resist their deployment have been demonstrated through the successive processes of the structural reorganisation of local government which have taken place since 1945.

THE OBJECTIVES OF STRUCTURAL REFORM

Controversies about central–local relations concern the conflict between two sets of values. On the one hand, the central government exerts control to enforce its policies and economic management as well as securing the equitable provision of services across the country. On the other hand, local democracy is the expression of local choices about whether or not to provide local services, as well as at what level and by what methods they should be provided.

At least since the early 1960s, repeated structural reforms have also highlighted conflicting values and political interests. The most fundamental debate about the structure of local government has been summarised by Ken Newton:

> On the one hand, large units of government are necessary in urban-industrial society in order to achieve efficiency, economies of scale, functional effectiveness and an adequate capacity to plan and organise; on the other hand small units of government are necessary to preserve the attributes of grass-roots democracy, including a sense of community and political efficacy on the part of ordinary citizens, an ability to participate directly and individually in community affairs, a reduction of the social and political distance between leaders and citizens and a limitation of the growth of large and inflexible government bureaucracies (Newton, 1978, p. 1).

These differing values were crucial to the dilemma which the Royal Commission on Local Government of 1966–1969 faced between unitary and two-tier local government structures. The majority on the Commission came down in favour of a single-tier or unitary structure except in the largest conurbations, while one member, Dr Derek Senior, proposed a two-tier system.

This conflict was again reflected in the controversies about the reorganised local government structure which was established by the Local Government Act of 1972. The local authorities established then are very large, especially when compared with their equivalents in other European democracies. Also, in some cases the new boundaries did violence to existing local loyalties. They have been repeatedly attacked as inefficient and top-heavy bureaucracies which are insensitive to local opinions and feelings. In consequence, there have been repeated pressures for further reorganisation.

In the late 1970s the larger district councils in the 'shire' counties lobbied vigorously for the return of the control over education, social services and public libraries which as county boroughs they had previously enjoyed. The then Secretary of State for the Environment, Peter Shore, was on the point of conceding an 'organic change' in local government which would permit this to happen when Labour lost office in 1979 (DoE, 1979). In the 1980s, as we have seen, seven large local authorities were abolished because their actions had brought them into severe conflict with central government policies. In the 1990s the Commission for Local Government has been established which presages further major reorganisation to establish unitary local authorities throughout the country.

Reorganisation is addictive (Elcock, 1991). We shall see in the next chapter that local government reorganisation was regarded as necessary from the end of the Second World War but it took until 1972 to bring it about, because of the extent of resistance to it, by the existing local authorities and many others. However, that reorganisation inevitably left a number of dissatisfied interests whose grievances could only be remedied by further reorganisation. Furthermore, changing political values changed the nature of central–local government relations. Turbulent local authorities were disposed of by abolition. The addictive nature of reorganisation can be seen also in the National Health Service, which underwent a fundamental restructuring in 1973, was radically restructured again in 1982 and is now being threatened with yet further restructuring, in the form of the abolition of the fourteen regional health authorities in 1996.

Furthermore, the judgement as to whether small or large units are more desirable is incapable of satisfactory resolution. E.F. Schumacher argued in the context of large industrial corporations that we should:

> Strive to find structures which need *minimum* administration. Very small structures administer themselves; there is no problem. It's not a matter of abstractly framing rules because the human mind encompasses the whole thing and can make decisions *ad hoc* and consultation of course is very easy.
>
> (Schumacher, 1979, p. 69)

He proposed that large organisations should be divided into units which can fall within the span of control of a single individual, instead of having to be operated by lengthy hierarchies (Schumacher, 1973). This argument finds a sympathetic echo in many debates about local government structure. It also underlies some changes which local authorities themselves have made in their internal structures, as we shall see in the next section.

However, Newton argues that large local authorities cannot be shown to be less efficient or to give rise to more citizen alienation than small ones. They may also be able to provide more and better services, as well as greater scope for public consultation, than small ones (Newton, 1978). The 'small is beautiful' thesis is, in short, not proven in the context of local government. Nonetheless, the post-1972 local government system, together with the Regional and Area health authorities and the regional water authorities which were established at the same time, were repeatedly attacked as being remote and unresponsive, providing secure havens for vast armies of unproductive bureaucrats.

The arguments that have been advanced in favour of large units of local government are three in number. The first, which was advanced by the reorganisers of the 1970s, was that larger units would attract more capable people to stand for election as local councillors. John Dearlove (1979) argued that this was intended to be a means of returning local government to the control of business and property interests; he believed that this had in fact happened since the 1972 reorganisation. However, subsequent research carried out for the Robinson (1977) and Widdicombe (1986) Committees cast doubt on this contention because although they indicate that some more younger and more highly educated councillors have been elected in recent years, the majority of councillors are still recruited from among the same type of people as when the Maud Committee (1967) carried out its study of councillors in 1966. The effect of reorganisation was marginal in terms of altering the calibre of councillors.

A second argument is that larger local authorities can be more economically administered because larger numbers of service personnel can be managed by a proportionately smaller number of administrative staff. This argument has been widely challenged in both local government and the NHS, with frequent allegations being made, predominantly but not exclusively by Conservative politicians, that these reorganisations produced a considerable increase in both the numbers and the salaries of the administrators employed in local government and the NHS. Newton (1978) shows that the evidence, such as it is, is inconclusive but he made an interesting point in a comparison between British local government, with relatively few large units, and the American system, which has an enormous number of small units. After the number of British local authorities was reduced by the 1972 reorganisation, the Department of the Environment, which is the central government department with the chief responsibility for overseeing local government, was able to reduce its staff by 4,000. By contrast, the two federal agencies mainly responsible for overseeing United States local government increased their staff by between 10 and 23 per cent in the same period. What is lost in terms of increased staff numbers at the local level when local government units are reduced in numbers and increased in size, may be at least partially compensated for by a reduction in the number of central government staff needed to administer local government's affairs.

The final argument in favour of larger units is simpler and less contentious: that a large unit can provide a wider range of services and a greater variety of specialist officers than a small one. Larger authorities can allow more specialisation of roles in services like education and social work. A related benefit will be greater equality of service provision, since large authorities will ensure that the variations in service standards which were established by smaller predecessor authorities will be eliminated, at least gradually. On the other hand, large units are less accessible to their citizens but internal measures may be adopted to counteract their remoteness. This forms part of the subject matter of the next section.

THE MANAGERIAL PERFORMANCE OF LOCAL AUTHORITIES

This section considers the controversies generated by the need to improve the quality of local authority management, as well as providing some indication of the increasing variety of methods being adopted to secure such an improvement.

In the 1950s and 1960s the main concern of local authority managers and their advisers, was with improving the co-ordination and central control over the departments and committees which are responsible for the execution of a local authority's policies and functions. During the 1960s these issues were considered by two official committees. The first, under the chairmanship of Sir George Mallaby (1967), was concerned with the staffing of local government. It recommended enhancing the status of personnel management within local authorities, including the appointment of a central, specialist personnel officer. It also urged the recruitment of more graduates to the local government service and more training for local authority staff. The second committee, the Maud Committee on the Management of Local Government, was more concerned with internal structural changes in local authorities. Its principal recommendations included the creation of a small management board of between five and nine members to co-ordinate the local authority's policies and service provision. It also recommended more centralised control at officer level. At the same time, many individual councils called in management consultants to review their internal management and structures (Greenwood and Stewart (eds), 1974). Individual academics, notably Professor J.D. Stewart of the University of Birmingham (1971), advocated greater co-ordination and control through new management structures and attitudes.

This movement became known generically as corporate management. Greenwood and Stewart (1974, pp. 1–3) described it as a move from traditional to federal structures within local authorities. The traditional approach was that each department and committee operated largely independently of the others and there was little co-ordination of their activities. This produced conflicts between departments in service provision (Donnison, 1962) and the duplication of resources such as vehicle repair and maintenance facilities. Such co-ordination as did occur was largely carried in party groups and their executive committees. This gave way in many authorities, to a greater or lesser extent, to the federal approach in which local authorities established central organs to make major policy decisions, co-ordinate service provision and provide common services such as purchasing and supplies, vehicle maintenance, reprographics and personnel management. This move towards more co-ordination was the central purpose behind the development of corporate management in local government, including the establishment of policy and resources committees to control the council's policies and resource allocation, the reduction in the number of committees formed in each local authority and the appointment of a chief executive officer who would run a management team of chief officers.

The second development which began at around this time was the development by local authorities of what Greenwood and Stewart (1974) called the 'governmental' approach to their role, which involved concerning themselves with the general welfare of the inhabitants of their areas, instead of confining themselves to providing the services and discharging the functions for which they have been given specific responsibility by statute. The idea that local authorities should accept a wider role in managing their community's affairs was developed by, among others, the Institute of Operational Research, members of which have argued that local authority decision-making should be a continuous process of exchange between the local authority and its economic and social environment. Also, it should co-ordinate the activities of other public, private and voluntary organisations which have interests in its area. Hence, the local authority as a whole or particular departments within it should play a 'reticulist' role, providing channels of communication among other organisations as well as with themselves, trying to stimulate new initiatives and in turn being stimulated by them (Friend and Jessop, 1969; Friend, Power and Yewlett, 1977). Such a wider approach was also advocated by the Redcliffe-Maud Royal Commission on Local Government (1969), which argued that local authorities have 'an all-round responsibility for the safety, health and well-being, both material and cultural, of people in different localities' (quoted in Greenwood and Stewart, 1974, p. 2). However, this approach involves increasing intervention by local authorities in the economic and social affairs of the community and it is therefore regarded with suspicion by many Conservative politicians.

Controversies concerning the 'governmental' local authority became acute in the early 1980s. After the 1979 General Election defeat, the Labour Party moved to develop local strategies so that socialism could to some extent be implemented locally during the party's exclusion from national office. This process became much more evident as Labour gained control of many more local authorities in the early 1980s, which in turn brought many new councillors to council service and office within their authorities (Lansley, Goss and Wolmar, 1989). This development has been described by John Gyford as the rise of the 'new urban Left' (Gyford, 1984).

These new politicians sought in particular to develop two forms of intervention. The first was to develop local authorities' increasing activities in the field of economic development by the introduction of local economic strategies which were intended to bring about the development of new industries and the establishment of new plants, especially in those local authority areas which were suffering from declining employment and industrial activity (Lansley, Goss and Wolmar, 1989; Moore and Richardson,

1989; King and Pierre, 1990). Some of the more ambitious of these local strategies were also conceived to be attempts to test out the Labour Party's 'alternative economic strategy' at the local level preparatory to its eventual national implementation. One manifestation of this new local economic interventionism was the establishment by a number of local authorities of enterprise boards charged with encouraging industrial development in their areas by investing local authority funds in local businesses (Cochrane and Clarke, 1990).

The second major form of intervention which developed during this period was an attempt to increase the opportunities available to minority groups and reduce discrimination against them. Apart from adopting equal opportunities policies for their own staffs' recruitment, employment and career development, many local authorities made grants to organisations which were concerned with assisting minorities and disadvantaged groups. These activities attracted unfavourable comment from the tabloid press and occasionally resulted in controversies, for example where employees were penalised or dismissed for making allegedly racialist or sexist remarks.

The intensified controversy over local authorities' economic development and equal opportunities policies resulted in a debate about what a local authority can properly spend its money on. The tradition was that local authorities only undertook those functions for which they were given specific legal authority. However, Section 172 of the 1972 Local Government Act permitted local authorities to spend up to the product of a 2-pence rate for their areas on anything which was, in the council's judgement, in the interests of all or some of the authority's inhabitants. This section was used to justify many of the economic development and equal opportunities activities of which many Conservatives complained. In consequence, this was one of the major issues which the Widdicombe Committee (1986) on *The Conduct of Local Authority Business* was asked to consider when it was established in 1985. However, in its final report, the Committee recommended that local authorities should be specifically empowered to undertake activities concerned with promoting economic development and that the Section 172 discretionary powers should be extended (Widdicombe, 1986). The first proposal has been implemented but not the second. The concept of the 'governmental' local authority is still controversial, both within local government and more generally. Its adoption provides a further pressure for the strengthening of the central control of the local authority's policies and service provision because they must be co-ordinated to meet the community's wider needs. Also, the 'governmental' local authority needs to have visible political and administrative heads who can be seen to be co-ordinating the activities of the council and other organisations. Hence, the roles of the leader of the council and the chief executive officer are likely to become more dominant in 'governmental' local authorities.

LOCAL AUTHORITIES AND THE PUBLIC

Local government has never had a very good public image. Its legitimacy has always been weak and this is reflected in relatively low turn-outs at local elections, although they have increased somewhat in recent years. Also, the results of local elections are usually determined largely by the national political struggle rather than by local personalities or issues (Newton, 1976). The creation of larger local government units in 1972, together with the establishment of some local authorities whose boundaries violate traditional local loyalties, has caused local government to seem more remote from the public. In town and country planning especially, local authorities have long had to face the problem of securing public participation in their decisions, both where this is required by statute and where local authorities are anxious to obtain expressions of public opinion, but they have often been faced with public apathy which has denied the local authority any meaningful results from its public participation exercises.

For example, in 1969 the Skeffington Committee produced a report entitled *People and Planning*, which recommended the incorporation of public participation into the town and country planning system, which has long been criticised for remoteness from the public and insensitivity to citizens' wishes (see, for example, Gower Davies, 1972). Its recommendations were enacted in the Town and Country Planning Act of 1971.

The nature of public participation depends on the kind of decision involved. At the strategic planning level, county councils are required to stage a series of public participation exercises during the preparation of their structure plans. Furthermore, at the level of individual planning applications various statutory requirements have been imposed to advertise applications, as well as giving those individuals and organisations who are affected by them an opportunity to comment on them. However, increased participation has not prevented protest demonstrations or even disorder breaking out at committee meetings, public enquiries and other planning procedures, generated by local residents who are opposed to a proposed development. The Department of Transport faced a series of particularly aggressive campaigns against a number of major road proposals in the 1970s and was forced to modify its public inquiry procedures to permit wider debate about whether a proposed new road was needed or not, as well as about the details of the proposed route (Levin, 1979). However, such participation procedures tend to be used by the middle rather than the working class. Kenneth Newton found in his study of local politics in Birmingham, for example, that:

> joiners (of groups) tend to be concentrated very heavily in the middle and upper class strata. Not only this but middle and upper class people are even more heavily over-represented among the ranks of office-holders in voluntary organisations.
>
> (Newton, 1976)

In E.E. Schattschneider's (1960) classic statement, 'the interest group heavenly chorus sings with a markedly upper class accent'. Working-class participation occurs chiefly through the Labour Party, the trade union movement and a narrow range of other groups, notably tenants' associations (Newton, 1976).

A more radical change which increases citizen participation in local decision-making and service provision, is to develop decentralised structures within local authorities which permit greater contact between local authority staff, the people they are serving and community leaders. Individual local authorities have experimented with such structures for some considerable time and these experiments have sometimes been encouraged by the central government but the results have not always been productive. Cynthia Cockburn (1979) has described how an experiment by Lambeth London Borough Council with neighbourhood councils was launched with a great deal of enthusiasm on all sides and the new councils were given direct rights of access to the borough council's leading decision-makers. When some of the neighbourhood councils began to attack established borough council policies, however, the latter responded by cutting off their direct access to leading decision-makers. It also imposed reforms which were intended to reduce the neighbourhood councils' radicalism and reduce their competition for attention with ward councillors, officers and the other longer-established channels of communication between council and citizens.

Similarly, the Home Office experiment with community development projects (CDPs) between 1969 and 1976 produced conflict because many of the CDPs argued that urban deprivation could not be remedied without a shift of economic power away from national and multi-national corporations. Remedies for such social pathologies as social deprivation and poor housing would not by themselves significantly improve the lot of residents in deprived inner-city areas (Community Development Project, 1974). In consequence of such unwelcome arguments, the Home Office ran down the CDP initiative after the mid-1970s. Nonetheless, in the late 1970s the Department of the Environment launched a new series of area management initiatives in a number of towns and cities. Again, service provision was decentralised and subjected to the influence of area committees (Harrop et al., 1978).

These fairly small-scale initiatives were developed in the 1980s into a bewildering mass of internal local authority decentralisation schemes, all of which were intended to decentralise control over service provision and render local authority services more attractive and accessible to the public (Hoggett and Hambleton, 1987; Hambleton, 1992). There is no space for a detailed account of these initiatives; it must suffice to say that they may be divided broadly into three types (Elcock, 1988):

Departmental decentralisation: where the services provided by a single department, usually social services or housing, are devolved to teams of staff covering relatively small parts of the council's area. Social workers have developed 'patch' working in many authorities, for example (Payne, 1979; Elcock, 1986).

Corporate decentralisation:, where neighbourhood offices containing staff from several departments are established. This might be seen as the development of corporate management from below, as opposed to corporate management at the top through policy and resource committees and chief executive officers. The relatively junior staff who are directly responsible for the provision of services to the public learn to collaborate with one another in neighbourhood offices, instead of communication and co-ordination occurring at the top of the authority through a policy and resources committee and a chief executive officer (Hambleton, 1979).

Political decentralisation: where neighbourhood offices report to committees consisting of ward councillors and other community leaders. The danger here is of conflict developing with the central organisation of the local authority. Newcastle upon Tyne's Priority Area Teams report repeatedly that their views and needs are not sympathetically treated at the Civic Centre (Elcock, 1983). However, Islington London Borough Council has launched a major initiative to secure through its neighbourhood committees increased participation from disadvantaged sections of the population, including women, racial minorities, the disabled and gay people. To this end, for example, standard procedures at meetings may have to be radically modified (Islington, 1986).

These decentralisation schemes are part of a wider move to improve relations between local authorities and their citizens. During the 1980s much encouragement has been given to local authorities to 'get closer to the customer'. The means they have adopted to do so range from new and more attractive offices to carrying out surveys of citizens' perceptions and use of local authority services (Gyford, 1991; Hague, 1989). John Gyford has analysed the changing relationship between local authorities and consumers in terms of three objectives. The first is to transform consumers into *local shareholders*, whereby their interests become the efficient delivery of services by private contractors. The local authority's role is reduced in this case to letting and monitoring the delivery of contracts for services delivered by private companies or voluntary organisations. Second, local authorities may seek to improve their relationships with the *local consumers* of their services, rendering them more responsive to the needs of individuals. Third, they may seek to encourage their consumers as *local citizens* to participate more in decision-making and the monitoring of services. Here, the citizen accepts a share of responsibility for the collective welfare of the community, in addition to securing better service delivery to him or herself individually (Gyford, 1991, see also Hambleton, 1992). However, the impact of the last two approaches may be restricted because local authorities are being compelled to contract out more of their services to the private sector.

CONCLUSION

In this first chapter we have drawn a preliminary sketch of local government as it stands in the early 1990s. We have raised a large number of issues and posed questions about them, which we will seek to answer later, by looking in turn at the work of councillors and officers, the way services are provided, the management and planning of local authorities' activities and resources. Before doing so, however, we need to look in greater detail at the history of local government and the reasons why it has acquired its present structure, functions and powers.

Chapter 2

The development and reform of local government

THE ORIGINS OF LOCAL GOVERNMENT

The first question that arises from the discussion of local government's uncertain place in the British Constitution is how we acquired the present system. Its origins are lost in the distant past. Many boroughs have governed themselves under Royal Charters since mediaeval times. Newcastle upon Tyne gained its first charter from Henry II in 1175. Kingston upon Hull was granted its first charter by Edward I in 1229, while the nearby market town of Beverley received a charter from Archbishop Thurstan even earlier, in 1129. Outside the boroughs, local services were administered from Norman times by Knights of the Peace; they became Justices of the Peace – a local judicial office which survives to this day – as well as by parish bodies which were responsible for matters both ecclesiastical and secular. Common lands were administered by commissions or benches of citizens, some of which still survive. These and other single-purpose bodies provided such services as highways, drainage and charitable education. Specific projects were undertaken by commissioners charged with their execution; this method was used to enable improvements to be made to urban environments when the local authorities then in existence were debarred by law from undertaking them themselves. Such special-purpose commissioners multiplied in number during the nineteenth century as improvement works were undertaken in the rapidly expanding industrial cities (See Chandler, 1991; Kingdom, 1990).

During the nineteenth century, however, this maze of parishes, commissions and other public bodies were almost completely replaced by multi-functional local authorities of the kind with which we are now familiar. This change was implemented by three major pieces of legislation. The first was the Municipal Corporations Act of 1835, which reformed the election of borough councillors in the ancient boroughs and introduced a standard electoral procedure in place of the many different ones provided for in the old charters, where different qualifications existed both for the franchise and for council membership. Many of these old councils had been riddled with corruption because they were dominated by a small fraction of the towns' populations, who constituted self-perpetuating oligarchies. This reputation for corruption earned local government the suspicion of the Victorian public service reformers and survives among civil servants to this day (see Crossman, 1955; Chandler, 1991; Kingdom, 1991).

In 1888, the county councils were created and in 1894 urban and rural district councils were established wherever a borough council did not already exist. In the major cities, county borough councils were created which became responsible for all local government functions within their areas, including education, the police, the fire brigade, water and sewerage. The rest of the country had two tiers of local government: county councils and district councils (including the smaller boroughs), within rural areas a third tier in the form of parish councils. These became democratically elected bodies with standard powers and duties prescribed by legislation. In the smallest villages, these powers are exercised by the parish meeting: the only example of direct democracy in modern Britain. The franchise for all these local authorities was extended in parallel with the successive Parliamentary Reform Acts.

They were all financed by the rates – a property tax levied on the basis of the value of land or property and set at so many pence per pound of the rateable value of each property. The council's rate income was thus the rate in the pound set by the council, multiplied by the total rateable value of the properties in each authority's area. One tier of local government actually collected the rates and the others levied precepts upon that rating authority. Inequalities in the resources available to local authorities were redressed through a system of central Exchequer grants to individual councils (see Stanyer, 1976, Chapter 2).

By 1894, then, the framework of local government was substantially that which existed until 1 April 1974. However, after the end of the Second World War there was an increasing feeling that

this local government system, created as it had been in the nineteenth century when the role of government generally was far
more limited and less complex than it became with the creation of
the Welfare State and the managed economy, was unable to cope
satisfactorily with the new demands being made upon it. Furthermore, the functions of local government before 1945 were concerned chiefly with the provision of such public utilities as gas,
electricity, water supplies and telephone services. These were
increasingly replaced by welfare services, beginning with the
development of education from the 1902 Education Act onwards
and vastly expanded after 1945. From this time on, too, local
authorities increasingly lost control of their public utilities to
nationalised public corporations. Kingston upon Hull's municipal
telephone service is a rare exception to that general rule (Loughlin,
Gelfand and Young (eds), 1985). The functions of local authorities
had therefore changed radically by the 1950s.

PRESSURES FOR REORGANISATION

Apart from the change in the dominant functions of local authorities, from the provision of public utilities to the provision of
welfare services, there were also increasing geographical pressures for reorganisation. Perhaps the most fundamental was
the country's shifting population, which radically changed the
relationship between towns and countryside, as well as producing
wide – even wild – variations in the populations of local authorities which were responsible for exercising the same powers. In
consequence, there were huge variations both in the resources
available to local authorities in the same tier and in the scale of the
demand for their services.

In 1961, the largest county borough, Birmingham, had over a
million inhabitants while there were thirty-three county boroughs
with populations below 100,000. Again, the largest county council,
Lancashire, had 2.2 million residents, while Rutland, the smallest
county, had a mere 23,000. The smallest municipal borough in the
country was Bishop's Castle in Shropshire, with only 800 inhabitants but nonetheless possessing a mayor, a bench of alder-
men, a mace and more important, the full range of municipal
borough functions. Hence, by the 1960s population movements
had brought about great anomalies which were urgently in need
of correction, since the smaller authorities could not hope to

provide the same services at the same standards as the larger ones in the same category. Either the smaller authorities should have their powers reduced or they should be amalgamated to form larger units. By the same token, the larger authorities could be given greater powers, including more control over small second-tier authorities in their areas. Other changes were needed too, including an increase in the minimum size for county boroughs. This had been set at 50,000 inhabitants in 1888 but was increased only to 75,000 in 1926.

A second geographical problem arose out of the housing needs of the larger towns and cities, especially following the destruction of houses caused by the blitz. Many city councils needed to replace slums or bomb-damaged houses with new estates on their peripheries, so that central areas could be redeveloped. In any case, these new housing developments would not have more than fifteen houses per acre, compared to between sixty and eighty in nineteenth century terraces. However, frequently the county and municipal borough councils had no land available for redevelopment within their own boundaries and when they sought to use land in neighbouring counties and districts, they frequently met with resistance, including refusals of planning permission. Farmers opposed encroachments on agricultural land, fearing that townspeople living near their holdings would disturb their crops and animals, either through ignorance or by deliberate vandalism. Often there was suspicion that 'big brother' in the form of the city council was about to take over leafy suburbs or rural areas. Furthermore, an influx of working-class city dwellers would threaten the seats of existing councillors and the political balance of suburban and rural councils. Middle-class householders feared that the value of their properties would fall and that the former slum dwellers would damage the amenities of their suburbs, towns and villages. For all these reasons, city slum clearance programmes were often delayed or even halted because city councils could find nowhere to rehouse the inhabitants of the slum areas they wanted to clear. Such conflicts were often long-standing and bitter, the more so since they were often partisan, involving a clash between a Labour-controlled county borough with county and district councils controlled by Conservative or Independent councillors. This friction was exacerbated by the increasing dependence of rural areas on the towns and cities for employment, facilities and services.

This constituted the third main pressure for reorganisation. In the nineteenth century, rural communities were still largely self-sufficient, with their inhabitants making their living and providing their food from agriculture and related industries but in the twentieth century, the proportion of country people who work as farmers, farm labourers and in other agricultural industries has declined rapidly. The agricultural workforce is now less than a third of its size after the Second World War and less than 3 per cent of Britain's population is engaged in agricultural production.

As the farm workforce has shrunk, the better-off townsfolk have moved into the countryside, a trend encouraged by the development of the railways and subsequently the general availability of motor cars (Wells, 1908; Perkin, 1970). In consequence, not only do more and more of the people who live in the country work in the towns; also country dwellers increasingly rely on towns and cities for many services and facilities. They shop in the towns, use their libraries, theatres and cinemas. They depend upon them for many social and educational services which tend to be provided at higher standards in urban areas, by both private suppliers and the public sector. Frequently, rural county and county district councils depended on neighbouring towns or cities for the provision of such specialist services as remedial education and accommodation for children taken into local authority care. The rural local authorities paid their urban counterparts for these services on the basis of the number of people who used them, which may or may not have been a true reflection of the cost of providing them.

For all these reasons, the argument was increasingly advanced that urban and surrounding rural areas should be merged, so that all those who depended on a town's facilities and services should contribute fully to them through local taxation. Town and city rate poundages were usually considerably higher than those levied in the surrounding rural and suburban areas, a state of affairs which aroused resentment among town and city councillors and inhabitants but which was jealously guarded by rural and suburban authorities.

The state of local government finance has also given rise to increasing concern. Local authorities have three principal sources of income. The first is local taxation, the second is the charges made for certain goods and services such as literature sales, entrance charges to swimming pools, municipal theatres and many other facilities. Fines for overdue library books also provide a significant amount of revenue. The third source of income is also the largest: grants from the central government. The proportion of local authority income which comes from the central government has shown an inexorable tendency to increase for many years. This carries with it the implication that local authorities are losing their independence from central control because they cannot support the cost of the services they provide from local sources alone. Thus, the proportion of local spending financed from the centre rose from 28.9 per cent in 1938 to 40 per cent in 1963, with a corresponding fall in the proportion financed from local sources. By the mid-1970s the proportion of local spending that was financed from central grants had risen to around 60 per cent. This in turn aroused concern that there might be little point in local democracy if the extent to which local authorities could control their revenue and spending decisions became marginal (Griffith, 1961). The Layfield Committee on *Local Government Finance* (1976) advised that if local authorities were to retain their autonomy from central control, the proportion of their spending financed from the Exchequer ought not to exceed 40 per cent.

Between 1979 and 1991, the proportion of local spending financed by Government grants fell to around 48 per cent but it then increased once more because the Government decided in 1991 to transfer part of the burden of local spending from the much disliked Community Charge to central taxation, in the form of a 2.5 per cent increase in value added tax. In consequence, the proportion of local authority spending which is financed centrally returned to its 1979 level.

The final issue which confronted local government in the 1950s and 1960s is easy to state but hard to describe and elaborate. It was – and is – that the public, as well as politicians and civil servants regard local authorities with distrust, suspicion and even contempt. Tales of corruption and bumbledom abound and in the 1960s they were reflected in a television comedy series about a fictitious borough council with the evocative name 'Swizzlewick'. This problem was recognised by the Maud Committee on *The Management of Local Government* (1967), which remarked at the beginning of their report that 'Parliament, Ministers and the Whitehall departments have come increasingly to lose faith in the responsibility of locally elected bodies' (Maud 1967, para. 5). Reform was therefore needed in both the structure and management of local authorities in the hope that Government and public confidence in them could be restored. Reform has been undertaken but these objectives have not been achieved.

ATTEMPTS AT REFORM

Although local government reorganisation was clearly necessary after 1945, it took a very long time to achieve because of the powerful coalitions of resistance that built up whenever change was proposed. The first attempt, by the wartime coalition Government, was the establishment of a commission to review local authority boundaries and recommend changes but when it reported in 1948 the then Labour Government rejected its proposals because they would have put the Labour Party at an electoral disadvantage. The commissioners argued that a change in boundaries would be futile unless it was coupled with a review of local authority functions but this was excluded from their terms of reference. However, they recommended that many county boroughs should be merged with neighbouring counties and this would have been to the disadvantage of the Labour Party, which controlled many of the county boroughs but would not have gained control of the proposed combined authorities.

The problem was tackled afresh in 1958 by the creation of a second boundary commission to review county and county borough areas. Once these boundaries were settled, the higher-tier authorities would then be required to reorganise the districts within their new boundaries, often amalgamating small district authorities to form larger second-tier units of local government. The 1958 commissioners had to deal with two major issues. First, the extension of county borough boundaries where previous attempts to do so had generated hostility in the neighbouring counties and districts. Such hostilities frequently erupted at the public inquiries which the commissioners had to hold where they proposed reorganisations which entailed merging county districts with neighbouring county boroughs. In many of these cases the minister refused to confirm the boundary commissioners' proposals in the face of determined local resistance. He also rejected the commissioners' proposal to merge Rutland with neighbouring Leicestershire in the face of a public campaign against it. In some cases, mergers were resisted in the courts (see Elcock, 1969, p. 303). Local boundary reform aroused a great deal of hostility and there were no votes in it for the minister's party. Back-bench MPs fearful for the loss of their seats when the boundaries were withdrawn to match the new local authority boundaries were another potent source of resistance (see Crossman, 1965).

The second issue was that once a county council began to reorganise its districts, they too would resist reform. The 1958 Boundary Commission quickly decided not to change the boundaries of the county of Shropshire. The county council then proposed the merger of a number of small districts, including Bishop's Castle but these proposals met with stubborn resistance, including a threat by the citizens of Bishop's Castle to invade Shire Hall in Shrewsbury. To save the day, the county council made a truly Gilbertian proposal: to create a new type of local authority – the rural borough – which would have the powers of a parish council but would retain its mayor, freemen, borough council and mace but not its aldermanic bench. Local pride was saved and the necessary reorganisation carried out without rural resistance but at the cost, according to Peter Richards (1966), of creating 'a new category of local authorities ... which has no *raison d'être* other than tradition. Rural boroughs have no relevance to the effective modernisation of local government' (Richards, 1966, p. 89).

The present Government has created the new Local Government Commission which, like its 1958 predecessor, is expected to tour the country carrying out successive reorganisations in order to bring local government boundaries more in line with local sentiment. It is also assumed that in most areas the two-tier system of local government will be replaced by a single tier. However, the way in which the 1958 Boundary Commission ran into the sands of local opposition may provide an indication that the 1992 Local Government Commission will run out of steam, probably after a few well-publicised successes in abolishing some of the less popular counties created in 1972.

The extent of local resistance to the reorganisations proposed by the 1958 Boundary Commission, coupled with resistance from back-bench MPs, caused Richard Crossman, who became Minister of Housing and Local Government in 1964, to decide that the commission's step-by-step approach to reorganisation was never going to succeed. He told his diary that 'the more I looked at what the Commission has been doing, the more futile I found their work' (Crossman, 1975, p. 65). His fellow Ministers were also pressing him not to implement reorganisation proposals which would eventually jeopardise their Parliamentary seats. On 20 November 1964 Crossman had 'a very challenging meeting with the local government section of the Ministry at which I said that I would like to see genuine local government reform on the agenda of the Government' (ibid). From this point on, the idea of a nationwide reform of local government's boundaries and functions grew and the commission's days were numbered: it was wound up in 1966.

There was also an example of the effectiveness of comprehensive as opposed to piecemeal reform already to hand. Between 1957 and 1960, the government of London had been reviewed by a Royal Commission chaired by Sir Edward Herbert, whose report had been implemented by the London Government Act of 1963. This replaced the old London County Council (LCC), which had been created in 1888, with the Greater London Council (GLC), whose area covered the whole London conurbation. At the same time, thirty-two Greater London boroughs were created as the lower tier of local government. Of the old LCC, only the Inner London Education Authority was retained in order to avoid breaking up the London Education Service. This was abolished in 1990 and education was then devolved to the London borough councils.

This reform created a new authority whose borders incorporated 8 million people. The creation of the GLC had been widely resisted, especially by the London Labour Party, which feared that it would not gain control of the new council, whereas its control over the LCC had been secure for many years (Rhodes and Ruck, 1970). However, in the 1980s the GLC became a centre of Labour opposition to the Thatcher administrations, to the extent that the GLC was itself abolished in 1986.

The successful reorganisation of London's local government encouraged Crossman to embark on comprehensive reform for the rest of England. His chosen instrument was a second Royal Commission, appointed in 1966 and chaired by Sir John Maud, later Lord Redcliffe-Maud. He was already chairing the Committee on the Management of Local Government, which had been set up in 1964; another committee, chaired by Sir George Mallaby, had been established in 1963 to review local government's staffing. These last two committees proposed major changes in the staffing and management of local authorities, many of which were taken up afresh by the Royal Commission. A separate Royal Commission under Lord Wheatley was appointed to review Scottish local government.

Reorganising local government in Wales, however, was dealt with by the Welsh Office, which produced a White Paper in 1967 proposing the creation of new and larger county and district councils throughout the principality. The two-tier structure was to be retained except in the county boroughs of Swansea, Cardiff and Newport, which were to be retained as all-purpose authorities. However, these proposals were changed after the Redcliffe-Maud Commission reported on English local government in 1969.

The Royal Commission recommended radical change. In the largest provincial cities, Birmingham, Liverpool and Manchester, two tiers of local government were to be retained. Elsewhere, fifty-eight unitary authorities should be created to carry out all local government functions in their areas. However, one of the commission's members, Derek Senior, issued a dissenting report which advocated two tiers of local government throughout England.

Both these sets of proposals were based on Mr Senior's concept of a 'city region' (Senior, 1966). This concept accepted the essential unity of town and country and defined the appropriate areas of local administration as those whose inhabitants depended substantially on a large town or city for government and commercial services, industrial products and employment. Both the majority and minority reports also recommended the creation of a regional or provincial tier of government in England, but this proposal was referred to yet another Royal Commission, the Commission on the Constitution, which was established in the year Redcliffe-Maud reported. Its principal concern was the devolution of government to Scotland and Wales in the face of by-election successes by the Scottish and Welsh National Parties against the governing Labour Party. It was thought appropriate that it should also review proposals for English regional government.

When the Redcliffe-Maud Commission reported in 1969, its recommendations were more or less accepted by the Labour Government, but before they could be implemented Labour lost the 1970 General Election and the new Conservative Government under Edward Heath, rejected its predecessor's plans. A new reorganisation plan was prepared and enacted in the Local Government Act of 1972, which established a two-tier structure throughout England. The structure is shown in Figure 2.1.

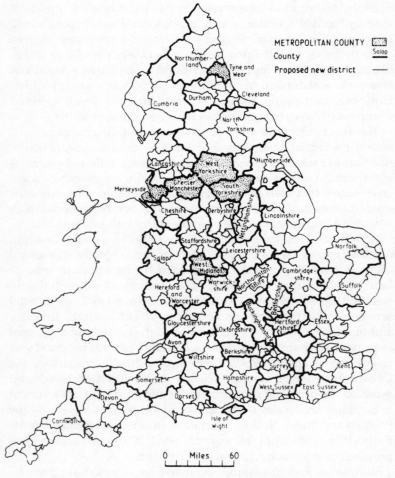

Figure 2.1 Local Government Act, 1972: proposed districts in the non-metropolitan counties in England
Source: HMSO

The distribution of powers and functions among the new local authorities was also redefined. In the six largest conurbations outside London, most service functions were allocated to the new metropolitan district councils, with the metropolitan county councils having strategic planning responsibilities and responsibility for a few services which were thought to require large areas for their efficient administration. These included the police, the fire service, public transport and refuse disposal. The metropolitan county councils were responsible for about 20 per cent of local government spending in their areas. In the rest of the country, however, the county councils were given responsibility for the major local authority services, notably education, the personal social services, highways and public libraries. In the 'shire' areas the district councils controlled only some 15 per cent of local government spending and the larger districts bitterly resented the loss of their former county borough status and powers. Only housing was a district function in metropolitan and 'shire' areas alike.

A few functions, such as the provision of entertainment and leisure services, were concurrent, discharged by county and district councils alike, while some others were shared. Thus for the first time, both tiers of local government were given responsibility in the field of town and country planning but their roles were separate. County councils were responsible mainly for strategic planning while most development control functions (but not all) were allocated to the district councils. The functions allocated to the different local authorities in 1972 are summarised in Table 2.1. These concurrent and shared powers have been the subject of many time-wasting disputes between county and district councils which have made co-ordination difficult. In 1980 almost all development control functions were reallocated to district councils.

It is often forgotten that one tier of local government has survived the 1972 and subsequent reorganisations largely unscathed: the parish councils. Indeed, they emerged from the 1972 reorganisation with their powers somewhat enhanced. They exist only in rural areas and small towns, although there have also been experiments with neighbourhood councils in some cities, which have sometimes been seen as a means of extending the parish tier of local government into the larger towns and cities.

Parish councils have some powers of their own, including the management of village halls, playing fields, footpaths and cemeteries. In common with all other local authorities, they also

Table 2.1 Distribution of principal local authority functions and powers, Local Government Act, 1972

	County councils	District councils
Metropolitan	Planning: Structure planning	Education
	Transport planning with control of Passenger Transport Authorities	Social services
		Libraries
		Museums and art galleries[1,2]
	Some development control	Housing
		Planning: Most development control and local plan-making
	Highways, traffic and transportation	Refuse collection
	Refuse disposal	Environmental health
	Consumer protection	Parks, open spaces[1]
	Fire service	Coastal protection
	Museums and art galleries[2]	
	Parks, open spaces[1,2]	
	Police	
Non-metropolitan	Education	Housing
	Social services	Planning (as metropolitan districts)
	Libraries, museums and art galleries[2]	Refuse collection
	Planning: Structure planning	Environmental health
	Transport planning but no responsibility for transport operation	Museums and art galleries[1,2]
		Parks, open spaces[1]
	Highways, traffic and transportation	Coastal protection[1]
		Municipal bus services
	Refuse disposal	
	Consumer protection	
	Fire service	
	Parks, open spaces[1]	
	Coastal protection[1]	
	Police	

Notes: 1 These are concurrent powers exercised by both county and district councils.
2 These services are often grouped together in leisure services committees and departments.

were given the power under the 1972 Local Government Act to spend up to the product of a 2-pence rate for the general benefit of their inhabitants. Parish councils also provide an important communication link between country people and the relatively large county and district councils established in 1972. They must be consulted on proposed structure and local plans, as well as on planning applications in their parishes. They are also consulted on such matters as the siting of bus stops and post offices, as well as on the pattern of rural bus services. They will resist attempts to alter public services when such alterations are seen as being to the disadvantage of their residents.

Parish councils are in a sense the most democratic of local authorities, in that their smallness allows easy access to parish council members, as well as openness in the conduct of their business. They are not only periodically elected but they are also accountable to an annual parish meeting. The smallest parishes are governed solely by parish meetings which all residents are entitled to attend. Like all local authorities, parish councils must admit the public to their meetings but some go further, allowing them to ask questions and speak in debates but not, of course, to vote.

Parish council areas were largely left untouched by the 1972 reorganisation, although small ones have been encouraged to amalgamate. They range from small bodies spending only a few thousand pounds a year to quite large organisations employing some full-time staff. Some former municipal boroughs have established town councils under the 1972 Act, which have the same powers and functions as parish councils. In order to do this, the proposal to establish a town council has to be approved by a local referendum.

Local government reorganisation in Scotland and Wales was less controversial than was the case in England. No change of mind was needed about the relative merits of single or two-tier systems. The Wheatley Commission reported on Scottish local government in 1972. Its recommendations resulted in the creation in 1975 of nine large regional councils with fifty-three district councils below them. In the three island areas all-purpose authorities were created. Although these proposals were accepted at the time, there has been periodic pressure for the abolition of the regional councils, the largest of which, Strathclyde, covers half the population of Scotland and is the biggest local authority in Western Europe.

In Wales, the Welsh Office's 1967 proposals were accepted except that Cardiff, Newport and Swansea were created as districts within the new county council areas of Gwent, South and West Glamorgan respectively. These new Welsh counties were much criticised as making neither geographic nor economic sense. Cardiff became the county town of two counties.

However, reorganisation once carried out has proved to be addictive (Elcock, 1991, Chapter 3). First came the bitterly contested proposals for Scottish and Welsh devolution, which led ultimately to the Labour Government's defeat in March 1979. In the late 1970s too, the larger 'shire' district councils, which had formerly been county boroughs responsible for all local authority services in their areas, commenced an agitation for the return to them of the functions they had lost to the 'shire' county councils after 1972. This agitation was led by the 'big nine' cities: Bristol, Derby, Hull, Leicester, Nottingham,. Plymouth, Portsmouth, Southampton and Stoke-on-Trent. In March 1977 Peter Shore, as Secretary of State for the Environment, indicated that he was inclined to accede to this demand by carrying out an 'organic change' in local government. Under this proposal, the larger 'shire' district councils who wished to do so would be allowed to assume control over some county council services, including education and social services. In 1978 this proposal was considered by a Cabinet committee and a White Paper was produced in January 1979 (DoE, 1979). The plan was abandoned by the Conservative Government when it won office in May, along with Scottish and Welsh devolution. However, the 'big nine' and other 'shire' district councils have not ceased their agitation for the restoration of their lost county borough powers.

At first, the Thatcher administration showed little interest in structural changes in the machinery of government. However, in 1982 the National Health Service was reorganised to remove its area level of management in the hope that this would reduce administrative costs. The following year, the Cabinet decided, apparently very suddenly, to include the proposal to abolish the GLC and the six metropolitan county councils in its election manifesto. The official reason given for this hasty proposal was that these authorities had few functions and were therefore redundant; however, it was significant that in 1981 the Labour Party had won control of all seven of these authorities (it had retained control of only South Yorkshire and Tyne and Wear in the previous elections in 1977). The GLC in particular had emerged as a focus of opposition to Margaret Thatcher and all her works.

The seven authorities were abolished after a massive Parliamentary and public campaign against their abolition, ceasing to exist on 1 April 1986. Their powers and functions, as listed in Table 2.1, were either taken over by the metropolitan district councils or are administered by joint boards consisting of members nominated by the district councils in each metropolitan county. This structure has proved inefficient and it causes problems for the co-ordination of those services which need to be planned for and provided over areas larger than the geographically small metropolitan districts.

Reorganisation in the 1990s: England

In the 1990s, yet further reorganisation is being carried out. This has developed partly because of the continuing agitation of the larger 'shire' districts for greater powers and status and partly because of public hostility towards some of the new counties created in 1972, notably Avon, Humberside and Cleveland. The Government has therefore appointed a Local Government Commission to review the English local government structure county by county, with a view to developing a single-tier structure in most areas based either on the counties or the district councils. A lively debate as to whether county or district government is superior has developed. The first reports are appearing in the summer of 1993 and it is likely that the commission will quickly achieve the abolition of some or all of the unpopular county councils, although the district councils are by no means always emerging victorious either. However, the obstruction suffered by its 1958 predecessor is likely to recur and this is rendered more likely by the procedures being adopted by the commission.

It has been charged to review local government in the English counties, which have been divided into four groups, dubbed *tranches* by the Secretary of State. Each *tranche* contains ten counties. The process of review begins with the preparation of bids for future arrangements by the county and district councils in each county in the *tranche* currently being reviewed. Not surprisingly, the district councils have almost invariably urged that they be allowed to assume all the local government responsibilities in their areas, thus becoming unitary authorities. However, it is likely that two-tier systems will be retained in some areas, notably geographically large counties like Northumberland. These bids are then to be considered by the Commission, which must then submit its recommendations to the Secretary of State after carrying out a process of public consultation. After a further six weeks for comments and objections, the Secretary of State will lay the final orders before Parliament for debate and approval.

The criteria to be considered by the commission include community identity and convenient and effective government. Size is not considered relevant, first because many services are now contracted out and second, because large authorities can decentralise their service provision by establishing local 'one stop shops' – the new name for neighbourhood offices. The process of reorganisation is intended to be completed by 1998. However, precedent suggests that piecemeal reorganisation will be at best slow and at worst be abandoned some years hence. In the summer of 1993, the review was nearing completion in only one area and this was of the Isle of Wight, where there has been widespread support for a unitary island authority for many years. Where county and district councils produce conflicting bids, the process of reconciling them or favouring one set of bids and rejecting the other is turning out to be fraught with protest and delay. This has now become apparent in a series of proposals published by the Commission during the Summer of 1993, some of which are exciting considerable opposition. The county of Cleveland should, according to the commissioners, be divided into four districts but in Durham, the county council is the survivor with the exclusion of Darlington, which would become a separate unitary authority under the commission's recommendations. Similarly, in Derbyshire the city of Derby would become a unitary authority, with the rest of the county forming a second such authority. Hence, all but one of the present Derbyshire district councils would disappear – a proposal they are vigorously resisting.

The unjustly unpopular Humberside County Council is to be abolished and replaced by new unitary authorities in the former East Riding of Yorkshire, together with two in South Humberside, despite the evident need for the coherent planning of the Humber Estuary. Avon County Council too is expected to disappear, to be replaced by an enlarged Bristol City Council and a pattern of unitary authorities extending into Somerset.

The proposed demise of the unpopular counties created in 1974 has provoked few tears but in few areas is there ready agreement to the Commissioners' proposals. More generally, they do not consistently favour either the case put by the county councils or that put by the district councils that they should form the basis for the new unitary authorities. Instead, the commission has proposed a variety of solutions, including the retention of two-tier local government in Lincolnshire although not, surprisingly, in the larger and more sparsely populated county of North Yorkshire. The passage of the commission's recommendations towards approval by the Secretary of State is therefore likely to be stormy, both because of local opposition and because there is no consistent basis on which the Association of County Councils or the Association of District Councils will support them. In late 1993 the commission was also disputing its remit with the Secretary of State himself.

Scotland
Reorganisation is also being executed in Scotland, where there has been much criticism over the years of the regional councils in particular. They are regarded as too large and remote from the people they serve, especially in the case of Strathclyde Regional Council, which provides local government for half the country's population. The Secretary of State for Scotland declared of Strathclyde in October 1992 that 'It is self-evident that a local authority which covers half the population of the country does not constitute local government' (*The Scotsman*, 14 October 1992). The Government has therefore produced a range of proposals for reducing the total number of local authorities in Scotland from sixty-five to a figure ranging between fifteen and fifty-one councils, by developing a single-tier structure. The Scottish Office also hired the independent consultants Touche Ross to estimate the cost savings and transitional costs which are likely to result from the adoption of each of the four options for change which the Scottish Office has developed, in a bid to reassure MPs and citizens alike that real cost savings will result from reorganisation (*The Scotsman*, 13 October 1992). The Government's claim, supported by the Touche Ross analysis, is that the fewer the number of authorities that are created, the bigger the savings will be, but some academic observers remain sceptical that reorganisation is desirable in itself or likely to increase efficiency. Arthur Midwinter (1992) has pointed out that the regional councils have low bureaucratic costs and small district councils have high ones. He

argues that 'the case for change is still assumed rather than demonstrated' by the Government's proposals. He therefore shares other observers' scepticism about whether structural reorganisation is an effective means of improving organisations' performance and increasing their efficiency (Elcock, 1991). The case for reorganising Scottish local government would be more convincing if democracy north of the border were to be increased by granting the long-standing demand for a Scottish Parliament, but this proposal is not on the Government's agenda at present, although the Prime Minister has indicated that some degree of increased Scottish access to its MPs, perhaps through sittings of the Scottish Grand Committee in Edinburgh, might be introduced. However, a White Paper announcing the Government's choice of a reorganisation scheme appeared in the summer of 1993. It proposes a structure based on twenty-eight council areas, so falling between the extremes of the options offered in the Spring.

Wales

On St David's Day 1993, the Secretary of State for Wales announced the Welsh Office's intention to replace the eight county councils and thirty-seven district councils established in the Principality in 1974 with twenty-one unitary authorities which will restore many but not all of the former Welsh county names, including Pembrokeshire, Flintshire and Denbighshire but not Montgomeryshire, after a two-year consultation exercise (*The Guardian*, 2 March 1993). Although the reintroduction of the traditional county names was widely welcomed in Wales, paradoxically the new system was criticised by the Welsh Language Society on the ground that several of the large county councils established in 1974 had vigorously encouraged the teaching of Welsh throughout large parts of Wales. Some of the Secretary of State's proposed smaller authorities are likely, in the society's opinion, to be less enthusiastic supporters of Welsh than their predecessors. Not for nothing, for example, has Pembrokeshire long been known as 'Little England beyond Wales'. Hence, there may be sown the seeds of discontent which could grow into a demand for yet further reorganisation in the future.

As between 1969 and 1974, then, the ministers responsible for local government in England, Scotland and Wales have adopted different approaches to reorganisation. English local government is being reorganised by a roving commission which is beginning its work with the review and presumed abolition of those new authorities which failed to win popular approval after 1974. The Scottish Secretary has offered a range of options, with carefully calculated price tags attached to each of them, while his Welsh colleague has presented a single scheme which claims to be the result of extensive consultation and which is also claimed to reflect local loyalties more closely than the 1974 reorganisation. The Prime Minister claimed in a speech to the 1993 Conservative Local Government Conference that the new local government systems to be introduced by his administration will last 100 years. However, the previous twenty years demonstrated that reorganisation, once embarked on, is highly addictive, which must arouse acute scepticism as to whether anything like the durability of the work of the Victorian founders of multi-purpose local authorities can ever be achieved again.

OTHER DEVELOPMENTS

The reform of the structure and management of local government were the major tasks which the central government addressed in the 1960s and 1970s but in the 1980s, the focus of the centre's attention changed, first towards financial restraint, then back to reorganisation and finally to changing the ways in which local authorities provide their services. The 'enabling' local authority, which provides services to citizens by organising their provision through a range of private, voluntary and public suppliers, should now become the 'residual' local authority, carrying out only those functions which cannot be provided elsewhere. As a consequence of this tide of reform, major changes have occurred in local government, three of which may be explored in the remainder of this chapter. These are the increasing complexity of local governance; improving means of access and redress for consumers and – most controversial of all – changes in local taxation.

Local government and local governance

The general system of local governance has become increasingly complicated, especially as functions have been removed from local authority control and handed over to an increasingly wide range of other organisations. This process began in the 1940s, with the removal of local authority gas and electricity undertakings to national public corporations with no local government influence over them, which have since been removed altogether from the public sector by privatisation. In 1948, too, many local authority health functions were removed to the new National Health Service authorities; this process was continued in the 1972 NHS reorganisation, as a result of which local authorities now have only a few health-care responsibilities (Loughlin, Gelfand and Young (eds), 1985; Stacey, 1975). Health care is now the responsibility of regional and district health authorities, whose members are appointed by the Secretary of State for Health and which receive their funding almost entirely from the Exchequer (Brown, 1975, 1979). Public transport in the major cities largely ceased to be under local authority control after the abolition of the GLC and the metropolitan county councils in 1986. At the same time, when bus services were deregulated, municipal bus services were transferred to private companies or (more usually) to publicly funded companies which were given a degree of autonomy from council control.

Water, sewerage and drainage services were removed from local government in 1974 (see Stacey, 1975) and then privatised in 1982. More recently, many planning and development control functions in the inner cities have been transferred from councils to urban development corporations, with board members appointed by the Secretary of State for the Environment. One must add to this the range of private firms and voluntary agencies which are increasingly taking over the provision of local services as a result of compulsory competitive tendering and the development of the Government's community care reforms, under which the local authority social services departments are charged to secure the provision of services for elderly and disabled persons but to do so wherever possible through contracts with other agencies, rather than by the direct provision of services and facilities by local authorities themselves.

Two trends can be detected here. The first is the increasing removal of functions and services from local authority to central government control, often with the intention then of carrying out a further transfer of control to the private sector. It can thus be argued that Loughlin, Gelfand and Young's (1985) municipal decline has accelerated since 1985. The second is the creation of an increasing range of public and private sector organisations with which local authorities need to collaborate and whose activities needed to be concerted in order to ensure coherent policies and service provision in local communities. We shall discuss some means for achieving this coherence later. Here we can note that local authorities remain the only multi-functional organisations within this system and are hence the obvious agencies to co-ordinate the activities of the others. However, the Government has been reluctant to accept this, as was demonstrated by the long delay in accepting the recommendation of the Griffiths Report (1988) on community care, that local authority social services departments were the most appropriate agencies for the co-ordination of community care. Securing the acceptance of this principle by the Prime Minister (Margaret Thatcher) and others took some eighteen months.

In this connection, we can also note a tendency to remove councillors from playing any role in the control of organisations other than their own. They were deprived of their seats on regional water authorities in 1988, some years before the water industry was privatised. More recently, local authorities have also been excluded from nominating their members for membership of regional and district health authorities. Between 1976 and 1982, local authorities nominated councillors for one-third of the seats on health authorities. The Conservative Government reduced that number to four after winning office in 1979 and councillors were excluded altogether in 1991.

Since 1982, health authorities have been required in any case to participate in a hierarchical process of annual reporting, DHAs to the RHA Chairmen and the latter to the Secretary of State for Health. Health authority chairmen are specifically required to demonstrate that they are implementing Government policies. The scope for local choice by health authorities as regards the implementation of central government policies was thus reduced. Hence local authority influence was first reduced by the intro-duction of the review meetings and then removed altogether by the removal of councillors from membership of health authorities.

Consumer relations

On another front, the public has been granted more channels to complain about local authorities' activities and seek redress against them when they feel aggrieved. One major change, for which there was widespread demand based on increasing mistrust of local authorities, was the introduction of local ombudsmen in 1974. Britain's first ombudsman, the Parliamentary Commissioner for administration, was established in 1967 but the exclusion of local government from his remit was widely criticised (Stacey, 1971). Demands for the creation of local ombudsmen was intensified by local government reorganisation, which was alleged to have created larger local authorities, both in terms of their geographical size and the number of their employees, which were more distant from their clients than their smaller predecessors had been (Newton, 1978). Furthermore, a precedent was set in 1969 by the establishment of the Northern Ireland Commissioner for Complaints, whose remit and the bulk of whose work covers local authorities (Elcock, 1971). Hence, in 1974, after reorganisation had been completed, local commissioners for administration were established to investigate complaints of maladministration by local authorities which had resulted in injustice, the same principle that governs the work of the Parliamentary commissioner (Chinkin and Bailey, 1976; Marshall, 1973).

There are three such commissioners for England, one of whom has a headquarters at York and covers the North of England, plus one for Wales. There is a separate commission for Scotland (see Thompson, 1991). They have proved their usefulness in increasing citizens' ability to seek redress where they feel wronged by the action or inaction of a local authority (Chinkin and Bailey 1976; Thompson, 1991).

The work of the local commissioners has been subjected to a series of restrictions which are in many respects similar to those which apply to the parliamentary commissioner (Stacey, 1978). Initially, access to a local commissioner could be sought only through a councillor of the authority complained of; only if the councillor failed to act could a citizen then approach the local commissioner directly. This 'councillor filter' has now been removed. Also, like the parliamentary commissioner the local commissioners are confined to investigating 'maladministration resulting in injustice'. However, this phrase now seems to be of little significance as a restraint upon British ombudsmen, a result of commissioners having broadened their remit by reinterpreting this phrase so that it includes all decisions or rules which appear bad or oppressive (Marshall, 1973).

As is the case with the Parliamentary Commissioner for Administration, many complaints have to be rejected because they are inappropriate or wrongly submitted. However, ombudsmen do attempt to advise complainants on how to correct such mistakes (Chinkin and Bailey, 1976; Thompson, 1991). Again, like the parliamentary commissioner, those departments whose activities have the most impact on members of the public generate the most complaints. They include planning, housing, education, social services and environmental health – all services with which the individual member of the public is likely to come into relatively frequent contact (Chinkin and Bailey, 1976). In Scotland, housing generates half of all complaints submitted to the commissioner: this is a function of the high level of public sector housing provision in Scotland (Thompson, 1991, p. 55f).

Finally, like the parliamentary commissioner, the Local Commissioners have no power to compel a local authority which they have found to have been at fault to grant redress. Most authorities do so voluntarily but where a local authority refuses, the commissioners do have a degree of sanction. When a commissioner reports on a case concerning a local authority, the latter is required to give publicity to the commissioner's findings. If the local authority fails or refuses to grant redress, the commissioner may issue a further report, which the local authority is likewise required to publicise. Only a small minority of authorities are determinedly recalcitrant but the commissioners have from time to time expressed the view that they should be given power to enforce their judgements (see the annual *Reports of the Local Commissioners for Administration*). The local commissioners have established their usefulness to the public, although as with the parliamentary commissioner there is room for doubt as to whether their existence is widely enough known. However, the local commissioners are energetic in advertising their existence.

In the 1980s, and 1990s, the ability of citizens to be able to complain about the activities of local authorities and seek redress against them has been extended, first by the rise of 'consumerism' in local government and more recently by the development of the Citizen's Charter (see Gyford, 1991). These developments have been concerned chiefly with recognition of the complainant as a customer who ought to be able to expect a certain level of courtesy and efficiency in dealing with his or her enquiry, request or complaint. The development of 'consumerism' ranges from the cosmetic to considerable exercises in bringing services 'closer to the customer' (Stewart, 1986; Fenwick and Harrop, 1989; Hague. 1989; Gyford, 1991). The latter include service decentralisation to provide services at the neighbourhood level (Hoggett and Hambleton, 1987; Elcock, 1986; 1988). Local authorities are now expected to take part in the Prime Minister's Citizen's Charter initiative. (Cabinet Office, 1991) The aggrieved citizen now has a wide range of formal and informal channels available to him or her through which to pursue a grievance against a local council – apart from the traditional remedy of complaining to a councillor. However, the extent and range of the remedies available varies considerably from one council to another.

Local taxation

Local taxation has been radically reformed twice in the last three years: financial as well as structural change seems to be addictive. The speed of change can be judged from the fact that when the second edition of this book went to press, the Government had stated its intention to introduce a community charge by around the year 2000 (DofE, 1986). By the time the book appeared and was in use, that date had been brought forward to 1990! The Community Charge had been introduced and abolished by 1993.

The main reasons why local taxation has been so contentious for so long are three in number. The first is that successive local taxes have been regressive: they have borne more heavily on the poor than on the wealthy. This feature was shared by the old system of rates and the Community Charge; it may well be the case with the Council Tax too. Second, none of these taxes is fiscally buoyant: revenue from them does not rise automatically with inflation, as with income tax and value added tax. In consequence, local authorities faced with increasing costs must resolve to increase the amount of their rate poundage (before 1990), their Community Charge (until 1993) and now their Council Tax. Councillors must therefore incur an annual political opprobrium of a kind the Chancellor of the Exchequer escapes as long as he does not need more revenue than is provided by the automatically rising yield of his two biggest earners: income tax and VAT (see Likierman, 1988). For example, in 1975 most local authorities were compelled to increase their rates by 25 per cent because national inflation rose by that amount (see Dell, 1991). In consequence, protest associations were formed, some of whose members withheld payment of the increased rates. The rise was widely and wrongly blamed on the costs of the recent local government reorganisation.

This increase led the Government to establish the Layfield Committee on Local Government Finance, which reported in 1976. Its report recommended a reform of the basis on which properties were valued for rates, coupled with the supplementing of the rates with a local income tax. However, although the Layfield Report was both impressively documented and well argued, its recommendations were never accepted. The eventual consequence was the rise and fall of the Poll Tax (see Midwinter and Monaghan, 1993).

A third issue is the basis for the valuation of property. Valuations get out of date but when they are revised, increases in the valuation of some properties evokes widespread protest. It was such a protest over a Scottish revaluation in 1986 that caused Margaret Thatcher's Government to make its hasty commitment to the speedy introduction of the Community Charge at the 1987 General Election – a commitment which the Government hailed as the flagship of its legislative programme after the 1987 election victory. Having nailed its colours to the mast-head of a flagship which then sank, the Government then reverted in the main to a new property tax: the Council Tax. This time, houses have been valued in nine bands, labelled A (the lowest value) to H. Doubts have been expressed about the accuracy of the valuations carried out for the Council Tax. Also, there is widespread anxiety about its impact in the South of England, where property values are highest and hence, householders are likely to have to pay more in Council Tax than they did under the Community Charge. An element of taxation relative to the number of people occupying a house has been retained in the form of a 25 per cent discount from the Council Tax for single occupiers. Local authority treasurers and many others will hope that the Council Tax will remain with us for longer than its predecessor.

For many observers, a local income tax has long been the obvious solution to the problems of the regressiveness and lack of fiscal buoyancy that have characterised local taxation in modern times. However, it has also long been clear that this tax is unacceptable to the Treasury and the Inland Revenue. Richard Crossman came to office as Minister of Housing and Local Government in 1964 with an enthusiasm to reform local taxation and introduce a local income tax. In this he was supported by a clear commitment in the Labour Party's election manifesto to do so. Faced with resistance from civil servants both from his own department and the Treasury, he failed almost completely. He introduced rate rebates for poorer ratepayers which reduced the regressive impact of the rates. For the rest, he told his diary that:

> I had the idea that we could abolish rating by substituting for it a more progressive local tax. The Department and in particular the Accountant-General, disliked this because they knew the Treasury was passionately opposed to it. In the end, they won.
>
> (Crossman 1975, p. 620)

In a lecture at Harvard University, Crossman commented that, 'If Whitehall gangs up on you it is very difficult to get your policy through or even get a fair hearing for a new idea' (Crossman 1972, p. 73). For the remainder of the 1960s and well into the 1970s reform of the rating system was a dead issue. During the 1970s it revived after the 25 per cent rates increase in 1974–1975, producing the Layfield Report but little Government action. In the early 1980s, too, the question was reconsidered but a Government paper concluded in 1982 that the system of local taxation could not be radically changed or fundamentally improved. At this stage the notion of a community charge was briefly dismissed. There matters rested until the Community Charge legislation came before Parliament in the late 1980s.

CONCLUSION

Local government reorganisation and reform have been dogged by political and administrative resistance to change from powerful people and groups, both within local government and on the national political stage. Resistance by powerful local figures, by the local authority associations and from civil servants present ministers with a series of obstacles which require a clear policy focus as well as much determination to overcome. For much of local government's recent history, the career advantage to ministers pressing for radical change have been small. This changed under Mrs Thatcher, when radical changes became more acceptable but the risks were also great of generating a confrontation either with an individual local authority or the local government policy community as a whole, or of the policy proving to be a disaster, as with the Community Charge. Nonetheless, much of the present local government system is unsatisfactory and talk of further reform is often in the air.

Part II

The dramatis personae

Chapter 3

The local councillor

The supreme decision-makers in any local authority are its elected members. All decisions taken anywhere in a local authority are formally those of the council and all the staff employed by the authority are ultimately responsible to it. Although the public image of councillors is generally poor: they tend to be regarded as pompous, corrupt and extravagant in their spending of other people's money – nonetheless, thousands of councillors devote many hours of their time and a great deal of energy to their service on local authorities. These councillors and the parties or other systems that recruit them, procure their election and organise their activities, constitute the main political elements in each local political system: the only other major factor to consider is pressure group activity, which tends to be related to officers rather than members (Newton, 1976). Councillors and their parties supply the policy guidelines within which their officers must work. They reflect more or less adequately the demands and needs of the citizens whom councillors are elected to represent.

Although the vast majority of local authorities are now controlled by one of the major national political parties, the local structures and processes of those parties vary widely and this is reflected in the ways in which decisions are taken by individual local authorities. Furthermore, few councils are now controlled by Independent councillors, although a few still are, the 'hung' authority, in which a smaller party (usually the Liberal-Democrats) holds the balance of power between the major party groups, became increasingly common in the 1980s, especially among county councils (Leach and Stewart, 1988). The operation of 'hung' authorities has again become of major importance after the 1993 county council elections, in which the Conservative Party lost control of all but one county council, retaining control only of Buckinghamshire. In consequence, many county councils now have no overall majority and they must therefore develop the means to get their business done without a single party being able to conduct it.

BECOMING A COUNCILLOR

Almost every adult can become a local government councillor. If a person is over 21, is not disqualified from voting in local elections and either has lived in the area of a particular local authority for twelve months or is on the register of electors in that authority's area, he or she can stand for election to the county or district council, provided also that he or she does not work for that authority. Since even local government employees work for either the county or the district council, they can still stand for the authority by which they are not employed – except in the former GLC and metropolitan counties, where the district councils are now the only local authorities in their areas. No deposit is required, unlike Parliamentary elections: all the aspirant councillor is required to do is to obtain a proposer, a seconder and eight assentors who are prepared to sign his or her nomination paper.

However, although the requirements for candidature are so slight, the political parties constantly complain that they cannot attract sufficient candidates of the right quality and in rural areas especially, seats often go uncontested. In parish council elections there may be insufficient nominees to fill the vacancies available. The problem is that public interest in local government is relatively limited in Britain, most of the time. Only about one-third of the electorate normally votes in local elections and Britain has long been unusual among West European countries in that the turn-out in local elections is substantially lower than that in general elections (Maud Committee, 1967, Volume 1, para. 37; Goldsmith (ed.), 1986, p. 146). One can speculate as to whether this is a consequence of a relatively homogeneous British political culture or because electors perceive local authorities as having little power, although their actions affect citizens' daily lives far more than do those of the central government. There has been some evidence in recent years that turn-outs in local elections are increasing but it is limited. (Gyford, Leach and Game, 1989, p. 249). More often than not, the prevailing public mood at local election time is apathy.

What is more, few people embark on a career of political activism with the intention of becoming a councillor. In their pioneering study of the members of Barking Borough Council in the early 1960s, Rees and Smith (1964) found that four-fifths of the council members they interviewed had had to be asked or even persuaded to stand for the council initially. This finding has been replicated in many studies of councillors since (for example, Newton, 1976; Dearlove, 1973; Maud Committee, 1967, Volume 2, p. 34; Barron, Crawley and Wood, 1991, pp. 42ff). The considerable literature now available on the career patterns and motivations of local councillors include three major official studies, carried out for the Maud Committee on the Management of Local Government (1957), the Robinson Committee on the Remuneration of Councillors (1977) and the Widdicombe Committee on the Conduct of Local Authority Business (1986). There is also a welter of academic studies of the councillors on individual local authorities or samples of authorities. In what follows, we shall draw on both the official surveys and the academic studies.

The likely career progression of a councillor begins with a person joining a political party and becoming active within it. Often, this activity in turn occurs because parents or siblings are or have themselves been politically active but it may also develop because of growing convictions or the impact of major political events. Once a person is a party activist, he or she is likely sooner or later to be asked to stand for the party in a local election – at first in a hopeless seat but later in a marginal or even a safe one. In consequence, that person suddenly finds that he or she has become a councillor.

Once this happens, their initial apathy or even antipathy towards local government changes. The new councillor becomes absorbed in the activity of the council and its committees, and councillors stand for re-election again and again because they have discovered that council service is interesting and fulfilling. However, their ambitions are usually confined to becoming a committee chairman or mayor or chairman of the council. Relatively few councillors stand for Parliament and when they do so, it is usually in hopeless constituencies as a necessary service to their parties. Although rather more MPs now have council experience than used to be the case, they give up their local government seats and offices on or soon after their election to Westminster. Even such leading local government figures as David Blunkett and Ken

Livingstone abandoned their local authority seats and offices after being elected to the House of Commons (Lansley, Goss and Wolman, 1989). Activity on the national political scene is a career path which is largely separate from local government (Ranney, 1975). There is no equivalent of the overlap between local and national political office-holding which is common in the rest of Europe and which the French describe as *le cumul des mandats*. There, as in most countries in Continental Europe, the major national politicians also hold local offices; not so in Britain.

Where (as is usually the case) local politics is dominated by the national political parties, the processes of political recruitment are conducted in accordance with the procedures laid down by those parties. Local party organisations prepare lists of approved potential candidates, from among whom the ward parties choose a shortlist of candidates who appear at selection meetings to speak and answer questions, after which one of their number is selected to contest the seat.

The procedure is different in some respects between the major parties. In the Labour Party, admission to the panel of candidates can only be obtained by getting a nomination from a ward party or an affiliated organisation such as a trade union branch or the Co-operative Party. The individual ward parties then choose a shortlist from the panel. The shortlisted nominees are then interviewed in turn and one of their number is selected by exhaustive ballot to become the ward's Labour candidate for the council. In the Conservative Party the list of approved candidates is formed from individual applicants who will be interviewed by a committee of the local party organisation. It is common practice for an executive committee or similar body to interview prospective candidates for each ward and select a single nominee to go forward to a general meeting of ward party members for acceptance or (rarely) rejection. However, these procedures can vary from one local area to another. Some cities have a tradition, which may cross party lines, of maintaining some degree of central control over the selection of candidates by the ward parties, while in others the latter are left almost entirely to their own devices. However, political parties in most places follow the procedures outlined here more or less closely.

It is well known that the councillors produced by these selection procedures are not representative of the population in general or even of their particular wards. Councillors have traditionally been 'overwhelmingly male, middle-aged, middle class – and of course white' (Gyford, Leach and Game, 1989, p. 45). There was some evidence that more younger people and more women became councillors in the 1980s but in the main, the Widdicombe Committee's researchers (1986) reported that:

> perhaps the most remarkable aspect is the stability of the population (of councillors) particularly since the Robinson study (in 1977) . . . elected members as a group are still highly unrepresentative of the overall population.
>
> (Widdicombe, 1986)

There tend to be too many retired people, too many self-employed and professional people, not enough manual workers and not enough women. Ethnic minorities are usually heavily under-represented (Barron, Crawley and Wood, 1991; Gyford, Leach and Game, 1989). Councillors are in general older than the average of the population and hold more educational qualifications (Maud Committee, Volume 1, 1967, pp. 135–136; Robinson, 1977, para. 46; Gyford, Leach and Game, 1989 p. 47). This all follows from several factors, the most obvious of which is that only those people with the time and energy to spare for council work are likely to make themselves available as candidates. Thus professional men and executives in their thirties and forties are likely to concentrate on making their careers and will not wish to risk casting doubt on their devotion to their careers and employers by devoting a substantial amount of their time and energies to council work. Also, people in these age groups are often involved in the raising of young families and council work can have a disruptive effect on family life (see Barron, Crawley and Wood, 1991, Chapter 5).

The remuneration of councillors

It has been suggested that more generous financial rewards would cause more younger people to come forward to serve as councillors but no payment which is remotely likely to be contemplated will persuade anyone to put their promotion chances at risk and neglect their families. Nor is it likely to persuade employers to be more generous than they are at present in giving their employees time off from work to attend council and committee meetings. To this extent, the advocates of increased remuneration for councillors, including the Maud (1967) and Robinson (1977) Committees have missed the point. Nonetheless, the proper basis for the remuneration of councillors has long been a subject of heated debate.

Since the Widdicombe Committee reported, major changes have been made in the nature of the remuneration offered to councillors. Formerly, councillors were entitled to travel and subsistence expenses plus either a taxable attendance allowance or a loss-of-earnings allowance to compensate them for work income lost as a result of attendance at council and committee meetings. However, there were allegations that this system of remuneration encouraged councillors to call and attend an excessive number of meetings so as to maximise their attendance allowance claims.

As a result of the Robinson Committee's work, leading members, such as council leaders, committee chairman and the leaders of opposition parties, are now usually entitled to receive special responsibility allowances in recognition of the increased time and energy that they must devote to their council work: it is not uncommon for council leaders and committee chairmen to be virtually full-time politicians with little or no time to earn a living apart from their income from the local authority (Maud, 1967; Robinson, 1977; Widdicombe, 1986). All their various allowances have been determined by individual councils, within set limits determined by the Secretary of State for the Environment.

The Widdicombe Committee (1986) recommended that the system should be changed to one in which all councillors would receive in effect a part-time salary. Councillors now receive a basic allowance, plus an attendance allowance and where appropriate, a special responsibility allowance. The duties for which an Attendance Allowance is payable are specified by the Secretary of State for the Environment. They are still, of course, entitled to travel and subsistence expenses in connection with their council work. The maximum total amount to be distributed to councillors in the form of allowances is determined by the Secretary of State for the Environment but the amounts actually paid, as well as the allocation of the fund between the three types of allowances, is mainly determined by each local authority. The main constraint is that between 5 and 25 per cent must be paid as special responsibility allowance to the authority's leading members. Each councillor may receive up to £8,120 in special responsibility allowance (figures up to date in 1993).

There can be no doubt that this system recognises the realities of modern local government, in which all councillors must be generous with their time and energy and where leading positions impose great demands on their holders. Nonetheless, the impact of the new system in attracting different kinds of people to council membership is likely to be limited. The sums involved are not great: for example, in 1993 the total allowance per councillor in metropolitan district councils was set at £3,000.

The parties and councillor recruitment

The political parties have an important influence on the composition of most local authorities and the conduct of their business. Indeed, the Widdicombe Committee (1986) concluded that the spread of party politics to most local authorities after reorganisation in 1972 had affected the general character of local government. The politics of most local authorities are now dominated by the debates between the major national parties. When party leaders complain to academic researchers and others about the problems they encounter in finding sufficient candidates, they do not mention that neither they nor their party members are willing simply to go into the highways and byways to recruit anyone who is willing to become a candidate. They need to be satisfied that potential councillors are diligent, loyal to the party and of sufficient intelligence to carry out their duties without bringing disgrace on their party's head.

Party members who are considered suitable to be asked to stand for the council are likely to have served a political apprenticeship lasting some time. This apprenticeship includes holding office within the party, working in elections and being 'seen and heard at meetings.' Bochel (1966) and Gordon (1979) both found that in the Labour Party the requirement that aspirant councillors serve a political apprenticeship acts as an important control over who is asked or allowed to stand for election. The apprenticeship will probably also include standing in a 'hopeless' ward before being selected for a winnable one. Similar demands are made in the Conservative Party (Dearlove, 1973; Saunders, 1979). The demands of such a political apprenticeship vary with the number of potential candidates available and may become nominal when candidates are in short supply, especially in hopeless or marginal seats. C.A. Collins (1977) has produced a useful diagram (Figure 3.1) which summarises the process aspirant councillors must go through to achieve a seat on a local authority, especially where (as is usually the case) recruitment is dominated by the Labour and Conservative Parties.

THE AMBITIONS AND MOTIVATIONS OF COUNCILLORS

Although most councillors had no idea of wanting to become local authority members when they first became political activists and indeed often have to be persuaded to allow their names to go forward (Barron, Crawley and Wood, 1991), nonetheless, once elected they often become increasingly absorbed in their local authority work. Some become frustrated and leave the council after serving for only one term, especially if they are in opposition (Corina, 1974). The remainder continue to serve, often for very long periods. However, the Widdicombe Committee (1986) found that the advent of party politics had increased councillor turnover to 30 per cent at each election and had also resulted in a decline in the average political longevity of councillors.

There have been several studies of councillor motivations and ambitions, although these were more common in the 1960s and 1970s than recently. On the basis of the research that has been carried out, councillors can be classified in terms of five different complexes of motivations. They are not exclusive: an individual councillor can and usually will be motivated by more than one of them.

The first motivation is a desire to influence a local authority's policies, either in general or, more commonly, in a specific field of its activity. Most decisions are made in local authority committees, with the full council meeting formally ratifying the committees' decisions. The committee system compels most councillors to specialise in one or two fields within the council's functions. In any case, it is common ground among researchers that very few councillors – perhaps 5 or 10 per cent – nurse a desire to influence council policy in general. Some councillors go on to the council with this intention but many – indeed the majority – are motivated primarily by their desire to help individuals in their wards. One study found that only 5 per cent of a sample of councillors sought to influence general policy, a further 20 per cent sought to do so in a specific issue area but the remaining three-quarters of councillors were mainly concerned to represent and protect the interests of

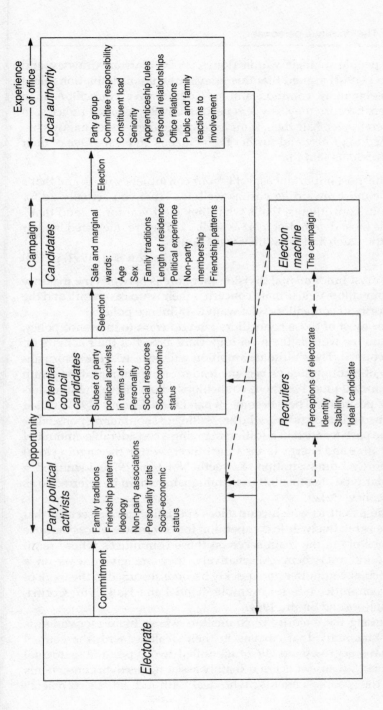

Figure 3.1 A model of councillor recruitment
Source: C.A. Collins, 'The social background and motivation of councillors', *Policy and Politics, 1977–8, 6: 444*

the people in their wards (Jones, 1973). Barron, Crawley and Wood (1991) argued that this grievance-chaser motivation might be even more common among Conservative councillors than others because they saw less need to develop council policies. In general, over half their sample of councillors were mainly concerned to protect and further their citizens' interests. One of their respondents said that:

> The most important aspect is your constituency work and that's the most rewarding part as well. It's what you actually do for your constituents, that's what they elect you for . . . and that's the most demanding part as well. . . . They're interested in their little patch and what they want done.
>
> (Barron *et al*; 1991, p. 160)

The most fundamental division therefore is between the majority of councillors whose main concern is their ward case-work and the minority of councillors who want to influence policy.

For most of those councillors who do want to influence policy, committee work is the most important aspect of their activity on the council. Their ultimate ambition will be to win the chairmanship of a committee or become leader of the council. This group will include most of those councillors who achieve these leadership positions. They become what Lewis Corina (1974) called politico-administrators, who are willing to shoulder responsibility in the party context in addition to giving a considerable amount of their time and energy to assisting officers within the ongoing local authority administration. Kenneth Newton (1976) identified a similar type of councillor in Birmingham, whom he referred to as the policy broker.

The extent to which councillors specialise can be seen in that there is relatively little competition for committee places because councillors in the main serve on those committees whose remit most interests them. Alternatively, they are given seats on a particular committee and quickly become absorbed in the work of that committee (see for example Blondel and Hall, 1967; Corina, 1974; Rees and Smith, 1964).

Among the majority of councillors whose main motivation is assisting individual citizens in their dealings with the council bureaucracy, Newton (1976) identified two types: the 'parochial member', whose concern is mainly assisting his own constituents and the 'people's agents', who deal with individuals' problems but on a city-wide basis. This motivation is especially common among female councillors (Rees and Smith, 1964). It means that these councillors will be most concerned to sit on those committees that deal with the provision of housing, social services and education, for example. Other more policy-orientated committees, such as planning, finance and even policy and resources, are likely to be less attractive to them (Maud, 1967, Volume 1, p. 35).

A third motivation is found among working-class councillors who failed to realise their intellectual potential during their education and therefore have jobs which they find insufficiently interesting or demanding. For such people, service on a local authority provides an alternative route to self-fulfilment, especially if they achieve a position of responsibility such as a committee chairmanship. Rees and Smith's account of this motivation cannot easily be bettered. A councillor who becomes a committee chairman obtains 'a most challenging and rewarding job' which:

> approximates to a senior management position in a medium-sized company. Almost all the Labour councillors in Barking (and probably most councillors in most authorities for that matter) have unexciting occupations with limited prospects. In contrast, membership of a council offers a worthwhile 'career'. The councillor meets people with similar interests to himself, he can play a part in taking important decisions affecting the lives of many thousands and in time he can play a leading role in such deliberations. For people with intelligence and ambition who find little satisfaction in their everyday jobs, council work provides an excellent outlet for their talents.
>
> (Rees and Smith, 1964, pp. 78–79)

The Maud Committee's survey of councillors made a similar point and demonstrated that it was more common among working-class councillors than their colleagues who were managers and professional men:

> Younger councillors in interesting and progressive jobs see council work as a kind of supplement in their lives, middle-aged councillors in more routine and undemanding jobs may see it as *compensation* and retired councillors may see it as a *substitute* (for work).
>
> (Maud, 1967, Volume 2, p. 163)

Councillors of all ages may use council service to express or develop their personalities and abilities but councillors from different age groups and backgrounds will do so in different ways.

These first three groups of motivations could all be said to redound to the credit of those members who are inspired by them; this might be less so of the final two, although there is nothing innately discreditable about either of them. Both relate to social satisfactions rather than a desire to influence policy or contribute in other ways to the work of the local authority.

For some councillors, the council becomes the centre of their social lives. The Maud Committee's survey (1967, Volume 2, p. 38) contains some wry descriptions of such members. One clerk 'wrote reproachfully of members who have no wish to go home' while a chief officer said that his council was 'a bit of a club for members. They actually seemed to like those interminable discussions'. Rees and Smith (1964, p. 79) concluded their chapter on councillor motivation that 'The Town Hall is the best club in Barking'. For many members of the council and especially for its controlling Labour group, the council had become their reference group. They had come to value their relations with their fellow councillors and to prize whatever esteem they had won in their colleagues' eyes. While most councillors enjoy the social life their local authority service brings, such a motivation will not necessarily ensure that a councillor will make a major contribution to policy-making, although he or she will be a regular attender at meetings, diligent in case-work and a loyal supporter of the party leadership.

The last motivation raises the question of whether and how much councillors see their local authority membership as conferring status on them. Most councillors are sceptical about their standing in the local community; the one who said that people who passed him on the street were likely to say 'There's that bloody twister Bill Blank. He's on the council. I wonder what he's on there for?' is probably typical (Rees and Smith, 1964, p. 78). However, it may sometimes be that councillor service and especially the ceremonial forms associated therewith, sometimes provides a much-needed boost to a member's self-esteem. Robert Baxter wrote of the unskilled workers, many of Irish descent, who made up the bulk of the Labour group on Liverpool City Council in the 1950s and 1960s, that:

A man may go on a council to do something, he may also go on to be someone. Membership of a council carries with it some social prestige but possibly more important is the prestige it brings to a councillor in his own eyes – the satisfaction of feeling important.

(Baxter, 1972, p. 106)

He argued that such men, not interested in policy but cherishing minor and perhaps less minor civic offices, such as committee chairmanships or seats on the aldermanic bench, formed the basis of support for autocratic leadership within the Liverpool Labour Group, since they would support through thick and thin a leader who could guarantee their continuance in their offices.

It follows from the range of their motivations that councillors for whom different motives for service are uppermost will have different opinions about policy and power within their authorities. A major interest in and concern about policy is the prerogative of a minority on most councils but that minority is likely to include most of the council's most powerful figures. Corina (1974) classified only thirteen of sixty councillors in Halifax as 'politico-administrators' and Newton (1976) classified thirteen of the sixty-six members he interviewed in Birmingham as 'policy brokers'. The Maud Committee observed that 'few members appeared to see themselves as policy-makers – only three or four of all the members, it was said, even is some quite large authorities' (Maud, 1967, Volume 2, p. 40). The remainder are content with lesser roles on committees, with helping their constituents and occasionally taking part in debates in the chamber. In consequence, perceptions of the relative power of leading individuals may differ, depending whether the question is power in general terms or in the context of a specific committee or issue area. In general terms, power may be perceived as being located in the hands of a small group of leading members, who are likely to be Corina's 'politico-administrators' or Newton's 'policy brokers'. However, in terms of specific issue-areas perceptions of power are likely to be dispersed, with committee chairmen and other senior members of each committee being perceived as powerful within their own specialities (Blondel and Hall, 1967).

COUNCILLORS AND THEIR PARTIES

The Widdicombe Committee (1986) argued that because most local authorities had become dominated by the political parties since reorganisation in 1974, their character had been significantly changed. The power structures and processes of the national parties largely determine the location of power within local authorities, as well as influencing the nature of local politics throughout the country. The number of councillors sitting as Independents has been greatly reduced, although there were still over 2,000 Independents sitting after the 1987 elections and over 10 per cent of councils were Independent-controlled (Gyford, Leach and Game, 1989, pp. 29f). Also, the proportion of seats which are filled without a contest fell dramatically. In Devon, fifty-nine out of seventy-five county councillors were returned unopposed in the last elections before reorganisation but in 1973, all ninety-eight seats on the new council were contested (Stanyer, 1976, pp. 63–64). Nationally, the 55 per cent of English county council seats which were uncontested before reorganisation fell by nearly three-quarters afterwards (Gyford, Leach and Game, 1989, p. 42).

The development of party politics

Organised and disciplined party politics in local government was originally the creation of the Labour Party. From its early days, Labour members on local councils as well as in the House of Commons have been expected to act in concert to promote the party's programme. In 1929, the Labour Party Conference adopted a set of model Standing Orders for Labour Groups on Local Authorities which still provide the basis for the rules of almost all such groups. They regulate relations between the group and the outside Labour Party organisation, provide for the election of group officers and an executive committee and most important in the present context, they forbid a Labour group member from speaking or failing to vote for a decision taken by majority vote at a Labour group meeting, unless they are permitted to abstain on grounds of conscience or a free vote is allowed on a particular issue. Some Labour groups have interpreted this standing order to mean that members are permitted a free vote unless the group decides to apply the whip on a particular issue, although this 'loose' inter-pretation is rare (Bulpitt, 1967). Most Labour councillors most of the time act in public as members of solid and disciplined groups, speaking and voting *en bloc* in support of their agreed policies.

The advent of these disciplined Labour groups on local auth-orities in the 1920s and 1930s led to the increased unification of other councillors in their own organised groups to resist the advancing Labour tide. In nearly all cases, such local groupings have now become Conservative groups although some local parties survived up to reorganisation in 1973 (see Bulpitt, 1967 and L.J. Sharpe (ed.), 1967). The 1974 reorganisation led to the spread of party politics to most (but not all) local authorities because rural areas which had escaped party domination were merged with towns and cities which had highly developed party machines.

The varying politics of local authorities

The nature of party politics in a particular local authority depends on a range of factors (Greenwood *et al.*, 1978). One is the security or otherwise with which one party controls the council. J.G. Bulpitt (1967) found that where one-party control was secure, as in Salford, the opposition was treated with scant courtesy: Labour councillors in Salford treated their Conservative opponents with 'ill-concealed contempt' (Bulpitt, 1967, p. 43). Where party control changes hands more or less regularly, as was the case in Manchester, party discipline is looser and party divisions are less general (ibid., Chapter 3). In Birmingham, Newton found a similar bipartisan approach on all but the most controversial issues in a city where control of the council tended to change fairly regularly. The opposition will be treated with greater consideration, in the expectation that when they obtain control they will reciprocate, or that they will grant support to a ruling party with a narrow majority at times of need. When Labour won control of Humberside County Council with an overall majority of only three in 1973, the Humberside Labour Group made its position more secure by being conciliatory towards the Liberal and Independent councillors, so gaining their support in some crucial votes in the chamber (Elcock, 1975).

The politics of 'hung' councils

Where no party has overall control, the outcome of debates will be uncertain and unpredictable. Small groups of Independent or minority party councillors hold the balance of power and their support will therefore be crucially important to both major parties. The consequence may be loose party discipline and an absence of much in the way of formal party organisation within the council chamber, since seldom can one party determine the result of votes there. This was the position Bulpitt found in Rochdale (1967, Chapter 4). Also decisions reached in committees will sometimes be overturned at the full Council meeting because of shifting political allegiances or divisions within the party groups. Thus Stuart Haywood (1977) reported of an Independent-controlled council that its policy and resources committee failed because the council lacked 'a group of members who can command a vicarious loyalty from colleagues' and because the committee failed to make 'an acknowledged and clearly understood contribution to the work of the council' (Haywood, 1977, p. 47). Decisions had to be taken on the basis of whatever alliances formed at the committees and the full council meeting: for instance an agreement to establish a gypsy site in a particular location which had been discussed with the county council, was 'decisively rejected by the councillors' (ibid., p. 52). Policy outcomes could not be guaranteed, either to officers or to the outside world, until the full council had met.

Equally, Andrew Blowers (1977) reported of Bedfordshire County Council that decisions could be reached only through 'a long process of negotiation among the parties' and 'at each stage the outcome could be uncertain and there were numerous instances of policies approved by committees being rejected by council or of conflicting recommendations by programme committees and the policy and resources committee which reflected different political values' (Blowers, 1977, p. 309). His view was that this resulted in council policy often being determined by the officers because councillors could not control the bureaucracy effectively.

The question of how to manage authorities where no one party has overall control has became more acute in the 1980s and 1990s, because an increasing number of local authorities, especially county councils, have become 'hung' in this period, with Liberal or Liberal Democrat councillors holding the balance of power between the two main parties. The absence of a controlling party can lead to considerable instability in decision-making, or to inertia because no decisions can be taken because no-one can command a majority in the council chamber (Blowers, 1977; Parkinson, 1985). This phenomenon has also emerged in studies of the budgetary processes of 'hung' councils.

In Liverpool City Council between 1974 and 1981, the outcome of the budget debate could not be predicted each year because the

Liberals held the balance of power and repeatedly used it to force compromises between Labour and Conservative views about spending and rate levels. In 1979, 1980 and 1983 two full council meetings were needed before a rate could be struck after deals had been done between the Liberals and other parties. When Labour gained control of the council in 1983, they argued that a rapid increase in spending was needed because the city's local services had become severely deficient because of Liberal-imposed spending cuts. This demand for increased spending was to result in a widely publicised clash with the Thatcher Government in 1985 and 1986 (Parkinson, 1985, 1987). However, studies of the budgetary processes in the 'hung' county councils of Avon and Lancashire indicated that the impact of bargains struck between the Liberals and the Labour Party had little effect on the councils' expenditure levels, changes being largely confined to making marginal changes in the levels of the councils' balances and rate levels (Barlow, 1987; Clements, 1987).

Alternatively, the Liberals or another minority party can agree to support one major party in office as a minority administration, in exchange for policy concessions, influence over policy or holding some offices, such as committee chairmanships (Barlow, 1987; Clements, 1987; Leach and Stewart, 1988). In these circumstances, rules or conventions may need to be prepared to enable the council's business to proceed smoothly and so that all actors within the council can be reasonably certain what decisions are likely to be accepted and how they are likely to be made (Barlow; 1987; Leach and Stewart, 1988; Widdicombe, 1986).

Leach and Stewart (1988) identified a range of procedures in councils where no one party has overall control. In some, partisanship is at a low level and consensus rules. In others, parties form a joint administration or, most commonly, the third party agrees to support a minority administration. Sometimes one party controls precisely half the council seats and may control the council through cross-party agreement or the mayor's casting vote, as was the case when Bradford City Council was Conservative-controlled in the late 1980s. If there is no administration, decision-making becomes unstable and committee chairmanships are likely to be filled on a rotating basis. The approach adopted will depend in part on whether the parties regard the lack of overall control as a temporary phenomenon or a long term reality. Where no party is able to control the council and hence determine its policies, the power of officers is likely to become considerable. The chief executive may play a crucial role in brokering an agreement among the parties on how to conduct the council's business (Widdicombe, 1986; Barlow, 1987).

Party policy and the role of the manifesto

Another issue to which party politics gives rise is the extent to which parties determine policy within the council and its committees, rather than serving as a vehicle for procuring the election of the party's councillors. At one extreme, in A.H. Birch's (1958) account of politics in Glossop in the 1950s, the parties functioned mainly as social organisations, played a marginal part in organising municipal elections and recruiting candidates to the council but they were of no significance in determining votes in committees or the council chamber. Again, Leach and Stewart (1988) identified councils where the level of partisanship is low and therefore the influence of parties on council policy is minimal. These authorities are likely to be found in rural areas. At the other extreme we might take Liverpool in the 1980s, where policy was determined by a small group of leading Labour councillors, led in practice but not in form by the deputy leader of the council, Derek Hatton. In this case, leading councillors with a new, Left-wing ideological orientation used the formal and even more the informal structures of a council with a long tradition of 'boss' politics to dominate policy-making (Baxter, 1972; Parkinson, 1985).

Between these extremes lie the bulk of local authorities, although research for the Widdicombe Committee revealed that party manifestos are not only being produced more commonly; they also serve as policy guides after election victories (Gyford, Leach and Game, 1989, pp. 107ff). Of councillors interviewed for the Widdicombe Committee 52 per cent said that implementing the manifesto should be councillors' 'first concern' after an election (ibid., p. 171). However, in many authorities, the manifestos are still largely forgotten after the election has been won or lost.

In developed party organisations, considerable time and effort may be put into preparing the manifesto. In the Labour Party, the local party organisation is responsible for preparing the election manifesto on which its candidates, including sitting councillors, must fight the election. It also prepares panels of approved candidates and oversees the selection process. Finally, the party organisation is entitled to send representatives to the party group meetings, at which they have speaking but not voting rights.

Leaders and followers: the Labour Party

The extent of freedom and discussion within council Labour groups varies quite widely; the party is not the disciplined monolith that is sometimes thought and in some groups a great deal of vigorous debate takes place before major decisions are taken. Victor Wiseman (1963) described the Labour group on Leeds City Council as having a tradition of vigorous debate. It also kept a wary eye on its leading figures in order to ensure that they did not become to powerful and arrogant: 'When a chairman begins to talk of "my committee" he should be watched with suspicion' (Wiseman, 1963, p. 137). The group elected an advisory committee (the Leodensian term for an executive committee) which manages the group's affairs between meetings and makes recommendations to the full group on matters coming before it. This advisory group contained the most senior and influential figures in the Labour group and therefore commanded a great deal of authority but an action or recommendation which is not acceptable to the full group would be rejected by it, as would a recommendation from a committee which was not acceptable, although this could cause considerable embarrassment to the committee chairman concerned, who would, in consequence, have to withdraw the offending minute at the meeting of the full council.

This group was clearly determined to keep its leading figures in check but in other cities this has not always been so. Liverpool has a long tradition of autocratic leadership in local politics, which is common to all the major parties on Liverpool City Council. When Alderman Jack Braddock was leader, there was no executive committee, Model Standing Orders notwithstanding and policy was made largely by Braddock himself, his deputy and the chief whip. This triumvirate also assumed responsibility for the allocation of committee seats, chairmanships and vice-chairmanships. Similarly dominant leadership existed in other Labour-controlled cities such as Hull, Sheffield and Birmingham, although Liverpool was always an extreme case (Jones and Norton (eds), 1979). Alan Norton has shown that the extent to which councillors are willing to delegate their powers to their leaders varies from one authority to another: he postulates 'a continuum between leaders who accept they are instrumental to the achievement of the Group policy and leaders who see Group policy as instrumental to their personal policy aims' (ibid., 1979, p. 216). Some leaders are more autocratic than others. This may be determined at least in part by the social origins of the members of the ruling group, which also influences their motivations for council service. In consequence, the power structure of the council is indirectly influenced by the social structure of the community (Elcock, 1981). Generally, Norton suggests that 'members have recently become less willing to contract out their power to the strong leader' (Jones and Norton, 1979, p. 221). One reason for this may be the arrival of more middle-class councillors, especially in the former county boroughs, where those persons who were employed by the only local authority in the area, such as teachers and lecturers, could not serve on the council because they were its employees. From 1974, when a two-tier system was introduced throughout the country, they could serve on whichever authority was not their employer.

This phenomenon also led to the controversial practice of 'twin tracking', whereby an officer of one council could serve on a member of a neighbouring council (Widdicombe, 1986). In consequence, most senior local government officers are now barred from council membership under the Local Government and Housing Act of 1989, which bars most staff earning over £23,733 from political activity. Chief officers, their deputies and other officers who report directly to the chief officer are excluded from political activity completely. Other officers who earn over £23,733 plus those who regularly advise councillors, are also excluded but can appeal against their exclusion.

Leaders and followers: the Conservative Party

Less work has been done on the structure of power in the Conservative Party. In rural areas authority has largely been vested in traditional leaders by councils which were dominated by Independents (J.M. Lee, 1963). Alan Norton wrote that 'traditional forms of deference are apparent in these counties. Leadership is a manifestation of the traditional community – a community still meaningful in terms of face to face relationships'. Council leaders would often be major landowners and their offices would almost be inherited with major estates (Jones and Norton, 1979; see also Holtby, 1936). In the towns, Conservative leaders have tended to be businessmen, shopkeepers or professional men with a more aggressive and competitive approach to politics. With the merging of town and country in the 1974 reorganisation, these men have tended to displace the landed gentry in most Conservative groups and Independent councillors have often had to accept the Conservative whip or face a Conservative opponent at the next election.

The Conservative Party tends to apply the whip to its councillors rather less freely than the Labour Party, more often allowing free votes in the chamber except when majorities are narrow. Disciplined Labour politics has forced the Conservatives to become more disciplined too, often to the regret of those Conservative councillors who formerly served as Independents.

One major study of a Conservative-controlled local authority was John Dearlove's study of the Royal Borough of Kensington and Chelsea (Dearlove, 1973). He found that the leader of the council and the committee chairmen were allowed very considerable powers by their colleagues. Equally, junior Conservative councillors were expected to know their places and not be too vociferous at committee meetings or in the council chamber until they had acquired sufficient experience: six months to speak in a committee and a year for the chamber was the norm. As in Labour-controlled authorities, councillors were expected to concentrate on one or two fields of the council's activities, to be assiduous in attending meetings and reading their committee papers and give loyal support to the party.

On the other hand, there were powerful mechanisms within the group to prevent any individual becoming too powerful. Committee chairmen can hold office for only two years and although this Group Standing Order is sometimes broken, it ensures a high turnover of committee chairmen compared to many other authorities. A chairman is usually replaced at the end of his two-year term of office by his deputy. There is also a hierarchy of chairmanships: a member must usually serve as vice-chairman and then chairman of a 'non-political' committee before he can expect to hold the same offices on a major committee, such as housing, town planning or works.

The leader of the Conservative Party enjoys great power. In the Conservative Party it is still common practice for the leader to serve also as the chairman of the party group – a practice which is officially discouraged in the Labour Party because it is felt that leaders who occupy both offices can arrogate too much power to themselves. In Croydon, another Conservative-controlled council, Saunders (1979) found that power was concentrated in the hands of a small 'political elite' composed of the seven members of the policy sub-committee – 'The Tory caucus with the Town Clerk there' (Saunders, p. 219). The committee chairmen enjoy considerable delegated powers but they are subject to a considerable measure of control by the policy sub-committee, through the budget and the need to obtain the approval of decisions by the finance and policy committee.

The concentration of power in the Conservative Party is related to the nature of leadership within it, at both the local and national levels. The leader is the embodiment of the party's policy and if the party is dissatisfied with the policies being followed, the ultimate means to change those policies is to dismiss the leader rather than attempt to challenge individual policies by resolution, as is common practice in the Labour Party. Robert McKenzie described national leadership within the Conservative Party as follows: 'When appointed, the Leader leads and the party follows, except when the party decides not to follow; then the Leader ceases to be Leader' (McKenzie, 1963, p. 63). A similar phenomenon existed in Kensington and Chelsea: one committee chairman told Dearlove that 'the only way one can stop the Leader marching too far ahead, short of a friendly chat and raising it at one or two party meetings, is to raise a censure motion' (ibid., 1963, p. 139). A former Conservative leader of Leeds City Council, when asked what members of his group would do if they were dissatisfied with council policy, responded, 'I suppose they would have to get rid of me'. The notion that the Leader is the custodian of Conservative policy thus operates in local as well as national politics, with its corollary that a change in policy entails a change of leader. There is a general tendency for council leaders to become full-time politicians, employing policy advisers and research assistants. To this extent they have become in effect local prime ministers (Cousins, 1984). The Widdicombe Committee also remarked on the increasing tendency for local authorities to employ political assistants for their leaders and recommended some curbs to restrict the possibility of nepotism and malpractice (Widdicombe, 1986).

Leadership and corporate management

The effect of efforts to centralise control over local authorities' policies and management, which form part of the movement towards corporate management discussed in Chapter 9, has further increased the importance of the leader of the council and other senior offices. The advent of party control in most local authorities has led to the formal establishment of the office of leader of the council (Cousins, 1984). He or she will chair the council's policy and resources committee and may become an increasingly dominant figure if the authority develops a 'governmental' view of the extent of its responsibilities. This dominance will be reinforced if the leader works closely with the chief executive officer, who similarly has a responsibility to co-ordinate the authority's management and the development of policy advice for its senior members. Over 90 per cent of authorities reported to the Widdicombe Committee that leaders and chief executives met to discuss policy and other matters at least once a week (Gyford, Leach and Game, 1989, p. 210). The Widdicombe Committee (1986) recommended that more equality of access to the chief executive and other senior officers, as well as the right to appoint research staff, should be extended to the leaders of opposition parties, but saw no reason to challenge the development of close liaisons between leaders and chief executive officers. This liaison was also identified as important to as well-managed local authority by Leach (1993).

More controversial is the relationship between the party groups and their executive committees with senior officers. It has become increasingly common practice for chief executives and other senior officers to be asked to advise party meetings, despite a general prohibition in their terms of conditions of employment against their doing so. Again, the Widdicombe Committee did not recommend the cessation of this practice, although it did note that officer briefings should be made available to all party groups, not just the controlling group.

It is also likely that corporate management has had the effect of strengthening the party executive committee, as well as other groups of leading councillors, because the party executives will usually meet to decide the line that is to be taken at the ensuing Policy and Resources Committee meeting. We shall see many examples of this later; here we need to note that it is another pressure leading towards the concentration of control in the hands of small groups of leading councillors.

This has led to suggestions that British local authorities should move towards the creation of a directly elected chief political executive figure, along the lines of the American 'Strong Mayor' or the South German *Burgermeister* (Gyford, Leach and Game, 1989, pp. 224–225; Lavery, 1992; Stoker and Wolman, 1992). In 1991, the Secretary of State for the Environment, Michael Heseltine, briefly suggested that such an office might be introduced into British local government but he quickly dropped the notion. Equally, the Government has not adopted the Widdicombe Committee's recommendation that the role and powers of the chief executive officer should be strengthened. Nonetheless, the nature of political and executive leadership in British local authorities is likely to be raised as an issue in the future.

IDEOLOGIES IN LOCAL POLITICS

Ideology has traditionally not been the most significant influence on the politics of local government, partly because many councillors are almost entirely preoccupied with their ward cases and local problems. The major policy battles over housing, education and other matters of political dispute tend to be fought at the national rather than the local level, with local politicians acting as spokespersons for their national party headquarters. Major changes in the management of local authorities, such as compulsory competitive tendering or the local management of schools, have equally been imposed from Whitehall, often through binding legislation and local authorities have no choice but to implement them. However, there is a common ideological cleavage, which is common to local politics on both sides of the Atlantic and concerns differences in attitudes towards local taxation and the provision of local services. Edward C. Banfield and James Q. Wilson (1966) described the ideologies of American city politics as being based upon two different views about what the local public interest is, related to the social classes and the parts of the city from which each party draws its electoral support:

> The first, which derives from the middle class ethos, favours . . .
> efficiency, impartiality, honesty, planning, strong executives,
> no favouritism, strong legal codes and strict enforcement of the

laws against gambling and vice. The other conception of the public interest . . . derives from the 'immigrant ethos'. This is the conception of those people who identify with the ward or neighbourhood rather than the city 'as a whole', who look for politicians for 'help' or 'favours', who regard gambling and vice as at worst, necessary evils and who are far less interested in the efficiency, impartiality and honesty of local government than in its readiness to confer benefits of one sort or another upon them. In the largest, most heterogeneous of our cities, the two mentalities stand forth as distinctly as did those which in another context, caused Disraeli to write of 'The Two Nations'.

(Banfield and Wilson, 1966, p 46)

The first view is characteristic of white, middle-class suburbanites and the Republican Party. The second is that of poor working-class inner-city dwellers, ethnic minorities and the Democratic Party.

In British local government similarly, Conservatives argue that local authorities' tax demands should be kept as low as possible, that councils should confine themselves to meeting their statutory obligations and to the support of voluntary groups and a few worthy causes. Local government should be apolitical ('keep politics out of local government') and the chief officers should be left to run the authority free of interference from members except when their decisions or activities are manifestly unacceptable to them or their constituents. Many Conservative councillors would concur with the Republican attitude described by Banfield and Wilson, that 'cleaning streets, running schools and collecting garbage ought to be no more controversial and therefore no more political, than selling groceries' (Banfield and Wilson, 1966, p. 20). To this can be added a belief that private sector management produces greater efficiency than public services can ever offer. Hence, wherever possible, services should be contracted out to the private sector and where this is not possible, private sector management methods should be adopted within the authority's own departments. Much of this approach to management is presented in apolitical terms which are to some extent a cover for an ideological commitment to the private as opposed to the public provision of services. Conservative councillors also argue that, where possible, individual citizens should be responsible for making their own provision for services and support, instead of relying on the local authority to provide them. John Gyford (1991) has characterised this approach as trying to convert local voters into local shareholders.

Councillors in the Labour Party, by contrast, generally believe that services must be provided for all who need them; that expenditure to help the needy, the disabled and the old, as well as to provide education, must be undertaken by the council and if this means increasing local taxation more than would otherwise be necessary, then so be it. Few Labour councillors have any very grandiose socialist *Weltanschauung* but most believe that increased expenditure on local services is necessary to help the poor and the disadvantaged as well as to protect citizens from exploitation by industry and commerce. Value for money should still be sought but not by the simple expedient of parsimony, which may result in mistaking economy for efficiency.

A strong commitment to developing equal opportunities for women, ethnic minorities and other groups such as gay people, has been characteristic of many Labour-controlled local authorities since the 1980s. The propensity of Labour-controlled local authorities to give financial support to organisations which are seeking to help or support minority groups, as well as a strong emphasis on changing attitudes and language in the interest of equal opportunities, has provoked widespread attacks on the so-called 'loony Left', especially in the tabloid press. However, the rise of the 'new urban Left' (Gyford, 1984) has produced a series of new policies, especially in the fields of equal opportunities and economic development but not a coherent new socialist ideology.

A further reason for attacks on Labour-controlled councils, both by their Conservative opponents and in the press, is that Labour councillors tend to hold more frequent council and committee meetings than do Conservative-controlled local authorities. This is because Labour councillors feel a greater need to ensure that the officers implement the policies they have laid down, through the election manifesto and the decisions they make in the Labour group. Committee chairmen and vice-chairmen should be in constant contact with their senior officers because some of them may not otherwise carry out Labour policies to the full. This in turn has led to Conservative accusations that Labour councillors call meetings simply to bump up their incomes from attendance allowances. The Widdicombe Committee (1986) found such accusations to be largely not proven but as we have seen, the Committee recommended a system of payment for councillors which does not produce increases in income with attendance at more meetings, recommendations that the Government has now adopted.

The Labour Party's electoral support is heavily concentrated in inner-city areas and council house estates. Labour supporters are thus in the main those people who are most dependent on central or local government for schools housing, help when in need, advice and other forms of assistance from the local authority. Labour councillors respond to these needs and demands, while Conservative councillors in the main represent people who are better able to help themselves and who resent the demands made on them by the poorer sections of society.

Political conflict in local government is essentially, therefore, between the representatives of those who are in most need of local authority services and who tend to bear only a relatively small proportion of the local tax burden, with those who bear a higher taxation burden and have less need of the services. However, it is often the case that the middle classes make more use of some local services such as libraries, cultural events, leisure centres and the provision of grants to students. They also make more use of opportunities to participate in decision-making, over such matters as planning applications and road routes. This can lead to a paradox among Conservative councillors, who will support rigorous economies in expenditure by their councils when these are couched in general terms while at the same time pressing for higher expenditure on public services in the wards they represent. They will also resist such consequences of expenditure cuts as the closure of local schools and libraries or the withdrawal of evening classes. This is not hypocrisy, although that charge is frequently levelled at Conservative councillors by their Labour opponents, but rather an instance of a conflict between the councillor's role as a policy-maker and the demand made on all British political representatives that they must protect and promote the interests of their constituents. This demand is stronger in the British political culture than in most others.

The considerable differences in the level and range of the services provided by local authorities provide many instances of the divide between Conservative and Labour beliefs. Conservatives believe in economy, minimal government intervention both in markets and in citizens' lives, together with the superiority of private over public provision. Above all, they must secure the lowest possible level of local taxation. Labour councillors, on the other hand, believe that public services are necessary for the support of the less wealthy and privileged groups in society and that they should, in the main, be provided by the public authorities. They will also favour more intervention in local markets and issues. In consequence, local taxation tends to be rather higher in Labour-controlled authorities, although increasingly Labour councils have been forced to pay more attention to increasing the efficiency of the council's departments in order to avoid their work being lost to the private sector through compulsory competitive tendering (Elcock, Fenwick and Harrop, 1988; J. Painter, 1991, Leach, 1992).

CONCLUSION

Studies of local councils and the political systems within which they operate reveal a wide range of differing political systems, whose variety has probably increased rather than diminished since local government reorganisation in 1974. At the same time, the domination of local politics by the national political parties has become general. It is a paradox that although the dominance of the national political parties has imposed an influence on local authorities which might be expected to render the conduct of their business more uniform, the reverse seems to have happened. The reasons for this will emerge later in this book.

Councillors are still largely the same kind of people as they were before reorganisation: they are still in the main white, male, middle-aged and middle class. However, they are a varied group of people who bring a wide range of knowledge and motives to service on councils. Some are anxious to develop or contribute to policy; others do not concern themselves much with this and are preoccupied with helping their constituents deal with their personal difficulties with the Council's or other public and private bureaucracies. Yet others find their principal satisfaction in the opportunities for social interaction that council service gives them.

Some councillors sit on only one local authority, others on several. It is quite possible to be a member of a parish, district and county council at the same time, although this practice is discouraged, especially in the Labour Party. because that party takes the view that multiple membership prevents a councillor doing justice to the demands each of his or her council seats makes upon him or her.

The local government councillor is constantly lampooned as a pompous fool who is concerned only with increasing his or her own importance in his or her own and other people's eyes and with making money in one way or another from council membership. Some councillors are undeniably self-important and a few are corrupt, although more efficient auditing coupled with the public exposure of corruption in some authorities act as effective deterrents to most of those who might be tempted. The Widdicombe Committee (1986) gave councillors a clean bill of health, asserting that malpractice was confined to a few individuals and authorities. Most local authority members are neither pompous nor corrupt. Their motives for service on the council vary and are not always completely creditable but generally they tend to be conscientious to a fault, especially in dealing with individual cases.

Party systems also vary widely. Some are autocratic, allowing the majority of council members little opportunity to influence policy independent of their leaders, while others adopt an open style of decision-making, under which they readily consider and accept proposals from individual members or even the opposition. Such open styles have been encouraged by the requirements to open meetings to the public and allow access to documents which were imposed by the 1986 Local Government (Access to Information) Act. Indeed, the obligations now imposed on local authorities to conduct their affairs openly are often cited as an example which the central government ought to be made to follow.

Local political systems have varying power structures, which affect the roles leaders, followers and opposition members can play in the decision-making and administrative processes of their local authorities. These political systems also influence the relationships between members and officers – the subject of the next chapter.

Chapter 4

The integrated roles of members and officers

Policy-making and management in local authorities are the responsibility of two groups of people. Councillors are elected on the basis of their party ideologies and programmes (or as individuals if they are Independents), to make the final decisions at committee and council meetings. In doing this they are advised by local government officers who have been professionally trained and who mostly hold office until they reach the statutory retirement age.

Two myths have long governed thinking about the roles of local authority members and officers and their relationships with one another. On the one hand there is the long-since discredited notion that politicians make policy and officials carry it out (Woodrow Wilson, 1887). On the other hand, there is Max Weber's (1975) thesis that the professional officers' views and influence must inevitably prevail over those of amateur politicians and therefore the dictatorship of the official is inevitable. It is frequently asserted that one view or the other should or does prevail: such simplistic statements are unrealistic. The reality of local government decision-making and management is both more varied and less clear cut than either legend suggests. It is that members and officers interact to take decisions and control the affairs of the authority. The roles of councillors and their senior officers are and must therefore be integrated.

The processes of decision-making and management in local government are determined by the characters of the senior actors among both members and officers. Councillors gain election and then attain such offices as committee chairmanships by a complex series of accidents which may or may not have any relationship to their abilities as policy-makers and managers. They join political parties, become active within them, stand for the council (often as a result of persuasion) and win a seat. Then, their advancement to a position of influence such as the chairmanship or vice-chairmanship of a committee will depend on whether a councillor retains a seat on the council for long enough to attain sufficient seniority; on the retirement, death or electoral defeat of incumbent chairmen; on the esteem or otherwise with which he or she comes to be held within the party group and on the council. Once appointed to a chairmanship or vice-chairmanship, a councillor's contact with officials will become close and frequent. He or she must learn to communicate with them and ensure that the wishes of the party group and the committee are carried out.

Officers for their part have to take care that their relationships with members, especially with chairmen and vice-chairmen, remain at the level required by their status and the ethics which control their conduct of their offices. Unlike civil servants, local authority officers are the servants of the whole council; they are not there to serve and advise only the party currently holding office. This is the reason for the prohibition in their terms and conditions of service on their being required to attend party group meetings. Where arrangements are made for them to do so, they must be voluntary (Widdicombe, 1986, para. 6:174). The Widdicombe Report (1986) defined officers' roles in terms of three functions. They must be:

- The professional *managers* of their departments, responsible for the efficient delivery of the services the council is responsible for providing.
- *Advisers* to councillors as the elected members responsible for policy, as well as for the acceptability of the council's policies and services to the public.
- *Arbitrators*, ensuring that the council's business is conducted fairly and in a proper manner. Thus the clerk or chief executive has the responsibility of advising the mayor or chairman of the council on conducting a fair and orderly meeting (Widdicombe, 1986, paragraph 6:133–135). To see how well or badly officers are equipped to carry out these three functions we need to look next at their backgrounds, training and experience.

Local government officers: recruitment, training and career structure

Traditionally the administration of local authorities has been divided into departments, each headed by a chief officer who is responsible to a committee of councillors. Before 1974, many authorities retained the traditional relationship of one department reporting to one committee but most of the present local authorities have streamlined their committee structures, with several departments reporting to a single committee (see Chapter 9). The nature of these officers has not greatly changed since reorganisation. They are in the main professionals, trained largely through working for qualifications awarded by professional associations or institutes. Some of these bodies award qualifications for use both in private practice and public service, such as the Law Society, the Institute of Civil Engineers and the Royal Institute of British Architects. Others are confined to the public sector alone, for example the Chartered Institute of Public Finance and Accountancy (CIPFA), a body which is separate from the professional associations regulating accountants in private or commercial practices. Again, town planners become qualified through membership of the Royal Town Planning Institute and most remain in public authorities, although a few become private consultants.

These professional officers have traditionally received relatively little training in public administration or management and what was available was until recently at a fairly low level. This situation is changing, with more local government officers taking Master in Business Administration (MBA) or similar courses. However, the senior local authority officer is still a professional architect, engineer, accountant, planner and so forth first and foremost and an administrator, manager or policy adviser very much second. He or she is a professional expert in his or her own field but such officers usually have little knowledge of what is involved in the specialisms of their colleagues working in other departments. Finally, like all professional experts, local government officers tend to believe that their expertise enables them to provide solutions to all the problems coming before them. They will therefore be reluctant to accept conflicting views from experts in other disciplines, or for that matter from councillors. Experts are easily persuaded that they know the correct answers and should discount rival solutions offered by members of other professions or, indeed politicians.

This highly specialised but narrow training also makes the co-ordination of proposals or actions hard to achieve. Departmentalism, or differentiation is very strong in British local government (Greenwood *et al.*, 1978). This departmentalism is reinforced by the weakness of the co-ordinating mechanisms available in local government. A basic reason for weak co-ordination is that local government, unlike the civil service, has no prestigious class of generalist administrators responsible for co-ordinating the work of the departments. In the civil service, the top officials are notoriously almost all generalist administrators (Fulton, 1968) who become preoccupied with ensuring the smooth working of the government machine and are less concerned with whether or not policies are soundly based on knowledge and expertise. The tendency among civil servants is to water down expert recommendations to the point at which all concerned can accept them and remain friends, regardless of the consequences for the quality of the policy concerned. Such an approach would be quite unacceptable to professional local government officers, who will ultimately be judged on the basis of reports put to committees and from whom clear recommendations are usually demanded by members. Their preoccupation with their own special fields means that in an issue involving several departments, officers may have difficulty in agreeing a coherent set of recommendations to present to members. Local authorities have therefore tended to 'remain in essence loose confederations of semi-autonomous empires' (T.A. Smith, 1966, p. 29) – a tendency reinforced by the preoccupation of most councillors and especially committee chairmen with the work of the committees on which they sit.

Co-ordination is made more difficult by the relatively low status accorded to administrative officers in local government. They tend to be relatively junior members of a clerk's or administration department which will usually be headed by yet another specialist professional: the council's most senior lawyer. Furthermore, until relatively recently lawyers had a virtual monopoly on the most senior officer post in a local authority: that of clerk to the council. The appointment by most local authorities since 1974 of a chief executive officer has reduced the dominance of lawyers at the top but many chief executives are still lawyers. Alan Norton (1991) found that 68 per cent of chief executives had a legal qualification.

The next most common professional background was accountancy, at 15 per cent. In any case, there is no obligation on a local authority to appoint a chief executive officer, although the Widdicombe Committee recommended that there should be.

Local government administrators can rise to become committee administrators, a role in which they do co-ordinate the departments that have to present reports to committees on particular matters. They also manage the relationship between officers and councillors, especially the crucial one between the committee chairman and his or her chief officer. Nonetheless, their status is inferior to the lawyers who are commonly located in the same department.

The result of this high level of departmentalism and weak co-ordination can be rigid policies and incoherent service provision (see Donnison, 1962). In consequence, there have been increasing pressures for changes to be made in the management of local authorities, in the recruitment and training of senior officers and for the creation of new posts such as that of chief executive officer. The first and last of these will be discussed in greater detail in Chapter 9, which deals with the development of corporate management in local government. Here we shall consider only the second issue – the recruitment, training and career patterns of local authority officers.

Until comparatively recently, relatively few university graduates chose careers in local government (T.A. Smith, 1966, p. 14; K.R. Poole, 1978, Chapter 7) but more are now doing so, to the extent that concern has sometimes been expressed by ministers and industrialists that too many highly educated people are going into the public services and not enough into industry (Bacon and Eltis, 1978). Be that as it may, the recruitment of more graduates means that officers are entering local government with a broader education than that provided where a person joins a local authority in his or her teens and then trains only for membership of a professional institute. They should therefore find it easier than their predecessors to understand the issues and problems with which other departments have to deal. Also, some of the professional institutes are encouraging the development of this wider vision by adopting new training regulations which include management or policy analysis. Also, more local government officers are taking management or public administration courses at degree or postgraduate level.

All these developments are encouraged by the Local Government Training Board (LGTB), which was set up under the Industrial Training Act of 1964, as a result of a recommendation made by the Mallaby Committee (1967). In 1992 it became the Local Government Management Board (LGMB). Since 1967 the board has supervised a wide range of training courses at universities and other centres, as well as supervising and administering the Certificate and Diploma in Municipal Administration (CMA and DMA) (Poole, 1978, pp. 157ff). In the 1980s an attempt was made to develop membership of the Institute of Chartered Secretaries and Administrators (ICSA) as a professional qualification for local authority administrators, under an agreement reached between ICSA and LGTB in 1981 (Wistrich, 1984). However, the present thrust in training for local authority officers, with which the board is intensively involved, is for the development of management courses within the contexts of the management charter initiative (MCI) and the developing national vocational qualifications (NVQ) movement.

Nonetheless, it is still often the case that professional qualifications remain the dominant goal for young local government officers; the pressure remains to become a specialist professional first and a manager or administrator second. Furthermore, cuts in training budgets are making it more difficult for local authority staff to enrol on training courses which are not a obligatory part of their career progression. Nonetheless, the need to raise the status and competence of local government administrators remains urgent, both to improve their own work and to increase their ability to secure co-ordination among the professional experts who must be brought together to advise councillors.

One development which may both increase the status of administrators and encourage better training is the obligation imposed on local authorities in 1989, as a result of the Widdicombe Report, to appoint two officers concerned with the arbitration function identified by the Widdicombe Committee. These are an identified head of the authority's paid service, who is usually the Chief Executive, and a monitoring officer whose duties are to identify possible breaches of the law by the authority and to identify possible maladministration which might give rise to a complaint to a local commissioner for administration.

As well as providing its recruits with a largely professional training which is thorough but narrow in its scope, local government rarely seeks to broaden its horizons by recruiting staff in mid-career from industry or other public bodies. If this could be done more frequently, ideas and methods from elsewhere could be introduced but superannuation regulations and rigid professional hierarchies are major obstacles to such freedom of movement. The professional institutes are also formidable obstacles to reform.

There is still an urgent need to give more officers a broader professional outlook but budgetary constraints make the necessary training difficult for councils to support. However, they can and do provide training courses for themselves, especially in the theory and practice of corporate management and planning. These courses provide authorities with a chance to 'sell' new methods of working to their employees, as well as to teach them something about the activities of departments other than their own. Not least in importance is the chance to meet and confer with colleagues from other departments. The most common point at which such training is provided is during the induction process shortly after an officer is recruited but ideally it should be made available fairly frequently throughout an officer's career. In recent years, demand from local authorities and their staff for training in how to improve consumer relations has become more popular as local authorities have developed new approaches to getting closer to their customers (LGTB, 1987; Fenwick and Harrop, 1989; Hague, 1988; Gyford, 1991).

Finally, career planning and expectations are important influences on the local government officer's approach to his or her job. Traditionally, the highest point to which most local government officers aspire is to become chief officers in their own professions, in charge of a department and responsible for it to a committee and its chairman. In order to achieve this goal, an officer will serve in a series of successively more senior posts in several local authorities, probably in different parts of the country. His or her career progression is thus a process of professional advancement in which the successful officer's identification with a particular authority is likely to be relatively short term. Officers at the top of their professions may then hope to become chief executive officers, although we have seen that a career in local government law is still the most likely route to this most senior of posts.

Attempts to introduce senior managers from outside local government have not met with great success; such persons and their local authority employers have usually parted company after only a few years. An early experiment with a city manager in

Newcastle upon Tyne failed when the experiment's principal sponsor, Councillor T. Dan Smith, left the leadership of the council to undertake another public office. In consequence, the post withered on the vine and its holder, a former Ford Motor Company executive, moved back into industry after a few years. He was replaced by the city treasurer (Elliott, 1971). The main point is that the professions still dominate the local government world. Not only does this make co-ordination difficult; it also inhibits the development of a common loyalty to the local government service of the kind which is, by contrast, a central feature of the civil servant's approach to policy-making (Sisson, 1959).

Decision-making processes: the interaction of members and officers

The role of the local government officer can be explored in greater detail by examining the processes by which local government services are managed and decisions about them made. In so doing, we can look in greater detail at the three officer functions identified by the Widdicombe Committee: policy advice, management and arbitration Since local authority services are provided by departments staffed largely by specialists, co-ordination tends to be difficult; departments have traditionally remained largely independent one from another. Modern pressures for better co-ordination and the more efficient use of increasingly scarce resources have in turn led to the introduction of new working methods, as well as new offices. The chief executive officer of a local authority is expected to undertake much of this co-ordination himself. In particular, he or she acts as the chairman of a management team or chief officers' meeting, whose main function is to agree proposals and recommendations for submission to the council, or policy and resources committee. The chief officers are expected to support such agreed proposals when they are discussed in the authority's committees and at the policy and resources committee meeting. The chief executive for his part must take care to ensure that they are acceptable to all the officers involved. These co-ordinating functions may have been strengthened by the designation now required by law of a head of the authority's paid service and of a monitoring officer with essentially arbitration functions. Management teams and chief officers' meetings may assist in improving co-ordination but they may also reduce the influence of councillors because advice agreed among and supported by an array of professional officers is even more difficult for members to challenge or reject than the advice of a single senior officer acting alone. On the other hand, securing such a common front may be difficult among officers whose professional standpoints and departmental interests will frequently differ.

Management team meetings may equally encourage officers to believe that theirs is the dominant role in the decision-making process. Stanley Blaydon, the leader of a metropolitan borough council, recalled in the *Municipal Review* (Blaydon, 1974) an occasion when he and his party colleagues met to determine their policy before a meeting of the authority's policy and resources committee. We have seen that this is a common procedure in authorities which are controlled by a party group but 'Our Chief Executive, seeing the paper minuting our decisions as he sat down, immediately insisted that these decisions were really only requests to the management team for a report and recommendations on the topics concerned'. Such experiences do not seem to be common but Blaydon's article does draw attention to the need for councillors not to be squeezed out of their rightful place in the decision-making process by officers, acting either individually or collectively in management teams. It is admittedly a brave lay person who will challenge a consensus arrived at by experienced professional officers but councillors must and in practice often do so. Their ability to do so is stronger where they have served on their committees for long periods and have hence gained knowledge through gaining long experience of the issues coming before the council and its committees.

The interaction between councillors and officers is central to democratic local government. On the one hand, stories abound among local government officers of strong committee chairmen and dictatorial party groups, while for their part many councillors suspect their officers of trying to get their way by using members as rubber stamps for their own decisions. Kenneth Newton interviewed members of Birmingham City Council and obtained from them a list of eleven tactics allegedly used by officers to get their way in spite or in default of instructions from members sitting on committees. He quoted one councillor's somewhat embittered comments about the officers' reports to committees as an example of an attitude common among members:

It is a subtle blend of bullshit and flannel and making sure that things go their way. And writing reports. Report writing, I would say, is the most important part of their job. They put out so many reports that you get swamped by it. You can't read it . . . It's all protective confetti for the officers.

(Newton, 1976, pp. 156–167, see also Corina, 1975)

If members are to avoid being thus overburdened and perhaps bamboozled, they must learn as much as they can about the subjects which come before their committees, carefully reading and scrutinising the papers they are sent in connection with committee and council meetings. Councillors are part-timers and they usually lack specialist expertise, so that they often have difficulty in dealing with the large volume of reports that come their way. Many of them remain members of their authorities and the same committees for long periods of time, however, and this enables them to acquire considerable knowledge of the services for which they are responsible and to learn to cope with the flood of paper that constantly flows through every councillor's letterbox. Newton (1976) found in Birmingham that it was normal for members to sit on the same committees for ten or fifteen years. The Widdicombe Committee (1986) found that councillors spend on average eighteen hours per month preparing for meetings and twenty-one hours per month attending them – hence preparation took almost as much time as attending council deliberations (see Gyford, Leach and Game, 1989, p. 62). Again, while many councillors have only limited formal education, many of them are men and women whose talents have not been fully developed or utilised in their working lives. These talents are developed by local government experience and many such members become effective at challenging officers' recommendations (Rees and Smith, 1964; Maud Committee, 1967). Lastly, some councillors are able to bring academic or professional knowledge and skills to their local authority service. For all these reasons, a local authority is likely to include among its members many who are capable of reading and understanding the officers' reports and challenging their conclusions when they see fit to do so.

One source of tension between members and officers arises from differences between what councillors regard as important and the professional concerns of their officers. Members usually attach considerable importance to obtaining help or redress for their constituents who have appealed to them or complained about some action or inaction of the council. Officers by contrast may be reluctant to make exceptions to established policies or procedures, for fear of stimulating further similar demands which they will be unable to meet. This highway engineers frequently come under pressure to abandon or modify long-term plans for new or improved roads in order that properties on or near the line of the proposed road do not lose their value and become unsaleable because of the road plan. The engineers tend to resist such pressures when they come from councillors on the ground that if the road line is not protected, development will take place along it and if the road ultimately becomes a necessity, comparatively new properties may have to be demolished in order to build it. This will not only involve the council in paying heavy compensation to the owners of the demolished buildings but will also give rise to a public outcry about the short-sightedness of the local authority in allowing development along the road line to go ahead, resulting in the wasteful demolition of new property. Councillors who respond to immediate electoral or political pressure therefore come into conflict with officers whose professional responsibilities require them to take a longer-term view of the issue. Apart from constituency pressures, of course, councillors come under pressure from colleagues and members of their parties as well as from pressure groups in such situations, the result of all of which is to generate tension and sometimes conflict between them and their officers.

Committee chairmen and chief officers

In these exchanges and conflicts between members and officers, through which both seek to influence the views, values and actions of the others in taking decisions and setting policy, the roles of committee chairmen and vice-chairmen are particularly important. Their importance has increased as party control of local authorities has become general, because committee chairmen and their deputies become the controlling party's leading spokespersons on the remits of their committees. Thus their roles become more akin to those of ministers, not only because they are the senior spokespersons on particular subjects but also because powers are delegated to them to take routine decisions between committee meetings, although these must be reported to the committee at its next meeting. The Widdicombe Committee (1986) concluded that 'As a result, the reality of local government business is often based more on personal authority than the corporate legal basis (of decisions) would suggest' (Para. 2:66, p. 37).

Not only will the chairman take the chair at meetings of the main committee, he or she will also chair sub-committees and attend many less formal meetings about the committee's functions and policies or on particular issues which need to be dealt with. The chairman must develop a close relationship with the chief officer and his or her immediate lieutenants and, like any successful minister (Boyle, 1965), the chairman will seek to discover what ideas are being floated and what debates are going on further down the departmental hierarchy.

In order to ensure that committee chairmen and vice-chairmen are fully involved in the development of policy recommendations, the Bains Committee (1972) recommended that before each committee or sub-committee meeting takes place, the agenda and papers should be discussed at a meeting involving the chairman and vice-chairman possibly together with the 'shadow' chairman or opposition spokesperson, with senior officers of the departments concerned. This agenda meeting creates a most important interface between officers and leading members. The officers can keep the chairman and vice-chairman informed about recent developments, consult them about issues which are likely to cause political controversy and discuss with them the recommendations they wish to make to the committee about whose political acceptability they are uncertain. The chairman and vice-chairman for their part must consider whether the officers' proposals are in accordance with their political views and those of their colleagues, if necessary advising or perhaps instructing the officers as to what their political masters wish should be done. The chairman and vice-chairman need, in short, to mediate between the officers and their fellow councillors to try and ensure that policy develops in the way desired by council members and their parties.

Above all, a close and trustful working relationship needs to develop between the chairman and his deputy, the chief officer and his or her senior subordinates and the committee clerk. The latter is responsible for organising meetings, taking the committee's minutes and advising the chairman on procedural points during committee meetings. The committee clerk will effectively control the chairman's diary and hence many of his or her waking hours. Here too, therefore, a trusting relationship is needed.

The committee's minutes record not merely the proceedings of the committee but also the decisions it takes, on those matters delegated to the committee by the council's standing orders, together with its recommendations to the policy and resources committee on matters lying within its terms of reference but not delegated to it. The latter recommendations may, of course, be amended or rejected by the policy and resources committee or the full council. Where party groups operate, as is usually the case, committee minutes are reviewed by the party group and its executive committee, as well as by group meetings of the party's members on the committee. These meetings will make demands on the chairman which he or she must then deliver to the officers; this will be done through the agenda meeting or other contacts between them. Failure to ensure the political acceptability of officers' recommendations may lead to the chairman being required by his party group to amend or withdraw them at meetings of the policy and resources committee or the full council – a process which inevitably causes embarrassment. In consequence, the Widdicombe Committee found that in party-controlled authorities:

> briefing meetings between the committee chairman and his chief officer provide an important forum in which professional advice and political objectives can be dove-tailed. It would seem, however, that the chairman is increasingly taking an active rather than a passive role in such meetings. Chairmen are increasingly initiating policy or acting as advocates for policies initiated in the party group.
>
> (Widdicombe 1986, para. 2:66, p. 37)

Indeed, with a critical party group watching his or her activities, woe betide a committee chairman who does not do this!

The importance of the role now played by committee chairmen and vice-chairmen, as well as by council leaders, has raised the issue of whether councillors should continue to be part-timers or whether some at least should become full-time and be paid a salary. A committee chairmanship is a very onerous responsibility to undertake on a part-time basis and one which carries with it a great deal of responsibility. In 1974, one member of Birmingham City Council left his job so that he could devote his energies wholly to his council work; he existed on unemployment benefit plus his attendance allowance and expenses as a council member. There were 'a good number of members (who) devote a full working day, five days a week, to public work' (Newton, 1976, p. 150). Such members were retired, self-employed or had tolerant employers, as well as partners. The Widdicombe Committee found that some 50 per cent of local authorities had some members whose involvement was effectively full-time and seemed surprised that this figure was not higher (Widdicombe 1986, para., 6:81, p. 126)

In 1980, special responsibility allowances were introduced for leading councillors, following the recommendations of the Robinson Committee (1977). This system was confirmed and developed as a result of the recommendations of the Widdicombe Report, which also secured effectively a part-time salary for all councillors. However, it is doubtful whether these measures will be sufficient to attract able, relatively young councillors to local authority work or encourage them to accept the risk to their careers entailed in taking on a leading role, such as a committee chairmanship, with its onerous and time-taking responsibilities. Their availability is likely still to depend on the toleration or encouragement of their council work by families, employers, business partners or associates or professional superiors (see Barron, Crawley and Wood, 1991). Nonetheless, it is unlikely that there will not be future pressure to increase the still relatively modest allowances paid to councillors, especially to committee chairmen and other leading members who must devote the lion's share of their working week to council business, including frequent – often daily – contact with the authority's senior officers.

The effect of party control on the power and relationships of members and officers

Party groups and their executive committees make collective decisions which can be imposed upon committees and officers. The party members on committees may also meet as a group to decide the party line on matters coming before the committee. Once such decisions are made, of course, members of the party are expected to support them in their speeches and votes and at committee and council meetings. They will be reported by the whips to the group for disciplinary action to be taken if they speak or vote against the party's policies unless excused for reasons of personal conscience (see Chapter 3). Victor Wiseman recalled that Leeds City Council's Labour Group met twice during each cycle of meetings, once to review policy generally and again to consider the agenda for the next council meeting. The mid-term meeting would consider major policy proposals and discuss the general policy of the council and its committees (Wiseman, 1963, Part 1). Thus, the group could ensure that its views were clearly known to members and officers alike. Kenneth Newton (1976) saw the party group as a major defence against excessive officer control since it enables councillors to state clearly what policies they collectively wish to follow. By the same token, Andrew Blowers (1977) argued that in a 'hung' council where the outcomes of committee and council meetings were unpredictable, the power of officers relative to members was increased. Again, in a rural district council where no party Groups existed, the officers were responsible for 'much of the co-ordination of present policy' (Bealey et al., 1965). In Wolverhampton, by contrast, 'the power of the Town Clerk has been quite severely curtailed by the rise of the group system' (G.W. Jones, 1973). Newton (1976) commented that:

> Officers may find it easier to control decision-making when they are faced by an array of individuals and independents; they may find it more difficult to divide and rule when committees are controlled by organised Groups with party policies and programmes.
>
> (Newton, 1976, p. 160)

The party system is thus an important means of ensuring that the will of the elected members is clearly stated and can be made to prevail, if necessary, against the officers' professional viewpoint.

The general dominance of party politics in local government after 1974, together with controversies over the conduct of business in individual local authorities, gave rise to new concerns, especially about whether, when one party controls the council, officers can maintain their politically detached status as servants of the whole council, not solely of the ruling party. These concerns were addressed in the Widdicombe Report (1986), which generally gave party politics in local government a clean bill of health, while noting some specific areas of concern, the main ones being the availability of officer advice to party groups, including one-party committees; the propriety or otherwise of appointing overtly political advisers to council leaders or majority groups and the appointment and dismissal of officers.

We have seen that, formally, a local authority's officers are prohibited by their terms of service from giving advice to meetings of party groups. However, this has sometimes been overcome on councils where one party was securely in overall control, by establishing a committee consisting only of the members of the ruling party; usually a policy and resources committee. More commonly, a variety of devices were developed which would allow officers on occasion to give advice to party group meetings at council or committee level.

The Widdicombe Committee recommended that these procedures ought to be regulated. They proposed that committees where decisions were to be made must be composed of members of all the parties represented on the council, in proportion to the number of members from each party serving on the full council (Widdicombe, 1986, paras. 5:43–5:54). However, if committees were established which were purely deliberative and not responsible for taking decisions, these could be composed of members from only one party and could legitimately be advised by the officers (ibid., para. 5:55–5:60). However, this latter recommendation was not adopted in the legislation which eventually followed the Widdicombe Report. Where party politicians or groups seek the advice of officers, they are now required to do so through the chief executive, who decides which officers should provide the advice requested and who must offer the same facilities to all other parties represented on the council.

A second, related issue considered by the Widdicombe Committee was the appointment of political advisers to leading politicians or majority party groups. Such advisers hold their posts only so long as the ruling party retains office. The practice of appointing political advisers was adopted mainly by Labour councils and their leaders in the 1980s, hence they were regarded with supicion by many Conservative councillors. However, the Widdicombe Committee recommended that this practice should be allowed to continue, although the number of such posts were restricted and the salary paid to their holders was set initially at not more than £13,500. Furthermore, officers earning over £23,733 in 1989 (except teachers) are barred from membership of political parties and all forms of political activity, in order to end the phenomenon of 'twin-tracking', whereby a person could serve as a councillor on one local authority while being employed as an officer by a nearby council. Hence, the Government has sought to reinforce the politial neutrality of local authority officers, especially those on the more senior grades. This has been still further reinforced by restrictions on the extent to which councillors can appoint or dismiss officers. However, the Government has not adopted the Widdicombe Committee's recommendation that the chief executive should enjoy special protection against dismissal by councillors, in the form of requiring that a two-thirds majority must vote for the dismissal of a chief executive officer.

The Widdicombe Committee had concluded that the 'tidal force of politicization in local government' (Leach, 1989) had produced few adverse effects on the proper conduct of local authority business, except in a few cases, despite widespread apparent concern that the party faithful were being rewarded with jobs or other favours; that officers were being appointed on the strength of their political views rather than their professional capabilities and that the political neutrality of officers in general was being destroyed. All these things may happen in an occasional authority but they are not general. Furthermore, party politics secures quicker and more consistent decisions from councillors, hence making their implementation by officers easier. The Government, however, was selective in its implementation of the recommendations of the Widdicombe Committee, accepting in the main those which would inhibit the work of political parties on local authorities and paying little attention to the remainder.

Pressure groups and the power of officers

Kenneth Newton (1976) made a very significant point concerning the other outside influence on local authority decisions: pressure groups. Pressure groups in local government have only come to the attention of its academic students relatively recently; in the late 1950s A.H. Birch and his colleagues could find little trace of organised pressure-group activity in the small Derbyshire town of Glossop (Birch, 1958). However, in the very different circumstances of England's second city, Newton found that pressure groups were of considerable significance: some 4,000 such groups were involved in trying to influence Birmingham City Council during the period of his study.

Newton argued that 'although the party system may have circumscribed the officers' room for manoeuvre, the pressure group system may have helped to expand it somewhat' (Newton, 1976, p. 162). The reason for this is that individuals or groups of citizens who wish to influence a local authority's policies or to protest against one of its decisions will tend first to approach officers rather than councillors. His interviews with the secretaries of interest groups in Birmingham showed that nearly 70 per cent of the initial contacts made by such organisations with local authorities were made at officer level and only 24 per cent at member level. In this respect, Birmingham appears to be fairly typical. The research project carried out for the Widdicombe Committee showed that, whereas 49 per cent of individuals contacted council offices with a complaint or proposal, only 20 per cent went initially to a councillor (Gyford, Leach and Game, 1989, p. 244).

The influence of pressure groups may be further increased where they provide services for the council. In some service areas, notably the social services, the provision of facilities or services by voluntary groups for local authorities has long been accepted as being advantageous to both sides. The voluntary group secures an income and access to the council's officers and facilities, while the local authority obtains the provision of a service at a cost less than that which it would incur by providing the service itself. Under the community care scheme, such contracting out of local authority services to voluntary groups, as well as to private firms, is being actively encouraged.

Two consequences for member–officer relations follow from the links that develop between officers and pressure groups. The first is that information, requests and demands from the groups are usually reported by officers to members and the former, therefore, largely control the flow of information to councillors about pressure-group activities and demands. Second, in their dealings with pressure groups, officers may prepare policy 'packages' which members can reject only at the cost of alienating the pressure groups concerned and causing a more or less lengthly delay in the implementation of the policy while a fresh 'package' more acceptable to them is prepared and negotiated with the groups. If members are to avoid such problems, they must make sure that they are aware of the work that is going on in the council's departments and the relationships that the staff employed within those departments have with pressure groups.

CONCLUSIONS

The relative power of local authority members and officers in their policy-making and administrative processes is hard to determine and varies from one authority to another – even between one councillor and another. The councillor sitting on a local authority committee is advised by officers who possess a high degree of specialist professional training and experience, who are unlikely to be particularly sensitive to the demands of political ideology or expediency. The officers also tend to be unaware of the demands of other departments and other local authorities, so that members can be presented at meetings with conflicting or even contradictory advice which they cannot always effectively challenge or reconcile. There may be no choice but to ask the officers to attempt to reconcile their differences and bring a united recommendation to a future meeting of the committee.

The increasing development of links between local authority officers and interest groups may strengthen the power of officers by providing them with information and interest-group support which they can use against their own authority's members. The officer can argue that it is dangerous for councillors to disregard the advice and views of interest groups who may resist or thwart the implementation of decisions they dislike. Finally, members are in constant danger of being submerged by large numbers of official reports which they are not always well equipped to challenge as they face a tiring round of committee meetings, often on top of their normal jobs.

Part III

The provision and delivery of services

INTRODUCTION

Having discussed the principal actors who are involved in policy-making and administration in local government, we next consider the functions of local authorities and the issues to which the exercise of those functions gives rise. These issues have changed dramatically over the last fifteen years or so. At one time, an account could have been given of a service which would have been at least partially valid for the provision of that service anywhere in the country. The provision of services was managed by specialist professional officers who ran their services according to their established professional orthodoxies. They reported to a committee of councillors who often had few differences among themselves about the management and provision of specific services. Labour councillors might be inclined to spend more in order to provide better services and more assistance to the more deprived members of the local community, whereas Conservatives would seek to reduce service provision in the hope of reducing the next year's increase in the local rates. Beyond that, however, there would be general agreement with the officers' advice about precisely how services should be managed and provided. Service management was a bi-polar relationship between providers and politicians, regulated by administrators (Public Finance Foundation, 1992 (annual), p. 9).

That began to change in the 1970s, when the consensus about how services should be provided began to break down. In general, we can suggest five main reasons for this. The first and most fundamental was the wider breakdown in the welfare consensus which had restricted the scope of partisan controversy after 1945 (see Elcock (ed.), 1982). Until the mid-1970s there was general agreement that the benefits accruing from the provision of an increasing level of public services were undeniable; political differences were largely confined to how much service could be afforded. Second, politicians and the public became increasingly sceptical about not only the efficiency of public services but also about their effectiveness in meeting citizens' needs and desires. Third and in consequence, new approaches to the provision of public services gained support, notably suggestions that public services could be improved by exposing them to market forces by privatising them or contracting them out to private firms. Where this was not possible, a surrogate for the market needed to be provided. More generally, management needed to be improved and the management function gained in importance, becoming an intermediate function between providers and politicians (Public Management Foundation, 1992, p. 14). Fourth, the boundary between local authorities and other providers of local services has become increasingly contentious as the Government has removed functions from local authorities and handed them over to new or sometimes existing bodies which are not controlled by elected representatives. This process had been apparent at least since the Second World War (Loughlin, Gelfond and Young (eds), 1985) but it accelerated during the 1980s. Many of the new local bodies are controlled by ministerial appointees, which led J.D. Stewart to warn as 1992 closed that Britain's public services were increasingly being run by a magisterial elite which was subject to no effective democratic accountability (*The Guardian*, 30 December 1992). Lastly, the deteriorating performance of the British economy has meant that the amount of resources available to local authorities, in common with other public service providers, ceased to increase as it had year after year since 1945. Instead, pressure was imposed for expenditure on public services to be reduced, although in practice expenditure reductions, as opposed to reduced expenditure growth, have seldom been achieved (Public Finance Foundation, annual).

These new controversies have had an enormous effect on the way in which local authorities provide their services. Hoggett and Hambleton (1987) indicated that two paradigms could be detected. The dominant influence on management and service provision in recent years, especially since the mid-1980s, has been the market-orientated one, with local authorities increasingly being compelled to submit their services to the discipline of competitive tendering or to that of a surrogate market. The result has been either that the provision of many local services has passed from staff employed by local authorities to contractors engaged by them, or that local authorities have retained the provision of these services themselves only by changing their management and in particular increasing their cost-effectiveness. To do this, local authorities have been required to devolve much of their service provision to autonomous direct service organisations (DSOs), which tender for the work required by the local authority in competition with private companies. Only if the DSO submits the lowest tender will it win the contract, although by the early 1990s they had been successful in around three-quarters of the tendering exercises thus far carried out (J. Painter, 1991). In all cases, however, the organisation responsible for supplying the service has been formally separated from the local authority which requires the service and purchases its provision from the lowest tenderer. In other cases, responsibility for providing services has been devolved to autonomous managers, such as school governors under local management of schools schemes within the terms of the 1988 Education Reform Act.

However, local authorities, along with other government organisations, have sought to restore public support for the services they provide by a range of measures which Hoggett and Hambleton separate into 'consumerist' and 'collectivist' approaches. The former are concerned with changing the relationships between local authorities and the many individuals for whom they provide services. The innovations thus introduced range from the cosmetic, like pleasant waiting rooms and telephone jingles, to substantial consumer research exercises. The latter include radical changes in the management of services, including the decentralisation of service provision to neighbourhood offices, sometimes controlled in part by neighbourhood committees.

We discussed these trends in general in Chapter 1; here we shall explore how they have developed in the context of particular services. Chapter 5 examines the services which are provided by the local authority either for individuals or for groups of individuals: these we combine under the generic heading of 'services for citizens'. Since this book is an attempt to discuss the realities of politics and management in local government rather than to chronicle all the functions of local authorities, some services are dealt with more fully than others because they best illustrate the issues and controversies that have arisen as approaches to local authority management and service provision have changed. The services and issues discussed most extensively here are hence those which bulk largest in the minds of councillors and their officers.

The problems raised by the uniformed emergency services are distinctive in many respects and it therefore seems right to discuss them in a separate chapter. The service which is most publicly visible and about which the severest controversies have been raised is the police. Its democratic accountability has long been in question (Marshall, 1965) and there is a possibility that the police will soon be removed from local authority control altogether. In this chapter the fire service is also discussed, since it gives rise to some of the same managerial and other issues as the police. Lastly, local authorities' responsibility for the provision of emergency services in civil disasters or under the threat of military attack are discussed.

In the provision of their services, local authorities make use of vast amounts of resources. Their budgets usually run into hundred of millions of pounds and collectively they account for between a quarter and a third of Britain's total public expenditure. Demands from ministers for expenditure cuts have significantly changed the methods by which local authorities manage their money. Local authorities also employ vast armies of staff, from dustmen and road-menders to chief executives. They own and administer large land and property holdings: the council is often the largest landowner in its area. It is therefore important to taxpayers that these various resources should be used as frugally as possible and deployed to the best effect. Their management is reviewed in Chapter 7.

Planning has become particularly contentious in recent times, although it has always been one of the less consensual areas of local government. Since the 1947 Town and Country Planning Act, local authorities have had extensive powers to control the use of land and its development or redevelopment. The planning system's supporters have always expected too much from it while its opponents never cease to resent the interference of 'the planners' with their freedom of action. In the early 1980s it appeared that the drive towards deregulation and free markets would emasculate the planning system; its influence has in any case been considerably reduced (Thornley, 1989). Even definitions of planning are controversial; suffice it to say that planning is concerned with the reduction of uncertainty about the future or, as Wildavsky (1980) has put it, 'Planning is . . . current action to secure future consequences; the more future consequences planners control, the better they have planned'. These benefits led in the 1960s and 1970s both to the strengthening of the town and country planning system but also to attempts to develop wider corporate strategic planning processes within local authorities. However, if the logic of free-market economics is accepted, increased uncertainty may be desirable rather than something to be reduced by planning: rival firms in a competitive market will compete harder if their information about their opponents is incomplete and the same will apply, so the argument runs, to public authorities which are compelled to work in competitive markets. The town and country planning system is still in existence, albeit much changed and rather reduced and it is discussed in Chapter 8.

Lastly, in Chapter 9 we take an overall look at the development of local government management since the late 1950s, when dissatisfaction with the incoherence of the administrative and decision-making procedures then generally operated led eventually to the adoption to a greater or lesser extent by most local authorities of corporate management. Corporate management too has suffered from controversies and has been supplemented or displaced by other approaches.

There has never been a more difficult time than the present to write in general terms about how local authorities provide their services and manage their affairs. Up to the 1960s you could have assumed that anywhere in the country, you would find in local authorities broadly the same committee systems, the same departments, the same administrative procedures and the same service providers. Now that has ceased to be the case. The Public Management Foundation (1992) has argued that public service management has altered from a dual relationship between politicians and service providers, through a management paradigm in which pressure on resources has stimulated demands for better and in particular more economical management, to a tripartite relationship between politicians, producers and customers or consumers who are reconciled and held together by managers. The ways in which this is done now vary widely and in consequence, local authority management has probably not been so innovative and varied since the mid-nineteenth century – a paradoxical statement to make at a time when the very existence of local government is being challenged more fundamentally than ever before in the twentieth century.

Chapter 5

Services to citizens

The main purpose for which local government came into existence and developed in the many forms it has taken since the Middle Ages, is to provide services for citizens. The relief of poverty, the provision of public education, the construction of sewers, the provision of hospitals, clean water, highways and public transport services, have all been local government functions, although many are now provided by bodies other than local authorities (Loughlin, Gelfand and Young (eds), 1985). They were provided by local bodies of various kinds, often responsible for a single function or a narrow range of functions, until multi-functional local authorities as we now know them were established throughout the country at the end of the nineteenth century (Chandler, 1991; Kingdom, 1991). The provision of such services absorbs most of the money paid to local authorities from local taxes and Government grants. It gives employment to the vast majority of their staffs and is the purpose of most of the buildings erected and maintained by local councils.

Many services must be provided by law, such as education for all children between the ages of five and sixteen, or accommodation and treatment for children committed to the care of a local authority by a court of law. Another example is the requirement to provided a free public library service. Books must be available without charge, unless they are returned late but the same does not apply to records, video tapes or computer software. Again, local education authorities are required to provide fees and a maintenance grant for all students aged eighteen or over who achieve two GCE 'A' level passes and obtain a place on a degree-level course at a university or college of higher education. These are usually called statutory services. Local authorities have no choice but to provide them, although this does not mean that they are mere agents of the central government with little opportunity to take independent decisions as to the nature and extent of the services they provide.

They often have considerable discretion over how these statutory services are provided. For example, the organisation of schools to provide education for children of the statutory school ages, including determining the ages at which a child moves from a primary school to a middle or secondary or high school, is left largely for local education authorities (LEAs) to determine. A small minority of Conservative LEAs managed to defy pressure, including legislation, from successive Labour Governments through the 1960s and 1970s to abolish the selection of pupils at eleven years old and have retained grammar schools for their abler children. These statutory services consume about 80 per cent of a local authority's budget, however, and in the case of major service committees, such as education or social services, the proportion of their expenditure thus committed may be closer to 90 per cent. Only the remaining 10 or 20 per cent covers those discretionary activities which the authority has a choice whether to support or not, such as adult education classes, pre-school playgroups and community centres. However, in 1979 local authorities were relieved of some statutory duties, such as the requirement to provide school meals and milk, which somewhat increased their discretion, both in terms of what activities to undertake and how much to spend on them.

The other services are not obligatory but are commonly provided by local authorities which are empowered to do so. There is a very wide range of discretionary functions. They include subsidies for the arts, adult education services and the provision of residential homes or day centres for elderly and handicapped people. These discretionary services are the most severely affected when budget cuts are required because they are not protected by any legal duty laid upon the local authority to provide them. Also, the extent to which they will be provided will vary widely, as for example does the extent to which social services committees provide aids for the physically and mentally handicapped under the Chronically Sick and Disabled Persons Act, 1970.

The importance of these services for citizens can be illustrated by looking at the proportion of a local authority's expenditure which is devoted to them. Newcastle upon Tyne City Council budgeted to spend £217,687,990 in revenue spending on all its services in the financial year 1992–1993, of which £109,588,930 was to be spent on education and £38,491,510 on social services. Of the council's 13,098 full time equivalent employees, 4,213 worked in education and 2,363 in social services. The largest employer of labour is 'Cityworks', the council's direct service organisation responsible for carrying out contracts for a range of services including refuse collection and street cleansing, which employed 3,674 people in the financial year 1992–1993. In non-metropolitan, or 'shire' district councils, housing constitutes the biggest commitment in terms of money and manpower. Newcastle upon Tyne's housing service employed 742 full-time equivalent staff in 1992–1993 and spent £3,404,590.

The provision of services for citizens is therefore the main preoccupation of councillors and officers. Decisions to increase or – more usually – to reduce local authority expenditure, whether taken locally or nationally, inevitably have an immediate effect on the quality and the extent of these services. Reductions imposed on 'shire' counties or metropolitan districts cannot but affect education and social services because they consume the lion's share of their budgets. By the same token, housing authorities are likely to be forced to increase rents or reduce their housing provision when expenditure must be reduced.

These reductions are also likely to bear more heavily on the discretionary than the statutory services. Thus, in social services much expenditure on child care is statutory, while much of that on the aged is discretionary, so that old people's homes and services suffer particularly severely when expenditure cuts are required. The consequences of this are likely to become sufficiently severe as the proportion of elderly people in the population grows.

Another important issue is that the efficiency or otherwise with which councils provide these services will considerably affect the council's overall finances. Increased efficiency results in lower costs which offer councillors the opportunity either to reduce local taxation or to provide more services for the same level of tax. However, a constraint on innovation or reduction of services in the past has been the influence of local policy communities (Richardson and Jordan, 1979) which include producer groups such as trades unions and professional associations. Their demands may be hard for a local authority to resist, although the pressure of Government reforms in the 1980s has greatly altered the relationship between local authorities and producer groups. Many established professional orthodoxies and restrictive labour practices have been swept away as a result of the imposition of compulsory competitive tendering, the local management of schools and other innovations designed to increase competitive pressures on local service providers and increase consumer power. Nonetheless, trade unions and professional groups are extensively consulted by local authorities about their policies, and resistance to them may provoke a protest to the Secretary of State or lead to industrial action. The changing nature of the relationship between local authorities, producer groups and consumers will be explored further in the context of particular services because their nature and extent varies from one service area to another.

These services to the citizen also provide councillors with much of their work as public representatives. Their ward cases are predominantly concerned with education, social services and housing. Parents who do not wish their children to go to a particular school; people seeking residential or day-care places for handicapped or elderly relatives; council tenants wanting to move to another part of the town or who are having difficulty getting repairs done, provide the bulk of councillors' postbags and the majority of visitors to their surgeries. Councillors in their turn need to be in frequent contact with their authority's officers in the education, social services and housing departments in order to seek solutions to their constituents' problems as well as taking opportunities to raise them in committee and sub-committee meetings. Councillors also have a part to play in monitoring standards of services. They serve on governing bodies of schools and other institutions; they visit children's and old people's homes to check on standards of cleanliness, catering and care; they consider proposals and planning applications for new council housing estates. In these and other ways councillors can keep a check on the quality of the services being provided for their electors. Most of them will be keen to serve on the committees responsible for these services; this applies especially to the many councillors whose principal satisfaction from their council duties comes from helping their constituents. A seat on the education, social services or housing committee carries with it some prestige in the eyes of those members who have not been so fortunate because it provides an opportunity to press constituency grievances. The chairmen and vice-chairmen of these committees are likely to be among the leading figures on the council and in the ruling party group. They will also be among the principal targets for attack by the opposition parties in the council chamber.

The manner in which these services are perceived by members of the public deteriorated in the 1960s and 1970s, despite the extent of council control over them and the diligence with which most councillors pursue their ward case-work. There was a widespread sense that those responsible for providing public services were inefficient and that they dealt unsympathetically with those who needed them. Public service was characterised as 'bureaucratic paternalism' by Hoggett and Hambleton (1987). Others have argued that professional public servants are more concerned to observe the demands of their professional orthodoxies than to act in the best interests of their clients or heed their wishes (Gower Davies, 1972; Illich *et al.*, 1977). In consequence, public support for the growth of public services declined. For instance, whereas in an opinion poll conducted in 1963, 80 per cent of those polled supported the expansion of the social services, by 1979 that proportion had fallen to only 30 per cent (Crewe, 1982). Among the public services, only the National Health Service has retained a high level of public esteem. In consequence, those responsible for the management of public services, including local authorities, have sought to change the way those services are provided in order to make them more responsive and acceptable to the public. Such changes have taken one of two approaches. They may have followed a market-orientated path in which the principle is to give the customer a choice of where he or she goes to obtain a service, so encouraging service providers to compete in becoming more attractive to potential customers. The alternative is public service reform, in which consumerist and collectivist solutions are developed in order to improve the relationship between public servants and their users, while maintaining the more or less monopolistic control over the service by public service organisations such as local authorities (Stewart, 1986; Hoggett and Hambleton, 1987). The remainder of this chapter will explore how these contending approaches to the provision of public services have developed in the context of a number of specific services.

In doing so, the accounts of the development of individual services will highlight one of the ironies of the Thatcher Governments' policies towards local government. The Governments which have held office since 1979 have pledged themselves to reduce state interference in the lives of the people, increase the choices available to citizens and hence reduce Government regulation of society. To do this, however, they have had to intervene to an unprecedented extent in how local authorities provide the services for which they are responsible. Until 1979, although the broad outlines of policy and overall levels of expenditure were set centrally, local authorities were largely free to determine the manner in which services were provided and their budgets spent. Particularly since 1987, however, local authorities' autonomy in this regard has been progressively restricted. They have been compelled to devolve control over school staffing and budgets to head teachers and governors under the schemes for the local management of schools introduced under the 1988 Education Reform Act. They have been forced to submit an increasing range of their services to compulsory competitive tendering since 1989. Under the community care scheme, they are under great pressure to dispose of residential homes and day-care facilities to private firms or voluntary agencies, then contracting with those firms or agencies for the provision of community care services. In consequence, although the choices available to individual citizens and the extent to which they can influence the provision of local services may have increased, the area of discretion available to councillors and officers in local authorities has been progressively reduced.

EDUCATION

Where local authorities are responsible for education, it consumes the largest proportion of the budget and is the field in which the largest proportion of their staffs are employed. The trends towards a combination of centralised control over policy and the devolution of powers to consumers which have characterised the development of local government since 1979, are well illustrated by the recent history of the education service.

Responsibility for education

Education has been a public responsibility since the passage of the Forster Act in 1870. Schooling became compulsory for children under thirteen in 1880 and local authorities assumed control of schools under the Balfour Act of 1902. At this time, the major political controversies in education concerned religious denominations and these controversies were not finally resolved until the passage of the Butler Act in 1944. This Act, which was part of the consensus reached about social policy by the wartime coalition Government, made schooling compulsory for all children between the ages of five and fifteen, the upper limit being raised to sixteen in 1972. It required LEAs, which were then the county and county borough councils, to provide efficient schools for all children in this age range. This responsibility passed to non-metropolitan county councils and metropolitan district councils after local government reorganisation took effect in 1974. LEAs also have discretionary powers to provide nursery education for the under-fives. Until recently, they also had the responsibility for further education colleges and polytechnics but these have now been removed from local authority control. LEAs are still responsible for sixth-form education in schools.

This system of local authority control over education survived largely unchanged from 1944 until 1988. Indeed, for the first two decades of this period, the politics of education were largely consensual. The 1944 Act had finally resolved the old religious controversies and had established an education system which was accepted by most people in all the major political parties (Jennings, 1977). It was a service also characterised by a strong professional hegemony. Because of the large size of local authority education systems and the wide range of their responsibilities, education committees and departments tended to enjoy a considerable degree of autonomy from the rest of the local authority. Robert E. Jennings found in a study of six LEAs that:

> Education is considered by many to be a strong semi-autonomous service of local government. This is regarded by most Education Committee chairmen to imply a greater responsibility than that which falls on other service committees because there are few real checks on education within the formal structure.
>
> (Jennings, 1977, p. 124)

Education was also heavily dominated by professional orthodoxies, values and interests. In particular, the chief education officer was a powerful chief officer whose word was often law (see Kogan and van der Eycken, 1973). Jack Brand wrote of one LEA that:

The fact that comes out of any study of education in Reading is that during the time of his office education in Reading was Percy Taylor. Without exception all recognised him as an outstanding administrator and educationalist who commanded loyalty of his staff and teachers and had a very clear idea of where he wanted education in Reading to go.

(Brand, 1966, p. 108)

One consequence of this professional hegemony in a large service was that chief education officers have often been reluctant participants in management teams and other forms of interdepartmental co-ordination, despite the many demands that the education service makes on other departments such as finance, the architect's and the estates departments. In 1976 the Chief Education Officer of Avon County Council resigned because:

I do not and cannot exercise the responsibilities the Education Committee and your schools and colleges expect of me and my departmental staff. The management of the education service is fragmented between so many committees and administrative departments of the council that there is no united or effective direction of it.

(*Guardian*, 6 December, 1976)

Education must be run as a single, self-contained service or it will lose its sense of direction and cease to operate effectively.

Its status is in part guaranteed by the statutory requirement for LEAs to establish an education committee, which tends to be large and prestigious. Until 1989, representatives of the teachers' unions and the churches had to be included among its members, the first of which obligations increased the extent of professional influence over the service. However, such co-optees are now denied voting rights. The Education Committee itself will spawn a wide range of sub-committees either dealing with particular aspects of the service, such as schools or further education and further sub-committees dealing with the educational needs and problems of divisions within the LEAs overall control.

The provision of education

Unlike most of the other major local authority services, education is not provided directly to members of the public. It is provided through schools and colleges which themselves have always enjoyed considerable freedom of action from the LEA and this has been further increased in recent years. They are controlled in part by boards of governors and managers appointed by the LEA but operate under their own instruments and articles of government which are prepared by the local authority and approved by the Secretary of State for Education. In consequence, the chain of command between the Education Committee and the teacher in the classroom is very long. Teachers often find the Education Committee impossibly remote and regard its decisions as high-handed and unrealistic. Equally, Education Committee members often have little feel for what is happening in the schools, unless they also serve as school governors. Their opportunity to do so has been reduced since 1986 by the reduction in the proportion of boards of governors who are nominated by the LEA. This reform was carried out with the intention of reducing the number of governors who are nominated by the party in control of the council but it also has the effect of reducing councillors' opportunities to learn about the schools they control (to some extent) as Education Committee members.

Intermediate between schools and the Education Committee is the education department and its chief education officer. Professional hegemony is also assured by the local and national inspectorates, which are responsible for monitoring standards and encouraging educational innovation (Kogan and van der Eycken, 1973). However, the inspectorate's role has also been changed by recent reforms The inspection of schools is now overseen by a national body, the Office for Standards in Education (OFSTED). The reforms have in effect abolished the national inspectorate but the new process of inspection will be more intensive than the old, with 6,000 inspections being carried out each year.

The extent to which the education service should be controlled nationally has long been a subject for debate because of the need to ensure that education standards do not vary too widely between one part of the country and another. The need to do this is indicated by the wide variations in expenditure on schools which are reported in Table 1.1 (see p 17). One chief education officer said that:

The job of the local authority is, on the whole, to implement national decisions – in doing this they interpret those decisions to suit their own particular area or parts of their area. I say this about strong national government because it seems to me quite wrong that educational provision should vary so much from area to area as it still does.

(Kogan and van der Eycken, 1973, p. 80)

To say that education is a national service locally administered understates the extent of the autonomy that LEAs enjoyed. They could determine the number of teachers they employed, the organisation of schools, the age of transfer from primary to secondary schools and whether sixth-form education should be offered within secondary schools or in separate tertiary colleges. However, national control of the service has been increased by the dominance on most LEAs of the national political parties (Jennings, 1977). It is probably also increased by the importance of interest groups in the education policy community (Richardson and Jordan, 1979; Rhodes, 1987). The teachers' and head teachers' unions, together with the professional organisations representing educational administrators, all have a powerful voice in the preparation of local and national education policies. A myriad of cause groups pressing particular issues, such as the abolition of corporal punishment, have had a more marginal but nonetheless sometimes significant influence.

Increased national control has resulted above all from the introduction of the national curriculum. This was foreshadowed in the 1970s, when the then Prime Minister, James Callaghan, called for a 'great debate' about what should be taught in schools, because of claims that pupils were leaving school lacking the knowledge and skills they needed to be effective workers and members of society. This 'great debate' ultimately came to a climax in the introduction of the national curriculum, together with national tests at ages between seven and fourteen during a child's schooling. The national curriculum and tests have been introduced without consultation with most educational interests and their introduction has been widely criticised by the teachers' unions and many others. However, Government concessions have been confined to reducing the proportion of the school timetable that must be devoted to the national curriculum, in order to prevent minority subjects such as Classics and religious education from being driven out of the state-school curriculum entirely. As a result of teacher resistance in the Summer of 1993, further simplification of both the national curriculum and the tests is likely to take place, but the principles underlying both are not to be abandoned. Hence, the introduction of the national curriculum and its associated tests constitute a considerable reduction in the autonomy of LEAs, as well as reducing the autonomy previously accorded to the teaching profession and hence its professional hegemony over education.

Controversies about education

This autonomy and professional hegemony were increasingly challenged from the 1960s onwards, because of a breakdown in the consensus which for twenty years had supported the education policies and structures enacted by the 1944 Education Act. The consensus began to break down after the Labour Party committed itself to the abolition of selective secondary education in the early 1960s. In doing so it was responding not only to a political judgement that the division between grammar and secondary-modern schools, together with the allocation of pupils to one or the other by the 'eleven-plus' examination, was socially divisive but also to a growing professional concern that significant numbers of pupils were being wrongly allocated and hence their talents were not being fully developed (Jennings, 1977). In consequence, the Labour Governments of the 1960s and 1970s adopted a series of increasingly coercive measures to enforce the abolition of selection for secondary education throughout the land. These began with Anthony Crosland's *Circular 10/65*, which announced in 1965 that capital building programmes for schools would not be approved by his department unless they had been prepared with a view to developing non-selective secondary education. The climax came in 1976 when Mrs Shirley Williams secured the passage through Parliament of an act which required all LEAs to abolish selection.

However, although Labour Governments and the professional consensus that the abolition of selection was desirable ensured that selection was abolished by most LEAs by the late 1970s, some Conservative-controlled authorities resisted vigorously. One such council, Tameside Metropolitan Borough Council, which passed from Labour to Conservative control in the 1976 local elections, carried its defiance to the Court of Appeal and won a judgment which secured the protection of its right not to implement a scheme for the comprehensive reorganisation of the borough's grammar schools which had been prepared by the Labour administration that had controlled the council before May 1976. The Secretary of State's attempt to compel the authority to go through with the scheme was rejected by Lord Denning and his two colleagues on the bench (Griffith, 1977; Loughlin, Gelfand and Young (eds.), 1985).

The general but not universal adoption of comprehensive education led to further controversy as concern was expressed about allegations that standards of educational attainment were falling. This concern was expressed particularly in the 'black papers', which were produced by a group of academics, educationalists and others who argued that the abolition of grammar schools, coupled with the adoption of 'progressive' teaching methods which moved away from the traditional didactic style of instruction, were threatening standards of attainment among pupils, to the detriment both of the pupils' development and the economic performance of the country (Cox and Dyson, 1971).

After Margaret Thatcher and the Conservatives won office in 1979, the Government's initial approach to education reform was incremental. The requirement to abolish selection for secondary schools was repealed, although Labour Party successes in the local elections of the early 1980s ensured that most LEAs continued to develop comprehensive secondary education. The Government offered an assisted places scheme, by which LEAs could purchase places for bright children from relatively poor backgrounds in independent schools. Financial pressure intensified as the Government imposed its increasingly severe financial regime on local authorities generally. One result was a period of bitter industrial disputes between teachers and their employers in the mid-1980s, including several lengthly strikes. Vocational education became a priority, which was in part developed by the establishment of 'competitors' with LEAs in the form of the technical and vocational education initiative and the developing vocational skills initiatives developed by the Manpower Services Commission and its successor, the Training Commission (McVicar, 1990).

The Education Reform Act and its aftermath

It was only after the mid-1980s that more radical reforms were introduced. The first stage was to reduce the influence of LEAs and in particular political parties on school boards of governors by reducing the number of governors appointed by LEAs and increasing the proportion elected by parents. The 1986 Education (No. 2) Act gave parents equality of representation with the LEA on school boards of governors.

The next stage was the removal of education institutions from LEA control, which was carried out largely through the Education Reform Act of 1988, which was piloted through Parliament by Kenneth Baker as Secretary of State for Education and Science. His objectives were to raise standards and to reduce the role of LEAs, while giving the consumers of education – mainly parents – greater control and more choice as to where they send their children to be educated.

The impact of the 1988 Education Act on LEAs has been two fold. On the one hand, it has had the effect of reducing their influence over educational institutions or removing them from their control altogether. Thus, polytechnics and colleges of further education were removed from LEA control and are now financed by national funding bodies which receive their income from the Exchequer. The polytechnics became universities in 1992 and are now financed in common with the older universities by the Higher Education Funding Councils for England, Scotland and Wales. Colleges of further education acquired their own funding council in April 1993 and were thus also removed from LEA control.

In the case of schools, there are two possibilities. The Government wished to 'increase the autonomy of schools and their responsiveness to parental wishes' (DES, 1987). To do this, they offered schools the possibility of leaving LEA control altogether and being funded, through their boards of governors, directly by the central government in the form now of the Department for Education. However, so far relatively few schools have taken advantage of this 'opting out' scheme, despite initial financial incentives offered by the Government to do so. The other possibility concerns the fact that LEAs have been required to develop schemes for the local management of schools, under which control over school budgets is transferred to boards of governors and head teachers. School budgets are allocated in accordance with an agreed formula approved by the Secretary of State. The LEA retains direct control only over the overall budget (which is in any case being increasingly heavily constrained by Government financial restrictions including its 'capping' powers) and the provision of a limited range of central services for schools, such as specialist advice and teaching, as well as administrative support and inspection services. The intention is that the school's customers, in the form of the parents of its pupils in particular, should become the main influence on school policy (McVicar, 1990).

The other main thrust of reform is to reduce LEAs' autonomy through increased central control of policy. The clearest example is the introduction of the national curriculum and its associated compulsory tests for pupils aged between seven and fourteen. These tests are intended to establish whether pupils are reaching nationally determined attainment targets and schools are to be ranked in national and local league tables according to how well their pupils fare in the tests. Before 1988, LEAs largely determined the school curriculum, subject only to a relatively few constraints, including an obligation to provide non-denominational religious education (except in the case of denominational schools) and physical training. However, pressure for the introduction of more national control over the curriculum taught in schools increased as concern about standards grew. In 1977 the then Prime Minister, James Callaghan, introduced his 'great debate' about the school curriculum, which led to an increasing consensus that the teaching of certain basic subjects to a prescribed standard should be made obligatory (McVicar, 1990, p. 132). To this the Conservative Government added the requirement to test pupils' attainment so that the performance of schools and individual teachers could be assessed and ranked.

The introduction of the national curriculum and its associated tests has generated much controversy, especially because of fears that the demands of the national curriculum would squeeze minority subjects such as Classics, music and religious education out of the school curriculum altogether. Also, the introduction of testing would force teachers to revert to traditional didactic and authoritarian teaching methods. League tables are to be published which will indicate how different schools are performing. The Government expects that these tables will in turn influence parents' choices about which school to send their children to. The league tables published so far are regarded as being of dubious accuracy. Thus, a consumer market will develop. Schools which perform poorly in the national tests will lose pupils and must therefore improve their performance or eventually close for lack of pupil demand. However, as Stewart Ranson has argued, the development of this form of market choice may have a major and undesirable influence on future generations of young people:

> individual consumerism in education is not only flawed as an instrument for achieving its purported objectives, it is mis-conceived in its conception of public choice. By defining the public as an aggregate of individual consumers in the market-place, it fragments and undermines the idea of the public as a collective whole. Individuals cannot alone achieve a 'public choice'. Can consumerism, moreover, achieve citizenship? A consumer expresses self-interest registered privately and with uncertain (though often malign) public consequences. A citizen, however, has a concern for the well-being of others as well as for the health of society and believes that both should become the subject of public debate in order to constitute a public choice. The challenge for more public participation and accountability requires different vehicles to support the objective of securing active citizenship.
>
> (Ranson, 1990, p. 195)

In the context of this book, the reduction in the role of the LEA weakens the right of local electors to make choices about how they wish to see the educational provision in their areas de-veloped, in favour of fragmented choices made by parents and governors which will take no account of the needs and problems of the more deprived areas of counties and districts. Education seems destined to be dominated by a set of national requirements which will reduce teachers' scope for creativity on the one hand and, on the other hand, will expose them to local pressures which may be short-term, prejudiced and ignorant. One particularly glaring example is the provision for schools to 'opt out' of LEA control. This decision is to be taken by a ballot of the parents of the children currently in the school. If the ballot result supports the opt-out and the turn-out in the vote is over 50 per cent, the decision cannot be reversed by a later group of parents who take a different view.

However, for the present the course of the development of the education system seems to be set by the 1988 Act, for better or for worse. In particular, central control over education, especially over the curriculum, is now much stronger than it was before 1988. On the other hand, the limited success so far enjoyed by the provision for schools to 'opt out' of LEA control may indicate that the public has a greater faith in and attachment to local government than ministers have allowed for.

THE PERSONAL SOCIAL SERVICES

The issues and problems facing the social services can be explored initially by considering their origins. Malcolm Payne (1979) argues that the modern social services department (SSD) has developed from two sources. The first he calls the 'social work tradition', which had its origins in nineteenth century charities, especially Christian ones and was subsequently influenced by the psychodynamic theories of Sigmund Freud and his disciples. In this tradition, the emphasis is on reform and self-determination for the client, to be brought about by an essentially creative process of interaction between client and social worker. A medical model of problem-solving – of diagnosis proceeding to treatment and cure – has been an important component of this approach. The second tradition, which has become increasingly dominant, is that of the local authority welfare services, which had their origins in the 1834 Poor Law. They were concerned primarily with the provision of accommodation and services for the poor as required by legislation. Payne remarks that 'Local government welfare has a strongly bureaucratic and hierarchical tradition' (Payne, 1979, p. 21). Such a tradition was unlikely to coexist easily with the more creative role required of field staff by the social work tradition. This uneasy coexistence is still causing management and other problems for the social work profession, which has only been fully unified since the merger of the former children's, welfare, health and other departments into SSDs as a result of the recommendations of the Seebohm Report (1968).

The problems involved in the provision of the personal social services are different in several respects from those of education. First, the services have been provided directly to clients by the local authority rather than through the medium of institutions like schools and colleges which have a degree of autonomy. Children's and old people's homes do not usually have their own boards of governors and their staff are responsible directly to the director of social services and the social services committee. However, where such homes are sold to private firms or voluntary agencies, the relationship will change to that of a service supplier providing the service to the council under a contract. Second, the social services cater for particular client groups who are in need, rather than for the population at large.

There are five main client groups, although an individual may fall into more than one of them. He or she may have multiple problems, handicaps or other difficulties which require the assistance of social workers with different specialisms or the combined support of several agencies, including the SSD, the health authority, voluntary groups and others. We have noted earlier that the extent to which provision for particular client groups is made under statutory requirements or under permissive legislation will determine the extent to which their services are protected or reduced in times of financial stringency.

The clients of social services

The first group of people with whom the social services are concerned is children who are in need of care from the local authority. There were some 90,000 children who were accommodated by local authorities in 1972–1973 (Holgate and Keidan, 1975) despite efforts to provide alternative means of providing for children in need, especially where family problems are only temporary. They come into local authority care for three main reasons. Generally, a child is in need if he or she is unlikely to achieve or maintain a reasonable standard of health and development or if these are likely to be significantly impaired unless the local authority intervenes. A separate category of need is disability.

First, local authorities have a statutory duty to accommodate children who have been orphaned or abandoned. Second, parents may request the local authority to accommodate children because they can no longer care for them themselves because of a parental illness or death, or as a result of a family breakdown; these placements are often temporary. However, such a case may lead the authority to decide that in the interests of the child the authority should seek a care order. This decision may also be taken as a result of observations of a family by social workers, NHS staff, teachers and the police which lead the social services department to the conclusion that the parents are unable to give the child adequate care or exercise sufficient control over it. However, as far as possible the social services must work in partnership with the parents: the social workers involved must be guided by the welfare of the child. The decision to issue a care order or assume parental control is taken by the Social Services Committee and may be challenged in a magistrate's court.

One area where the use of these powers has become increasingly controversial is when child abuse is suspected. In Cleveland, large numbers of children were taken into care in the mid-1980s because two doctors conducted an anal dilatation test which they claimed indicated that sexual abuse of the child was likely to have taken place. The subsequent judicial inquiry condemned the test as an unreliable indicator of sexual abuse and denounced the removal of the children from their parental homes as high-handed and unjustified (Butler-Sloss, 1988). On the other hand, social workers have been repeatedly criticised for not taking action where physical abuse has resulted in the death of a child. The first major controversy about such a case occurred over Maria Colwell in 1972 but sadly there have been many more since. In this field of practice in particular, social workers have to walk a very narrow tightrope between being condemned for high-handed, autocratic actions in removing children from their parental homes and being condemned for negligence if they fail to act on signs of abuse and the child subsequently dies.

Third, a child may be committed to the care of a local authority by a court of law, after being convicted of one or more criminal offences. The court may also prescribe particular courses of action short of taking the child into care, by making a supervision order or an intermediate treatment order under which the child continues to live in the family home but is required to engage in a programme of activities which will bring him or her into a new environment, provide new experiences and the opportunity to make contact with other children of the same age.

When children are taken into the care of a local authority after being convicted of an offence, they may be sent initially to an observation and assessment centre where their behavioural and other problems and needs can be assessed by specialist staff, in order to decide the appropriate provision for their future. However, practice varies considerably from one authority to another. Further action may include sending them to community homes (formerly approved schools) or family group homes – smaller establishments with less strict disciplinary regimes. Alternatively, placement with foster parents may be considered. Children taken into care for reasons other than delinquency are less likely to be sent to observation and assessment centres initially but this may become necessary where severe emotional or behavioural problems become apparent, for example because the child is stealing from other residents or from the staff of a community home or family group home.

The second and now the largest main client group, which is becoming increasingly the dominant concern of SSDs, is old people. Here, liaison with the National Health Service is of particular importance. Overcrowding and poor conditions in hospital geriatric wards became a national scandal in the late 1960s (Robb, 1967; Brown, 1975; Crossman, 1977). If old people who cannot look after themselves but are not specifically in need of medical treatment can be looked after in hostels or in their own homes instead of occupying hospital beds simply because there is nowhere else for them to go, pressure on the hospital service can be reduced and this would make more beds and resources available for those who need treatment and facilitate measures to reduce overcrowding. In the late 1980s the NHS embarked on a programme of closing down its large mental hospitals in the expectation that many of their often elderly patients could be cared for in the community. In practice, the failure or inability of SSDs and others to provide alternative forms of care have either imposed increased demands on family members or other informal carers, or have resulted in former inmates of mental hospitals joining the growing number of the homeless. There is hence a need for close liaison between hospital workers and SSDs to ensure that where old people are discharged from hospital adequate provision is made for them, but communications sometimes break down – occasionally with fatal results for the discharged patient.

Three main kinds of care are provided by the social services for the elderly. Residential homes are provided for those who need them either permanently or temporarily, while relatives are ill or on holiday. However, the provision of old people's homes is not a statutory requirement, with the result that local authorities have closed many such homes down to save money as Government restrictions on their expenditure have become increasingly severe. Second, day-care services may be provided, most commonly in the form of day centres which old people can attend during the day, which give them a chance to pursue activities and meet their fellows. Such centres may be attached to old people's homes or they may be entirely separate from them but again some are being closed to reduce spending. Third, SSDs provide domiciliary care, often working in collaboration with voluntary agencies such as the Women's Royal Volunteer Service, which delivers 'meals on wheels' to old people living in their own homes. Other domiciliary care services include day and night sitters. They are designed to enable old people to retain their independence rather than being taken into hospitals or residential care, which deprives them of their independence and is much more expensive, either for the local authority or the NHS.

In recent years, a great deal of emphasis has been placed on day and residential care because it is cheaper than providing residential care. It is also arguably more desirable in that old people can better preserve their dignity and independence for as long as possible. The principal disadvantages are that breakdowns in communication occur which can cause suffering or even death from hypothermia or illness because no-one realised in sufficient time that an old person needed help. This problem arises in particular because the care of the elderly is one of the principal components of the 'mixed economy of welfare', which is being further developed as a result of the Government's community care legislation. Large numbers of individuals, private companies and voluntary organisations are involved in the care of the elderly, as well as SSDs and the NHS. In consequence, services are liable to become fragmented and communications to break down.

In addition, community care makes the work of the staff in residential homes more difficult and less rewarding because increasingly, their residents are the most senile and infirm old people who can no longer be cared for in any other way, which makes these homes increasingly difficult and depressing places in which to work. It has also been increasingly recognised that relatives or friends who are caring for old people need periodic breaks from their labours and responsibilities, which may be met by arranging for a short stay for the old person, perhaps of two or three weeks, in a hospital or a residential home while the relatives take a holiday. This arrangement for respite care may avert the breakdown of family or other informal care by preventing carers being subjected to excessive and interminable stress which may cause a nervous breakdown or other illness. However, spending cuts are making such respite care less available.

The significance of the elderly as a client group for SSDs is increasing, not only because the proportion of elderly people in the British population is increasing but also because the numbers of the very old – the over-seventy-fives – is also increasing and they make much heavier demands for care than the remainder of the elderly population. Demand for social services for the elderly is therefore increasing at a time when SSDs' budgets are being cut. Furthermore, the full implementation of the Community Care Act is intended to strengthen the mixed economy of welfare by encouraging SSDs to dispose of their residential homes and day-care centres to the private or voluntary sectors and then negotiate contracts with them for the care of their elderly clients. SSDs also have a responsibility to inspect private care homes but they lack the resources to undertake this task as fully as they would wish. In consequence, not only are failures of communication among the various agencies responsible for caring for the elderly likely to become more common; also poor standards of care are likely to remain undetected. Indeed, Wandsworth London Borough Council contracted out its residential care for the elderly to a private contractor in the early 1980s, only to discover some years later that the contractor was maintaining his profit margin by reducing food portions for residents to near starvation levels. The problem was identified only when relatives complained after visiting their relatives in the homes. Ultimately, the contractor was discharged. Above all, increased pressure is being imposed on family members and other unpaid, informal carers. Neil Evans has commented that:

> While the Government might applaud the selflessness of famil-ies and neighbours what practical expression would this find? The Government, it was claimed, especially by feminist writers, sought a return to Victorian values of family life to cajole women into undertaking unpaid or poorly paid caring and domestic tasks.
>
> (Evans, 1990, p. 150)

Furthermore, many of the workers involved in residential or domiciliary care are themselves poorly paid, receive little training, are often unqualified and enjoy low status within their SSDs. Their wages and conditions of service are likely to deteriorate further when services are taken over by private contractors.

Many of these issues also affect the third main client group: the mentally and physically handicapped or ill. Here again there is an important area of overlap with the NHS. Pressure on nurses and hospital beds can be relieved if disabled or handicapped people can be accommodated in local authority homes or be enabled to live in their own homes with the assistance of domiciliary care workers and the provision of mechanical aids like stairlifts, special baths and toilets with the help of grants from the social services committee. Extensive powers to provide such assistance were given to local authorities under the Chronically Sick and Disabled Act of 1970. They also provide residential homes and day-care centres – including adult training centres – and as with the elderly, the balance between domiciliary and residential care is an important judgement for the members of social services committees and the staff of SSDs to make. Again too, these services have been reduced by budget cuts because many of them are discretionary and they are subject to the same pressure to contract out provision to private or voluntary providers under the community care scheme. As with the care of the elderly, there is a risk that provision will become patchy, that private or voluntary provision will not be adequately scrutinised and that the burdens imposed on informal carers will be increased. With the closure of many mental hospitals and the reduction in the number of hospital beds for the mentally ill and handicapped, families are increasingly being forced to care for severely handicapped children and young adults, with little support from state agencies, because of lack of provision for them elsewhere.

A fourth client group is more difficult to define at all clearly. It is made up of people who are failing to cope with their families or their own lives because of personal problems or environmental factors such as unemployment, bad housing or the loss of a parent or partner through death or desertion. In some cases it may become apparent that such a person is mentally ill and needs to consult a psychiatrist or enter a mental hospital as a voluntary or compulsory patient. Social workers have the power to order the detention of a person in a mental hospital, after consultation with medical practitioners. Many other people who have temporary or permanent difficulties may be helped by counselling or support services such as the provision of day nurseries to relieve hard-pressed parents, especially single-parent families of part of the burden of caring for their children. A major responsibility is laid on social workers who visit such clients to advise them and assist them in obtaining such support but again, much of this provision is discretionary and has been reduced because of financial stringency.

A final and very controversial set of client groups are ethnic, racial or other minorities. One such is travelling people or gypsies, whose needs involve several local authority departments but for whom the SSD is sometimes the main point of contact with local government, although sometimes the department's involvement may be confined to the employment of a liaison officer. Voluntary agencies may also be extensively involved. In any case, the problems of travelling people engage members of several other local authority departments. Planning authorities have to deal with the considerable problems involved in the establishment of caravan sites for gypsies. Under the Caravan Sites Act of 1968, county councils and metropolitan district councils are required to provide sites for 'people of nomadic habit' who 'reside in or resort to' their areas. The statutory duty to provide sites for gypsies is not, therefore, limited to those of Romany descent (Adams*et al.*, 1976; Elcock, 1979). Once established, the administration of such sites frequently falls to the SSD, which employs site wardens, ensures that children are properly cared for and provides help as needed if illness or other crises hit gypsy families. However, the education department is also likely to be quite heavily involved in the provision of schooling for the travellers' children. Education welfare officers must investigate cases where travellers' children are not attending school when they are required to do so by law. Above all, local authorities need to develop policies for gypsies which ensure that they can pursue their chosen way of life without causing undue nuisance or other problems for house-dwellers. If running water is not provided on a gypsy site, the travellers living there will be constantly asking to fill containers with water at nearby houses and this generates resentment among house-holders. Again, if they are not provided with the means to dispose of waste, unsightly piles of rubbish will appear and the travellers may burn it, so creating an unpleasant smoke. The provision of skips for rubbish collection and disposal will solve this problem at little cost to the local authority. Government policies are pushing more travellers into seeking houses, when the local authority housing departments are likely to become the main actors in trying to meet their needs.

Making provision for gypsies is not easy. Any suggestion that a site for travellers be established in a particular location invariably causes a public outcry and the process of obtaining planning permission becomes as a result controversial and protracted. Once a site is established, however, it causes few problems if it is properly supervised and managed (Adams *et al.*, 1975; Elcock, 1979). However, controversies about provision for travelling people has intensified as a result of the activities of 'new age' travellers in the late 1980s with the result that the Department of the Environment has been considering whether to remove the obligation to provide sites imposed on local authorities under the 1968 Caravan Sites Act. To do so would, however, deprive many travellers of any legal resting place, as well as increasing the nuisance and dangers caused by illegal camps.

Other minority groups who pose problems for SSDs which are in some ways analogous to those of travelling people include racial minorities, whose problems have come to be seen as increasingly important in SSDs. They tend to be concentrated in decaying inner-city areas and have more than their share of unemployment and other social problems, as well as sometimes possessing customs and ways of life which cause difficulties with employers, landlords and neighbours, or with white children and their parents in schools. Homeless people too need help from social workers, although their rehousing is the responsibility of the housing authorities.

Social services management

These client groups present a varied and formidable list of responsibilities. However, they have one thing in common. As Marian Barnes and her colleagues (1990) put it:

> In general, use of personal social services is concentrated in those groups within the population who have least power and opportunity to choose between different problem-solving strategies. Referral is made at a time in people's lives when they are experiencing severe difficulties in material circumstances, interpersonal relationships and ability to care for themselves or those dependent on them. The history of such problems may be lengthy and turning to social services may be a last resort, prompted in part by a wish to find someone else to share the burden. Involving social services staff often means the involvement of strangers in the most intimate aspects of life.
>
> (Barnes, Prior and Thomas, 1990, p. 106)

In consequence, social workers may have considerable power

over their clients. They must be careful and wise in their use of the powers and discretion vested in them. They must be sensitive to the wishes and needs of their clients in a formidably wide variety of situations. Also, the nature of the social worker's task means that he or she will possess a considerable area of discretion. When visiting clients, the field social worker is on his or her own and managers can check on their activities only *ex post facto*, through reports submitted when the social worker returns to the office. Social workers also face a dilemma between intervening too readily and too frequently in their clients' private lives, hence incurring criticism for being authoritarian and heavy-handed, or failing to intervene and being regarded as ineffective or being attacked for failing to prevent a possibly fatal disaster.

Problems of co-ordination and control

Before 1971, these clients' needs were met through separate local authority departments dealing with children, welfare work and health, but as a result of the Seebohm Report (1968), these functions were integrated into 'generic' social services departments under the control of statutory social services committees in 1971. Although most social workers are themselves formally generic, there is an increasing tendency to develop special interests and there is a growing number of specialised social workers working on alcohol or drug dependency, children, the elderly, the mentally ill or AIDS victims. Their activities need to be co-ordinated, therefore, within the department for which they work. Social services are now part of the functions of county councils and metropolitan district councils

Despite the development of these integrated SSDs, the co-ordination of policy and the treatment and care of individuals continues to be problematic. Failures of communication and liaison have led to widely publicised tragedies, including the deaths of children at their parents' hands and old people dying alone because no-one realised that they were ill or injured. Such problems of communication and co-ordination have been revealed time after time in the reports of official enquiries into child abuse and other crises. Thus, teachers may identify a problem child or one who is at risk of non-accidental injury by his or her parents because they notice behaviour problems, hunger and emaciation, listlessness or bruising. These signs need to be reported to social workers in good time in order to reduce the possibility of a tragedy developing. Other education staff, such as education welfare officers and educational psychologists also have important responsibilities for the care of children and liaison between these staff and social workers needs to be close. At another level, if a child is expelled or suspended from school, he or she may create family problems or resort to crime, creating problems with which social workers may have to deal. Again, the education committee and department are responsible for the provision of special education for physically and mentally handicapped children and the SSD will be able to assist in identifying such children and ensuring that they are properly cared for when they are not at school. The education department may be able to take children into residential schools and hence avoid the need for them to be accommodated elsewhere.

The education department and the SSD are invariably departments within the same local authority, yet problems of communication and co-ordination between their staffs occur. However, social workers and SSDs also need to communicate and collaborate with other services, notably the police and the NHS. Here liaison may become even more problematic – a problem identified very clearly in the inquiry into the removal of children from their families in Cleveland (Butler-Sloss, 1988).

The police have become increasingly aware of the need to become involved in the communities for the preservation of whose law and order they are responsible, including providing advice and assistance for those whose personal or social problems lead them, or are likely to lead them into conflict with the law. For instance, in his investigation into the Brixton riots, Lord Scarman (1982) identified poor relations between the police and racial minorities as a major cause of public disaffection in inner-city areas. In consequence, police forces have increasingly sought to improve relations with minority groups and with local communities more generally. However, problems of jurisdiction between the police and social workers may arise and cause difficulties. The police are reluctant to become involved in domestic disputes, although these may cause risks to children. In consequence, social workers may be compelled in effect to spy on families to ensure that their children do not come to harm. They feel, with some justification, that such an investigative role is not properly theirs and that it causes resentment among their clients, whose confidence they need to win and retain. Again, the Cleveland inquiry revealed that personal differences between senior police officers, social workers and pediatric consultants resulted in a failure to collate information which might have prevented the unjustified removal of children into the care of the local authority. A similar problem of poor communication and co-ordination was identified by the inquiry into the removal of children from their families in the Orkney Islands because Satanic abuse was wrongly suspected by social workers. On this occasion, the social workers concerned were accused of tyrannical behaviour in the form of dawn raids on families to remove their children into care.

Another service with whose members social workers need to work closely is the probation and after-care service, which is controlled by the Home Office but is administered and partly funded by local authorities. Its work involves the supervision of young people and others who have committed offences, as well as giving support and advice to newly released prisoners. The probation service's work therefore requires close collaboration with SSDs. Indeed, the Seebohm Committee (1968) was concerned about the relationship between these two services. In Scotland the probation service was merged with social work departments in 1969. In England and Wales it remains formally separate but often the same local authority bears responsibility for both, which ought to make co-operation relatively easy. This co-operation is both desirable and necessary but it has been seriously impeded by an obsession among SSD staff with the preservation of their clients' confidentiality. It is also hindered by a feeling among social workers of a need to establish and defend their autonomous professional status, which makes them reluctant to communicate with or learn from the staff of other departments or agencies. This concern with professional status may also produce an unduly authoritarian attitude in relationships with clients, who may be forced into passive and dependent relationships with social workers which in turn can lead at best to apathy and at worst to resentment.

SSDs also need to collaborate with other local authorities, especially in housing, which is always a district council responsibility and is thus separated from social services outside the metropolitan areas. The problems which can arise in this liaison can be illustrated by the case of homeless persons. A person who becomes homeless looks initially to the housing authority for assistance but social workers may need to liaise with housing officers in order to find them suitable accommodation. Private accommodation is rarely available for such people except in the form of expensive and cramped bed and breakfast hostels but in order to obtain council accommodation, a homeless person has to overcome two major obstacles. First, housing authorities may require evidence that the person is a resident of their area and has been so for some time, so that he or she has a legitimate claim to be housed by that particular authority. Second, most housing authorities have long waiting lists for council flats and houses and they are understandably reluctant to allow anyone to jump the queue. If this were to be too easily permitted, people might deliberately make themselves homeless in order to get council accommodation without spending time on a waiting list. Hence, the legislation has been altered to relieve housing authorities of their obligation to provide accommodation for people who are voluntarily homeless. Furthermore, the pressure on local authority housing has increased because many sitting tenants have exercised their right to purchase their council houses under the 1980 Act, with the result that the stock of houses and flats available to local authorities has considerably diminished. However, housing associations are increasingly helping to meet the needs of particular groups of homeless people, including single parents, the young homeless and the disabled.

The problems to which this gives rise are particularly acute outside the metropolitan areas because the county councils, which are responsible for social services, are not housing authorities, hence they own little accommodation which is suitable for accommodating homeless people. In consequence, they are compelled to pay for such people to live in hotels or bed and breakfast accommodation until permanent homes can be found for them. The passage of the Homeless Persons Act, 1977, which vested responsibility for rehousing homeless people in the district councils as the housing authorities, has not prevented lengthy wrangles occurring between district councils over which of them should accept responsibility for housing a particular family which became homeless in one district but has been accommodated by the social services in another. Meanwhile, these families must live in a hostel or hotel at the expense of the social services committee, often with families with children crammed into single rooms. Some such disputes between housing authorities have been resolved only in the High Court.

A third area of collaboration which can be difficult is with the central government agencies which have a responsibility for helping people in poverty or other forms of distress. These include the Department of Social Security (DSS) and the NHS. Social workers have to advise their clients on obtaining social security benefits, medical treatment and other assistance. They may represent their clients before appeal tribunals when their entitlement to benefits is disputed by the DSS or another agency (Bell, 1969; Elcock, 1969). Local authorities and Citizens' Advice Bureaux often employ welfare rights advisers who can assist people with their claims or represent them at tribunal hearings. Thus, Cambridgeshire SSD employs two such advisers, Cambridge City Council has an office staffed by a further three and the Citizens' Advice Bureau also employs welfare rights advisers. However, such generous provision is not always available in other areas.

The division of responsibility between SSDs and the NHS is particularly artificial. Hospital social workers are employed by SSDs but community nurses, whose functions are at least co-ordinate with those of such social workers, are employed by health authorities. However, in some areas both groups work together in health centres. At another level, the Government makes funds available for joint projects, under which the health authority pays for the capital costs of a project but the SSD progressively takes over its running costs. These jointly funded projects are managed by joint consultative committees which include representatives of the health authorities and the SSD. These schemes encourage the construction of hostels for old people or the handicapped. These jointly financed schemes work to the benefit of the SSD because they can acquire additional care facilities and to the health authorities because they relieve pressure on hospital beds.

The social services must also work with the courts of law because they are responsible for referring cases to SSDs and they impose duties on them as a result of the decisions they take about individual cases. Finally, social workers need to co-operate with voluntary organisations. Many of these provide services at less cost than if the local authority provided them itself. In consequence, social services committees make grants to a wide range of organisations such as MIND, the WRVS, Dr Barnardo's and many others. The use to which these grants are put must be monitored to ensure that public funds are properly and efficiently spent but too much and too vigorous probing into voluntary associations' affairs by local authority auditors may produce resentment and the withdrawal of badly needed voluntary services. The intervention of volunteers may also be seen as a challenge to social workers' professional status because it may indicate to the public that social work can be carried out just as well by amateurs as by professional social workers. On the other hand, voluntary workers and agencies do much to relieve the burdens on hard-pressed social workers, although voluntary agencies may not always exist in the locations where they are most sorely needed.

These voluntary groups also mount campaigns on behalf of the causes or client groups which they seek to represent and, in consequence, they may come into conflict with local authorities as well as the central government. The importance of co-ordination with voluntary organisations has been considerably increased by the community care legislation, which encourages local authorities to purchase services from voluntary organisations among others rather than provide those services themselves. Many social workers therefore have to work closely with voluntary organisations and assist them to develop initiatives.

Co-ordination and co-operation with other departments of the local authority, with other local authorities and many other agencies is a major policy and management problem with which SSDs have long been familiar but which will increase with the introduction of the community care policy. It is difficult to achieve in today's large and impersonal local authorities in which individual social workers tend to be isolated from one another and from colleagues elsewhere whose expertise and co-operation they need but do not know how to obtain. This problem is likely to become greater as the mixed economy of social care is developed under the community care legislation, which will require extensive liaison to be developed between SSDs – which are charged with the overall co-ordination of community care – and a large number of private and voluntary agencies who are increasingly becoming responsible for providing many forms of care. To do this, they have been required to prepare community care plans, which must be approved by the Secretary of State for Health, as the basis for the development of co-ordinated care in their areas.

Hierarchy, management and responsiveness

Apart from the difficulty of co-ordinating the provision of care with other agencies, SSDs face a number of other management problems. One is that the demand for social services is always greater than any conceivable supply of them and this problem has become more and more acute as a result of successive rounds of public spending cuts, especially since 1979. Harsh choices are unavoidable, as social workers and their managers are faced with the constant need to decide the priority to be accorded to different client groups, although many such choices are imposed by the requirement to provide statutory services. This can lead to conflicts within the department and with clients. Thus, a field social worker may feel that her or his colleagues at headquarters do not fully appreciate the needs of a particular client or client group, while headquarters may respond that they do but there are others whose need is greater. Some clients may approach councillors or MPs and thereby gain greater attention and a higher priority but most clients are insufficiently articulate and informed to do this. Equally, if all those needing the social services were to do this, a further way of assessing priorities would have to be found, given that the resources available are not unlimited. The assessment of need is difficult and may lead to reliance on what R.G.S. Brown (1975) called secondary criteria, which can be relatively easily quantified but may be misleading. The same problem applies to measuring the achievements of the social services. A greater number of children taken into care or of old people in residential homes may indicate more generous provision or the failure of other policies, for example to encourage families to stay together and look after their children, or to enable old people to live independently. More success with family support or domiciliary care can result in the provision of a more acceptable and cheaper service than opening yet more residential homes. The adequate assessment of needs and achievements pose major problems for social services managers but they must be attempted in order to try and determine the appropriate priorities and assess the cost-effectiveness of the provision made. A particularly difficult area is that of preventative work. It may be very cost-effective to put more resources into trying to prevent social problems developing and hence avoid imposing demands on remedial services but the effectiveness of preventative services is very difficult to determine because there is no means of measuring what would have happened without it. Furthermore, the demands of statutory obligations for the provision of remedial services often squeezes out preventative work (Brown, 1975, pp. 135–136; Judge, 1979).

Budget cuts may also stimulate innovation. The quality of service to the public may be improved within a static or declining budget by providing more cost-effective services or by developing better relationships with clients. Such innovations have also been stimulated by dissatisfaction with the hierarchical structures of SSDs and the resultant predominance of 'bureaucratic paternalism' (Hoggett and Hambleton, 1987). SSDs are commonly organised on a three-tier basis. At the centre is a headquarters unit containing the director of social services and other senior officers, who are responsible for advising the social services committee on matters of policy, for the overall planning of the service and administering the committee's budget. Below headquarters there will often be divisional or area offices responsible for the running of residential homes in each division or area and for teams of social workers providing field services, as well as domiciliary care workers. These three groups of staff used to be kept largely separate from one another but they are tending to work more closely together now. The divisional offices will also be mainly responsible for liaison with voluntary organisations. The divisional officers may report to sub-committees of councillors plus representatives of district councils and other organisations.

This fairly simple hierarchy raises important problems of accountability and control, however. Goals in the social services are notoriously difficult to set with any degree of precision and the measurement of achievement is almost impossible. To make matters worse, there is no fully agreed set of professional values in social work, partly because of the different traditions from which social work practice developed and the former specialisation of social workers in such fields as children's or welfare work, or work with the mentally handicapped. The Seebohm Committee recommended that social workers should become generic, being able to assist clients with all their social care problems, at least in the first instance.

In consequence, a wide range of knowledge and skills must be taught to social workers during their training courses. One consequence is the difficulty in agreeing the content of training courses because of the wide range of problems social workers must deal with and the situations for which they must be prepared. For example, there is a continuing debate about how much time should be accorded in training courses to issues of racial or gender discrimination. Furthermore, training opportunities for residential – and domiciliary – care staff are more limited than those available for field workers, although the development of three-year Diploma in Social Work courses to replace the former two-year Certificate of Qualification in Social Work course and other training courses for residential workers, is intended to reduce these differentials. The urgency of providing better training for residential-care staff has been stressed by inquiries into poor standards of care or systematic abuse in residential homes, such as that into the Staffordshire 'pin-down' scandal, where the development of an unacceptably cruel punishment regime for children in care was blamed partly on the lack of training for the staff in the council's children's homes.

Field workers in particular have to take responsible and difficult decisions largely on their own, although their seniors should be available for consultation if the social worker feels a need to discuss a case with someone else or is reluctant to take some responsibility for a case where a mistake may lead to a widely publicized tragedy. The accountability of SSDs to local authority members and the extensive publicity invariably given to such tragedies as deaths from baby-battering or hypothermia, continually force social workers and their managers on to the defensive. What matters seems to be to avoid making mistakes and the social worker's creativity is stifled by excessive supervision by superiors or the writing of lengthly reports for them. Another problem is that, although formally social workers are appointed to teams which are responsible for clients in a particular part of the local authority's area, each worker has his or her own case load and is rarely able to discuss cases with colleagues unless a formal case conference is called, when other workers such as probation officers, health service staff or teachers may also be present. The pressure of case work limits the frequency and value of team meetings. It may be that specialist teams could work together more effectively and such teams are sometimes created, for instance intake teams which deal with immediate crises and short-term referrals, passing clients to long-term teams where necessary.

A profession that lost its way?

The isolation which social workers tend to suffer is reinforced by the difficulties they have had in establishing a clear professional identity and forming effective interest groups. Professionalism was slow to develop among social workers and was retarded in particular by the generic responsibilities they acquired in 1971. Furthermore, whereas the teachers' unions play an important part in protecting and promoting the professional and other interests of teachers both in relation to the central government and local authorities, social workers largely lack such protection. They are for the most part members of the National Association of Local Government Officers (NALGO), in which their needs are dealt with along with those of a wide variety of other local authority staff. In 1993 NALGO merged with the National Union of Public Employees (NUPE) and the Confederation of Health Service Employees (COHSE) to form a new public services union, UNISON. Thus social workers' interests are now a smaller aspect of a much larger union's activities. They can also join the British Association of Social Workers (BASW) but many do not do so and few take an active interest in its activities. Many social workers lack formal qualifications, which makes it impossible for local authorities or BASW to enforce consistent professional standards. The latter has pressed for the creation of a social work professional council along similar lines to the General Medical Council to regulate standards and discipline among social workers, hence improving their somewhat ambivalent status. The status and role of the body responsible for the validation of social work training courses, the Central Council for Education and Training in Social Work (CCETSW) is also a subject of controversy. Also, lack of resources to send social workers on qualifying or post-qualification courses means that the existence of large numbers of unqualified social workers has continued to pose problems both of professional identity and competence.

The development of a professional identity among social workers is further impeded by the difficulty of defining their professional roles at all clearly. On the one hand, it can be argued that any person with sympathy and common sense can help another person in distress and one does not need a training course to acquire those qualities. On the other hand, social work training may be too general to enable them to undertake such specialist roles as counselling or psychotherapy to enable people to resolve deep-seated personal and social problems, the manifestations of which may be behavioural problems among children, truancy, marital stress and family violence. Social workers can treat the symptoms but not the disease; indeed some would argue that social work is inherently a form of social pathology, because it deals with the symptoms of social problems rather than attacking their root causes in the political and economic systems (CDP, 1974).

Such concerns, together with the failure of industrial action in 1978, led increasingly to social work becoming 'a profession that lost its way' (Dean, 1979), because although by 1979 as many people were qualifying in social work as in medicine, there was no agreement on what they should do. When no-one knows what they should do there is a tendency to accept responsibility for anything and everything (ibid.). In 1980 the Secretary of State for Social Services asked the National Institute for Social Work to undertake an enquiry into the role of social workers with a view to producing a clear and generally acceptable definition of their role. The majority of the committee's members recommended greater concentration on community work (Barclay, 1981).

Social workers are expected to be accountable at once to their employing local authorities and their clients. They must accept responsibility for the advice they give their clients and in doing so they have a considerable degree of autonomy but they are inhibited by the need to account to their superiors *ex post facto* for their actions. They also need to co-operate with others, such as the police or magistrates, who may or may not share their views. Within SSDs there may be conflicts of judgement, for example field workers may disagree with the disciplinary regime enforced in a residential home. Conflict over the priority to be accorded to individuals or client groups is likely to be endemic between field workers and headquarters. Greater professional autonomy for social workers individually or in teams might reduce some of these problems but the need to determine overall policies and priorities means that conflicts between individual social workers and teams dealing with their clients and the headquarters which sets priorities under the guidance of the social services committee, are likely to remain endemic.

New patterns of management

The hierarchical management structure also requires alteration in order to develop social services which are more responsive to social service clients and local communities, especially as 'bureaucratic paternalism' has become less acceptable. Increasing dissatisfaction with the established organisation of SSDs has resulted in the social services being at the forefront of experiments with decentralisation schemes in the 1970s and 1980s (Payne, 1979; Hoggett and Hambleton, 1987). These initiatives have also be used to break down the barriers between field-work staff, residential- and domiciliary-care staff – now more usually known as community care staff (Elcock, 1986).

Malcolm Payne (1979) identified three main types of social work team. The *traditional* team's members are responsible for the cases allocated to them but they are under hierarchical supervision by their superiors. They are hence unlikely to produce creative social work but they may develop into *transitional* teams with more support from voluntary and ancillary staff, with more collective action to deal with cases although formal responsibility for each case may still be vested in a single social worker. Ultimately, Payne argues that the *community* team should emerge, in which 'the social workers are involved in a network which can be described as part of the community support system' (Payne, 1979, p. 151). In a community team, cases are shared informally and team members develop extensive contacts with outsiders. Community teams both encourage more creative social work and provide social workers with more mutual support in a stressful profession which produces high levels of nervous breakdowns and marital stress among its members (Holman, 1979).

During the 1980s, many SSDs developed forms of decentralisation which developed the trends identified by Payne in his discussion of the community team. For example, in 1984 Humberside County Council replaced its seventeen Area Teams with forty-eight Neighbourhood Teams which were to develop responsibility for all social services in relatively small areas of around 5,000 people. These neighbourhood teams included residential, day-care and domiciliary-care staff and were given responsibility not only for the social services but also for developing links with other agencies, including voluntary groups. The teams were allocated funds which they could use according to their own discretion. The scheme resulted in better co-ordination of service provision at the neighbourhood level and better morale among staff, but its effectiveness was progressively reduced by budget cuts (Elcock, 1986). The Humberside scheme was modelled on a successful decentralisation scheme developed by East Sussex County Council and similar developments have taken place in other authorities (Hoggett and Hambleton, 1987) but their impact has been reduced by financial stringency. One problem has been that the increased accessibility of the neighbourhood teams has stimulated an increase in demand for social services while at the same time their availability has been reduced by spending cuts. In consequence, cynicism and dissatisfaction among clients whose hopes for help and services are dashed, negates the objective of decentralisation to make social services more responsive to clients.

The issue most likely to dominate social work is the co-ordination of the activities of numerous local authority services, Government departments, voluntary agencies, private companies and many others to ensure that the needs of various vulnerable or deprived groups within society are met as far as possible within limited and shrinking resources. The burden of statutory duties is also likely to increase as Parliament legislates to provide for intervention in more and more social problems. The increasing mobility of the population, the demise of the extended family and increasing materialism are all likely to add to the responsibilities of the personal social services, as is the 'age explosion'; particularly the increasing number of people aged over seventy-five. The decline in social budgets may force citizens to look after ageing or inform family members ourselves, which may not be entirely a bad thing but it nonetheless seems likely that the needs which must be met by the social services will continue both to diversify and to increase.

HOUSING

Housing has long been at the heart of political controversy in local authorities because it raises the fundamental political issue of how far Governments should intervene in order to protect citizens from the operation of market forces. Local authorities began building houses in order to replace the slums built during the Industrial Revolution with safe, comfortable dwellings: the commitment to do so dates from Lloyd George's pledge in 1918 to build 'homes fit for heroes' after the First World War. Most major cities still have areas of housing which are unpleasant and unhealthy, although since the early twentieth century local authorities have had the power to condemn houses as unfit for human habitation and close them.

The desire to eliminate the slums produced the garden cities of the late nineteenth and early twentieth centuries, the post-Second World War new towns and many other forms of public housing. The development of public housing has also played a major part in the careers of local and national political figures. In Leeds, for example, the drive to clear the slums in the 1930s was led by a legendary figure, the Reverend Charles Jenkinson, an Anglican clergyman. Appointed to a slum parish in Leeds in the late 1920s, he was so horrified by what he found there that he got elected to Leeds City Council and persuaded other Labour Party leaders to accompany him on a tour of Europe to study workers' housing developments, including the Karl Marxhof in Vienna, on which Leeds's innovatory Quarry Hill Flats were later modelled (Hammerton, 1952). Jenkinson's chairmanship of the Leeds Housing Committee in the mid-1930s produced massive demolition and rehousing schemes, of which his biographer commented that 'It may be that more than one vicar, in a moment of despondency, has wished his parish were wiped off the face of the earth. Never had a vicar been seen actually arranging for this to be done (ibid., p. 88). For this policy Jenkinson was repeatedly attacked by slum landlords and the Conservative Party, who denounced his policy as 'red ruin'. In other cities too, politicians gained local and national prominence by leading campaigns to clear the slums and provide decent houses for all (see Donoughue and Jones, 1973 for the example of Herbert Morrison on the London County Council).

Successive Governments since 1919 passed legislation which increased local authorities' powers to close, compulsorily purchase and demolish slum housing and replace it with new council houses to be let at subsidised rents. Under such legislation as the Slum Clearance Act of 1930 and the Housing Act of 1974, local authorities were given extensive powers to develop their housing policies and subsidise rents. However, major mistakes were also made. The Quarry Hill Flats in Leeds eventually became a slum and itself had to be demolished in the 1980s. In the 1950s and 1960s housing authorities erected a large number of high-rise developments with encouragement from the Government, many of which have deteriorated into unattractive slums themselves, becoming known to their tenants as 'Alcatraz' or 'The Piggeries'. Some such developments have had to be demolished long before the debts that local authorities incurred for their construction had been paid off. Also, the laying down of cost yardsticks for council housing by the Department of the Environment encouraged many housing authorities to build large housing estates on the edges of towns or cities because the cost per house was cheaper than developing smaller estates which would be more attractive to tenants and not oblige them to move miles away from the facilities of the city centre, as well as from established friends and relatives. Often the consequences of moving large numbers of former inner-city residents to large estates on the urban fringe have included vandalism, petty crime and social problems, including marital stress among tenants and their families living on bleak estates with few social amenities. On the other hand, some housing authorities have developed imaginative estates which have proved popular with their inhabitants because they were designed to meet the expressed social and other needs of tenants, instead of simply putting roofs over people's heads. A notable example is the Byker Wall in Newcastle upon Tyne, which was designed to encourage social integration among the residents, providing for their social and recreational needs. Furthermore, care was taken where possible to preserve existing social networks by moving relatively few residents at a time and keeping family and friendship groups together. However, like Quarry Hill Flats, the inspiration for the Byker Wall came from abroad, in this case in the form of a firm of Scandinavian architects.

Until the early 1970s, the judgement about the extent of rent subsidies was left to local housing authorities to make, but it was always a matter of party controversy. The Conservative Party always opposed locally and nationally, what they regarded as the extravagant and wasteful approach of Labour-controlled local authorities to council house building and rent subsidies. They recognised the need to help those who were truly in need but they took the view that general rent subsidies provided help at the public expense for many tenants who could afford to pay economic rents for their houses. In consequence, when Edward Heath won office in 1970 with a commitment to introduce more business-like methods to government, legislation was prepared which would force local housing authorities to raise rents until they reached an economic 'fair rent' level. This policy was enacted in the Housing Finance Act, 1972. This required all housing authorities to raise rents at six-monthly intervals until they reached an economic level related to house values in their areas. Most housing authorities complied with the Act, albeit more or less reluctantly but it led to a confrontation between the Clay Cross Urban District Council and the Government which became a local government *cause célèbre*. The Clay Cross councillors refused to raise their council house rents as required by the Act. In consequence, the district auditor ordered that they be surcharged with the amount of revenue which the council had lost because the rents had not been raised. The councillors were disqualified from office and most were rendered bankrupt by the large amounts of money they were required to pay. However, the Labour Government which was elected in 1974 repealed the Housing Finance Act and restored to local authorities the freedom to fix their rents as they saw fit. They also partially relieved the former Clay Cross councillors of the burdens imposed upon them.

In 1979, housing was at the forefront of the renewed and much more persistent exposure of public services to market forces which was required by the successive Thatcher administrations. In 1980, local housing authorities were once more required to raise their council house rents to market levels. Furthermore, they were required by law to sell council houses to those tenants who wished to purchase them, at a discounted price which was set at a lower level for those tenants who had occupied their houses for longer. This policy was initially resisted by many housing authorities. Norwich City Council and many others delayed the processing of conveyances of council houses to sitting tenants who had decided to buy them and pleaded that they had insufficient staff to process the conveyances quickly. In consequence, conveyances were held up for up to eighteen months. However, a threat that the Government would appoint a commissioner to take over Norwich's housing department if the sales did not proceed more quickly led to quicker progress. Nonetheless, many housing authorities have expressed anxiety that houses which are sold to tenants are then never again available for public housing purposes. This applies especially to those houses which were built or converted for the use of disabled people but the right to buy has been given to these tenants in common with all others.

The major, long-standing policy question for local authorities is whether and to what extent housing should be regarded as a social service rather than as an economic good. Since 1965, the supply of private rented accommodation has declined almost to vanishing point, for which many Conservatives blame ham-fisted intervention by Labour Governments in the housing market, especially in the Rent Act of 1965, which both controlled the rents landlords could charge and increased tenants' security of tenure. In consequence, in many areas local authorities became virtually the sole source of accommodation for rent rather than purchase. By the early 1980s local authorities owned between a quarter and a third of the country's housing stock; in Scotland the proportion was over a half. The costs involved in the construction, maintenance and replacement of this stock became a considerable proportion of housing authorities' budgets and constituted a significant proportion of national public expenditure. So, to the Conservative Party's traditional dislike of subsidised housing was added pressure to reduce public spending on housing by increasing rents, selling council houses and transferring part of the responsibility for providing houses to rent to other agencies, notably housing associations. Hence to an effort to reduce the role of local authorities as organs of the State in providing services was added another policy thrust of more general application: the removal of functions from local authorities to other agencies.

The development of alternative forms of housing provision has been encouraged by certain long-standing limitations on council housing, which in their turn resulted from their provision as a social service rather than as an economic good. One was the restrictions imposed on council house tenants, sometimes including such minor matters as the colours they were allowed to use to paint their front doors.

Some housing authorities have undoubtedly used such petty restrictions as a means of enforcing the Benthamite 'lesser eligibility' principle, in accordance with which houses provided at the public expense must be inferior to those obtainable through the private market, in order to encourage those seeking houses to purchase them or rent them from private landlords wherever possible. On the other hand, the standards laid down nationally by the Department of the Environment, such as the Parker Morris standard defined in 1968, have been regarded by some as too costly. Also, some housing authorities have developed imaginative schemes such as the Byker Wall in Newcastle upon Tyne, which for a long time escaped many of the problems associated with council housing estates, such as vandalism and petty crime and was very popular, although it is no longer as popular as it was. In the 1970s, renovation schemes for substandard or dilapidated housing were encouraged by government funding through general improvement areas or housing action areas. Renovation rather than clearance also has the advantage of keeping local communities together rather than dispersing them and destroying established family, friendship and neighbourhood support networks. Indeed, some local communities have vigorously resisted attempts by local authorities to break them up in order that the areas they live in can be redeveloped (Gower Davies, 1972).

Another persistent problem has been the restriction which the system of housing tenure, especially in the local authority sector, has imposed on the mobility of labour in Britain. Council house tenants cannot easily move from one local authority area to another because they will have to go on the waiting list for a new house in the new area. Even within a single housing authority's area, transfers from one part of the district to another are hard to obtain. This has inhibited many British workers from moving from areas where they are unemployed to areas where work is available: the inflexibility of local authority housing allocation policies has prevented many British workers from taking Lord Tebbitt's advice to 'get on your bike' and look for work, even if they had been inclined to do so.

The changing management of housing

Much discontent with restrictive bureaucracy and slow repair services, coupled with the continuing partisan controversy about the purpose for which public housing should be put, has led to attempts at radical change in the management of housing. As with other service areas discussed here, we can make a distinction between reforms whose intention is to remove housing from local authority control and transfer it either to the private sector or to an alternative form of control independent of councils and those with the intention of improving the management of housing within the overall management structures of local authorities. There is again a division to be made between market-based solutions and those concerned with public service reform (Hoggett and Hambleton, 1987).

During the 1970s, resistance to clearance schemes and discontent with council policies led to friction between local authorities and residents on council estates. In Lambeth, one frustrated politician declared of one of the borough's neighbourhood councils: 'Angell – I'd shoot the lot!' Indeed, several of Lambeth's Neighbourhood Councils became vocal opponents of council policy on such matters as squatting, the demolition of old estates which ought to be rehabilitated and rent increases (Cockburn, 1979). Resistance to clearance schemes was also encouraged by the Community Development Project (Community Development Project, 1974) and by local community leaders (Gower Davies, 1972). Hence, housing provided a good example of the problems that local authorities must face when they encourage increased public participation in their decision-making and management: they are forced to listen to things they do not wish to hear.

Nonetheless, in the 1980s, housing authorities, like the SSDs, were in the vanguard of developing internal decentralisation schemes (Hoggett and Hambleton, 1987). Often, neighbourhood offices were created, either to deal with housing problems alone or as part of a wider project of corporate decentralisation (Hambleton, 1979; Elcock, 1986). Often, area repair teams would be attached to these neighbourhood offices with the intention of ensuring a quicker response when repairs were requested, both because the repair team would not have to travel from a central depot and because the line of communication between tenant and repair team would be shortened because there was no need for the tenant's request to be sent to the Town Hall for approval and then be sent to the repair section. One result, however, has been an increase in demand which cannot always be met. Also, bureaucratic confusion can develop among the neighbourhood offices, as well as between them and the central housing department. In some cases, therefore, decentralisation has failed to deliver a satisfactory service. In any case, in housing as in other service areas, the effectiveness of neighbourhood offices has been reduced by budget reductions.

Market-based solutions have, not surprisingly, been favoured by the Governments which have held office since 1979. The early initiative of giving council house tenants the right to buy their homes was fundamental to the Government's aim of increasing home ownership. By 1988, over 1.1 million council houses had been sold to sitting tenants. (Atkinson and Durden,

1990, Table 8:1, p. 121). This radical policy change has since been supplemented by a series of further initiatives designed to remove houses from local authority control and subject their management to market forces or increased consumer pressure. In common with other public service reforms of this period, the aim was to reduce local authorities to a residual role in providing housing (ibid., 1990, pp. 118f). The areas of discretion available to local housing authorities have been steadily eroded both by legislation such as the 1989 Local Government and Housing Act, which introduced the 'ring-fencing' of local authorities' housing revenue accounts. In consequence, local authorities' power to subsidise these accounts from elsewhere in their budgets has been almost eliminated. Their discretion has also been reduced by the increasing stringency of the financial controls imposed on local authorities and by the establishment by the Government of performance indicators by which their achievements must be measured.

A major avenue of development has been the encouragement of housing associations as an alternative to local housing authorities which offer a more flexible, market-orientated approach to the provision of houses to rent than can be available through local authorities. Housing associations originated in the nineteenth century as charitable organisations but their development has been encouraged by the allocation of funds to them by the Housing Corporation. Under the 1988 Housing Act, housing associations are expected to become the future providers of social rented housing, with local authorities confined in this as in other services to an 'enabling' role of encouraging the provision of such houses by others, in particular housing associations.

Housing associations have also been encouraged where possible to take over estates from local authorities and in addition, most of the public money available for new housing has been given to housing associations through the Housing Corporation, rather than to local authorities. Although such takeovers have yet to happen on a large scale, housing associations have become increasingly involved in rehabilitation and improvement of rundown and unpopular council housing estates. For instance, the North British Housing Association has been involved in the rehabilitation of a notoriously dilapidated and unpopular council house estate at Cowgate, in Newcastle upon Tyne. In Scotland a national agency, Scottish Homes, has been given the task and the resources for the development and management of public housing in a country where about half of all houses are still rented from local authorities or other public sector agencies.

Further initiatives have included an attempt in the late 1980s to establish housing action trusts, where the Department of the Environment can transfer a run-down estate from the council to an approved landlord. Also, tenants on a council estate can be balloted to approve a change of landlord to a housing association or a private company. Indeed, under the 1988 Housing Act, tenants may initiate such a ballot but the new landlord must be approved by the Housing Corporation. However, few of these ballots to introduce a 'choose a landlord' scheme have produced a vote to desert the local authority, indicating – as does the relatively few schools whose parents have voted to opt out of LEA control – that public attachment to local authorities is stronger than ministers and their advisers have believed. However, ministers have persevered in their efforts to create autonomous agencies which 'effectively bypass local authorities and electorates and provide government with a way of pursuing particular policies regardless of local wishes' (Atkinson and Durden, 1990, p. 17). We shall see similar developments in other areas of local government, notably town and country planning.

Housing, then, has been a political football for many years because of attempts by successive Governments to impose their ideological preferences on local authorities and reduce their powers, especially when Conservative Governments have sought to impose the discipline of the market on public sector housing provision. There has been public resistance to unpopular local authorities but also wariness of radical changes in tenure proposed by ministers. There seems little prospect that housing will become any less controversial in the future and issues concerning it will continue to dominate debates in the council chambers of those local authorities which have responsibility for it.

LEISURE SERVICES*

Local government is the principal public service provider of leisure services but it has long shared with the private and voluntary sectors in a genuinely mixed economy of provision. The

* This section was contributed by Dr Ken Harrop, of the Department of Economics and Government, University of Northumbria at Newcastle.

services on offer include leisure and sports centres, festivals, country parks, camping and caravan sites, museums, art galleries, arts centres, theatres and orchestras, sports pitches and heritage centres. This diverse range of facilities and services is often described in three main categories – arts and culture, tourism, sport and physical recreation – although Travis (1986) has referred to ten 'identifiable sectors within the realm of local authority leisure services'. These are: sport and physical recreation, informal outdoor recreation, arts and culture, libraries, entertainment and catering, conservation and interpretation, tourism, youth and community, adult education and social services (for example, clubs for the elderly or social tourism). Apart from the statutory obligation to provide public libraries and other educational opportunities and that imposed upon some local authorities to manage national parks and areas of outstanding natural beauty, provision in this field is almost entirely discretionary and therefore particularly exposed to spending reductions.

The origins of local government's involvement in leisure services lie in distinctively nineteenth-century conceptions of civic philanthropy and municipal paternalism which preceded both the development of the leisure industry and in some senses the creation of modern British local government itself. Thus, public parks, for example, were opened in Preston and in Birkenhead in 1842 and 1843 respectively – developments consolidated in the Recreational Grounds Act of 1852 as part of an attempt to retrieve a lost sense of ruralism as well as for public health and sanitary reasons. With the latter consideration in mind, local authorities began to provide facilities such as slipper and swimming baths. In more recent times, local government's provision of sports facilities was assisted by the work of the Sports Council after its creation in 1965.

Investment in the arts gained momentum following the creation of the Arts Council in 1946 and the emergence of regional arts associations in the 1950s and 1960s. The establishment of regional tourist boards, partly as a result of the Development of Tourism Act of 1969, provided a local focus for tourism development.

The aims and intentions of local government in developing leisure services are multi-faceted and have also tended to change over time but they can be accommodated within a framework set out by Rapoport and Dover (1976), which suggests that leisure-providing organisations may be motivated by three principal concerns. First is the concern to meet the requirements of individual consumers and customers in terms of, for example physical fitness, the pursuit of excellence, entertainment and enjoyment, intellectual development or social and physical welfare, Second, is a concern to promote community well-being by way of economic development, reducing levels of vandalism and crime or the conservation of natural beauty and heritage. Third, there are the interests of the providing organisation itself including commercial profit and organisational image.

There are clearly many implied and explicit tensions here for compatibility. Mutuality of objectives may be difficult to arrange. The rehabilitation of a dilapidated inner-city area via a tourism development strategy, for example, may not obviously be perceived by locals as solving their problems. In the short term the development of high-class hotels, the capital-intensive restoration of former ship-building or other industrial waterfronts as marinas or waterparks may serve to heighten community tension and to lead to still further alienation and perhaps yet more crime as differences in material circumstances become even more obvious.

It is, however, the economic development potential of leisure, especially tourism, which has come to the fore in local government's thinking over the past decade or so. Leisure is seen as:

> a source of economic growth and job creation which can, at least in part, fill the gaps left by declines in older, more traditional industries. As such, it may be one key to the resolution of the social problems caused by the economic decay of inner cities, old industrial towns and rural areas.
>
> (Martin and Mason, 1988, p. 15)

Throughout the UK – in Belfast, Bradford, Chichester, Glasgow, South Tyneside and Swansea for example – local authorities have attempted to pursue integrated strategies of leisure and tourism development. Martin and Mason (1988) describe a frequent approach which borrows heavily from North American redevelopment schemes, especially those in Baltimore and Boston. Typically, the preferred model has three principal ingredients:

- The development of a major new physical facility such as a museum or conference centre in order to provide a focus and catalyst for developers, the media and locals and tourists alike. The National Aquarium and the Maryland Science Centre in

Baltimore and the National Museum of Photography, Film and Television in Bradford serve as examples.

- the upgrading of existing facilities and buildings, wherever possible highlighting any heritage or cultural elements, together with comprehensive thematic re-interpretation for publicity purposes. In extreme cases, places are marketed almost as somewhere else: South Tyneside becomes 'Catherine Cookson Country' and Durham 'Land of the Prince Bishops' (Barke and Harrop, 1993).

- the projection of the urban centre concerned as the ideal starting point for visiting and exploring surrounding geographical areas. Thus, Bradford is naturally the perfect base for exploring 'Bronte Country and 'Emmerdale Farm Country', Swansea likewise for 'Dylan Thomas Country'. Middlesbrough is promoted as the gateway to 'Captain Cook Country' as well as to James Herriot's Yorkshire Dales (Barke and Harrop, 1993).

The connection between tourism on the one hand, with the arts and popular culture on the other is clearly very close in these sorts of initiatives and has been actively encouraged by the national, regional and local arts development agencies with whom local authorities work in partnership.

For example, in launching the Arts Council's Urban Renaissance strategy in 1988, its then Chairman, Sir William Rees-Mogg argued:

> There is little awareness nationally of the important role which the arts are playing in revitalising depressed urban areas. The Arts Council has launched the 'Urban Renaissance' project to inform those involved in redevelopment – policy makers, property developers and inner city agencies – on the ways in which the arts can stimulate economic and social regeneration. Throughout Britain, the Regional Arts Associations are accomplishing much in inner city areas. 'Urban Renaissance' will provide a facility for sharing these successful formulas for regeneration, involving partnerships across the public and private sectors.
>
> (Arts Council, 1988)

The metropolitan district of Bradford was one of the pioneer authorities in these matters. The origins of its initiative can be traced back to the economic recession of the late 1970s when the authority's unemployment rate rose to 16 per cent as a consequence of the failure of its traditional economic base – particularly textiles and engineering – and the loss of more than 60,000 jobs. Its structural economic problems were compounded by a poor image:

> To make matters worse, Bradford was losing out on much needed investment to other West Yorkshire towns and cities, chiefly because of its poor image. Investors were reluctant to commit money to what they believed was a grimy, backward industrial area. Meanwhile, Bradford was making headlines on a daily basis as television documentaries reported high levels of social deprivation and the Yorkshire Ripper stalked the streets.
> (City of Bradford Metropolitan Council, Economic Development Unit, undated)

The local authority's decision in 1979 to establish the first of the modern generation of economic development units in the UK led to an analysis of Bradford's circumstances and its strengths and weaknesses.

On the credit side was a good range of hotel accommodation – under-utilised and under-occupied at weekends when the demand for short-break holidays was on the increase – as well as Bradford's proximity to Haworth, home of the literary Brontë sisters, to the model town of Saltaire and the Yorkshire Dales. Accordingly, despite the sniffing of snobs and the scoffing of cynics, Bradford developed its first two short-break packages, 'In The Footsteps of the Brontës' and 'Industrial Heritage', which established the city in the minds of the public and the travel industry as a popular visitor destination. The initial success led to other themed holidays including 'millshopping', 'television themes', 'Bradford entertains', 'psychic sightseeing', the hugely popular 'Flavours of Asia' and 'horseriding' and 'artlovers' Bradford'. Within a decade of the original launch, Bradford had become a market leader in short-stay and weekend breaks, attracting some 6 million domestic and overseas visitors annually and injecting £56 million per annum into the local economy. Bradford has become a by-word for marketing the industrial town, demonstrating that not only the seaside authorities can benefit from tourism. The conferment of prestigious awards such as the English Tourist Board's Sir Mark Henig award in 1983 as England's fastest growing tourist destination and again in 1987 for its 'Flavours of Asia' package, as well as Museum of the Year awards for the National Museum of Photography and for the Colour Museum and an RIBA award for the

Alhambra Theatre have all helped to relieve the psychological despondency of the late 1970s and early 1980s. Moreover, the benefits are not only for visitors, for by the end of the 1980s, the unemployment had been reduced to 8 per cent and in a quality of life survey, Bradford was ranked sixth out of the country's thirty-eight biggest cities, well above its rival and near neighbour, Leeds.

Another success story is Wigan where:

> There are many outward signs of the Borough's new confidence ... best known of all, the transformation of the Wigan Pier area from a derelict eyesore into one of the country's most exciting tourist attractions. With its heritage centre featuring professional actors, its canal water buses and display of working industrial machinery, the Pier now draws over ⅓ million visitors a year.
>
> (*Municipal Year Book*, 1992, Volume 2, p. 288)

There, total development costs of £4.13 million between 1982 and 1987 transformed a derelict industrial site into a major tourism, leisure, educational and commercial project involving the renovation of canalside warehouses, the conversion of a cotton-spinning mill and the provision of a complex accommodating offices, a heritage centre, a public house, a restaurant and concert hall, exhibition and display facilities. Funding was provided by Wigan Metropolitan Borough Council in partnership with the now abolished Greater Manchester County Council, urban programme funds, urban development grants, derelict land grants, the European Regional Development Fund, the Countryside Commission, English Tourist Board and private sector contributions and sponsorship. Such a complex mix of partners with inter-dependent interests and expectations has become increasingly typical of major leisure projects. This is a good example of the fragmentation of local governance which is discussed in Chapter 10.

Even within local authorities themselves, the organisation and management of leisure services can appear complex. For example, there may be a leisure services department or committee, but not necessarily so. Even if a leisure services department does exist, responsibility for tourism development may lie elsewhere – perhaps in an economic development unit, reflecting the potential contribution of tourism to that function. In any case, the terminology itself can be bewilderingly wide with labels such as leisure, recreation, culture, amenities as well as some more idiosyncratic historical oddities all appearing on the organisation chart. This complicated, fragmented picture is partly a consequence of the development of the modern all-embracing leisure industry out of a diverse range of earlier, separate activities and partly a result of the growth of leisure services within local government itself.

Of particular relevance in the latter context is the fragmented and piecemeal legislative basis. There exists no single, comprehensive local government (development of leisure, arts and tourism) act, for example, to provide a focus in the same way as the Education Acts of 1944 and 1988 have underpinned the public education service. Various legislative enactments provide the basis for leisure services provision. They include the Local Government Act of 1948 which permitted local authorities to establish information and publicity services for tourism, or the Public Libraries and Museums Act of 1964 which imposed a duty upon the appropriate local authorities to provide arrangements for a public library service and permitted all others to provide museums and art galleries. The Countryside Act of 1968 permitted local authorities to provide countryside recreation facilities. The Local Government Act of 1972 and the Local Government (Miscellaneous Provisions) Act of 1976 were all made use of as local authorities sought to develop their leisure provision. By the early 1980s, however, Travis was able to document the move away from the organisational fragmentation of the 1970s, which reflected the chaotic scatter of 'relevant' discretionary powers, towards the development of integrated leisure service departments with more influence within the authority and greater political muscle (Travis, 1983). A 1985 survey by the Audit Commission, the Local Government Training Board and the Institute of Local Government Studies confirmed the emergence of leisure/recreation groups, with 78 per cent of authorities having a committee with this remit (Audit Commission *et al.*, 1985).

More recently, as in other areas of local government service, the organisational effects of legisaltion relating to compulsary competitive tendering have been apparent. The Local Government Act of 1988 extended the operation of CCT beyond those activities originally designated in the Local Government Planning and Land Use Act of 1980. In November 1988, as a result of an order issued in accordance with that year's Act, local authorities were required to submit the management of certain sports and leisure facilities to competitive tendering processes. Included within the scope of this requirement were:

> sports centres, leisure centres, swimming pools, skating rinks, tennis courts, squash courts, bowling centres, pitches for team games, athletics grounds, cycle tracks, golf courses, putting greens, bowling greens, riding centres, artificial ski slopes, racecourses, centres for flying, ballooning or parachuting, and centres for boating and water sports on inland and coastal waters.
>
> (Audit Commission, 1990; Mallabar, 1991)

In respect of these facilities and venues, English local authorities were required to meet the provisions of a phased timetable which called for:

- 35 per cent of facilities to be subject to competitive tendering processes by no later than 1 January 1992;
- 70 per cent of facilities by no later than 1 August 1992;
- 100 per cent of facilities by no later than 1 January 1993.

Clearly, these major changes to the methods of service delivery raise important topics for consideration. These include, among others, the definition of explicit policies for these areas of leisure services, together with the setting of unambiguous objectives and targets as well as arranging the organisational and management split between client and contractor, issues explored in some detail by Mallabar (1991).

Another issue for leisure services concerns resource availability. In times of standstill or negative growth, the task of defending a largely optional or discretionary service, which critics can brand as an unnecessary luxury, may be particularly difficult. A recent survey of authorities in Northern England (Harrop, Rose and Cousins, 1993) attempted to assess the effects of the financial settlement for 1993–1994 on local authority services and jobs. Along with education, social services and central services, leisure was one of the four areas to be worst affected. Most authorities could readily provide examples of leisure services to be cut and associated jobs to be lost.

CONCLUSION

This discussion of several major local government services has indicated how new approaches to the management of public services, together with the Government's determination to challenge established professional orthodoxies, have changed and are still changing the way in which these and other services are provided for citizens. On the one hand, market-based reforms are decentralising service provision to private companies, voluntary agencies and consumers themselves – as in the case of the increased role of parent governors in the management of schools. On the other hand, the Government's determination to enforce nationwide policies on local authorities has increased the centre's dominance, as with the introduction of the national curriculum. Some ministers have claimed to regard as an ideal the possibly apocryphal American local authority which meets once a year to let contracts for the provision of the services for which it is responsible, then leaving the contractors to provide the services. This represents an ideal vision of the 'enabling' local authority as the Government – or at least some ministers – perceive it.

The increased central control over many local authority services has stemmed from the breakdown of the former political consensus which surrounded many of them and which often permitted the professional workers concerned with providing the services to dominate much of the decision-making about services for citizens. Public disillusion with 'bureaucratic paternalism' stems from two sources. The first is real or alleged service failures, sometimes leading to personal tragedies, such as child deaths from parental abuse, or collective failures, such as children leaving school illiterate. The second is the unsympathetic face often offered by local authority departments to the users of their services, for example petty restrictions or slow repair services imposed on council house tenants. As a result, the radical changes offered by the 'New Right', which challenged the professional orthodoxies long endorsed by most local authority politicians, have been repeatedly endorsed by the electorate. In consequence, political and professional consensus has been replaced by changes demanded by ministers and enforced by them on local authorities and their service-providers alike, despite spirited resistance by both professional groups and local authorities.

However, more long-standing issues also remain to be determined by local authority members and their officers. Four such long-standing issues can be identified and their continued importance indicates that although much is changing in local authority services, some problems are perennial and will ensure that local authorities remain recognisably the same kinds of organisations, dealing with the same kinds of issues, as they were before the Thatcher onslaught began in 1979.

First, access to services remains a major issue, whose importance has been increased by the efforts of local authorities to 'get closer to the public'. Client groups have to be identified and decisions made about whether officers should seek out people who need help or advice, or wait for people to come to local authority offices and ask for it. Decentralisation schemes make the latter easier and less stressful but unless staff also try to contact citizens in need, some groups may be neglected, especially ethnic minorities, women and the gay community. On the other hand, such proactive or investigative services are expensive to provide and may be regarded as intrusions on citizens' privacy. The increased demand for services created by such activities will also impose extra strain on the council's budget.

This leads to the second enduring problem: the need to set priorities for the provision and development of services. This is a neverending task for councillors and officers – to decide whom to help, how much and when. The total amount to be spent on each service must be determined and within that overall amount those concerned must decide whom to help. Inevitably, some of those who are not accorded a high priority will protest though their MPs and councillors, who are expected to pursue such grievances on behalf of their constituents. A study of local authority budgets in the mid-1980s detected not a single local authority which overtly declared its priorities – not surprisingly, because giving any service a low priority would provoke protests from service-providers and their clients (Elcock and Jordan (eds), 1987). The increasingly stringent financial climate of local government has made the need to determine priorities more pressing and the decisions that must be taken more difficult. Also, their grievance-chasing role prevents the removal of councillors from involvement in the details of service provision, despite the advice of a string of management reports that they should concern themselves with setting directions or broad policies (Barratt and Downs, 1988; Clarke and Stewart, 1988; Stewart, 1986).

The final two problems which are common to these services for citizens are the subjects of later chapters. Co-ordination and co-operation among departments, local authorities and other organisations are essential if needs are to be met, as well as clients being given consistent advice and assistance to meet their needs and solve their problems. However, securing such co-ordination has often been difficult. One of the main objectives of managerial change in local government has been to improve communication, co-ordination and co-operation both within individual local authorities and between the various local authorities and other organisations which are involved in service provision. Such inter-organisational co-ordination has become increasingly important as service provision has been devolved to a wider range of agencies, as is particulary the case in social services and leisure services, among the areas of activity discussed in this chapter.

Lastly, local authorities need to get the best possible value for the money they spend and from the people they employ in providing services for citizens. This need has become increasingly pressing as their financial room for manoeuvre has been reduced by cuts in central government grants and increasing restrictions on their freedom to raise money locally. Resource management has therefore become ever more important in the 1970s and 1980s.

Chapter 6

The police and emergency services

Before turning to the wider issues of the management of local government, we need to discuss a further group of services which raise particular problems for councillors and officers in local authorities: the uniformed emergency services. Although the police and the fire brigade are responsible, along with other service departments, for the provision of services for citizens, the nature of the services they provide and the ways in which they are organised present distinctive problems for local government. The police are distinctive in particular because they are involved in the enforcement of the law and regulations in the public's collective interest but this brings them into conflict, sometimes involving violence, with individual citizens in a wide variety of ways. The fire service also enforces regulations which bring its members into disputes with members of the public, especially entrepreneurs whose premises are found to be in breach of the fire regulations.

Like the police, fire brigades are subject to high levels of discipline. Their members must also work together closely and have confidence in one another because – again like the police – their work involves them in situations where they must sometimes face the imminent possibility of injury or death. The risk to their personal safety can be minimised by close teamwork and support one for another. Political controversy will also be restricted both at the local and the national levels because few politicians, either in Parliament or on local authorities, will wish to be seen attacking the forces of law and order or challenging the level of fire cover being provided. Hence, for example, these services are seldom likely to be at the centre of controversies about the level of public spending because few politicians will want to be seen to be reducing the resources available to them.

However, these services do raise some major issues in terms of policy and management. In particular, issues of accountability to the public and its elected representatives are especially acute, particularly in the case of the police. Furthermore, these uniformed, disciplined services tend to develop strong internal cultures which both make them resistant to outside accountability and render efforts to co-ordinate their activities with those of other departments and committees particularly difficult (Baldwin and Kinsey, 1982). The chief constable and the fire chief are often particularly reluctant to participate in meetings of management teams which take them away from their commands in order to discuss wider management issues which they regard as being of marginal relevance to them.

The relationship between the central government and local authorities is also different in these cases from that which prevails in other local government services and the policy communities associated with them. First, the number of interested parties involved in policy-making in these fields is relatively small and usually, the degree of consensus among them is therefore relatively high. Also, political controversy about them is usually muted. In applying Grant Jordan's (1982) analysis, therefore, the police and fire service policy communities are likely to be 'iron triangles' rather than 'elastic nets'. For example, relations between the Home Office and the trade unions representing police officers and firemen tend to be relatively consensual. The two unions representing members of fire brigades, for example, are given representation on the Home Office's Central Fire Brigades Advisory Council, which oversees the management of the fire service. Such trade union involvement in the management of the service for which their members work is highly unusual. Industrial disputes are rare and when they do happen, they are likely to arouse much public concern, especially as these services are essential to the assurance of public safety. Thus the fire service strike of 1977–1978 led to the establishment of a formula for settling firemen's pay which has survived into the 1990s because it provides a means of ensuring that further industrial action in the fire service is unlikely. The police achieved a similarly long-standing formula from the Edmund Davies review of their pay in 1979. However, the Home Secretary's failure to consult the police representative organisations on proposals for structural reform produced a surprised protest from the general secretaries of the three main police unions in March 1993 (*The Guardian*, 12 March 1993).

Attitudes to local government control may also be somewhat ambivalent within the police and fire services. Indeed, the Fire Brigades Union has argued as a matter of policy since 1977 that the fire service should be returned to national control (as existed during the Second World War) in order to ensure that consistent standards of fire cover are provided throughout the country, rather than fire brigades having to compete for resources with other local authority services. Although local control over the police is greatly valued, not least within the police service itself, considerations of efficiency have encouraged the creation of an increasing number and range of national and regional facilities, including regional crime squads, the Police National Computer and the National Co-ordination Centre at times of a national policing crisis, such as the 1984–1985 miners' strike was perceived to be.

The police

A fundamental principle of democratic public administration is that those employed in the public services must be held accountable for their actions to the representatives elected by the public – councillors in the case of local government. If social workers or teachers behave arbitrarily towards clients or parents; if incompetence results in harm to a child or an old person, we are entitled to complain to MPs and councillors. They in turn can demand an explanation and seek redress for their constituents from the officials concerned. In the case of the police service, however, special problems arise because their essential functions are the maintenance of public order and the detection of crime. Indeed, Lord Scarman (1981) pointed out that sometimes these objectives may come into conflict: the need to detain persons and search premises in order to detect crime may sour relationships between the police and the members of a local community, sometimes leading to severe public disorder of the kind that occurred in Brixton in response to 'Swamp '81' – a police search for illegal drugs.

If the police are to be able to carry out their duties effectively, they must be given powers and privileges denied to other public servants. Their activities and methods cannot be debated openly at committee and council meetings because criminals as well as honest citizens can attend or read press reports of such meetings. Policemen need powers to detain citizens, search property and ask questions which could never be granted to social workers or housing officers, but if policemen abuse their powers or cause damage and suffering through incompetence, they ought to be held to account by elected representatives like any other public servants. However, holding the police to account has become increasingly difficult in recent times. The result has been the introduction of major legislation to regulate police conduct, notably the Police and Criminal Evidence Act of 1984 and major debates about the governance of the police: above all whether the police should be a local service locally accountable or a national force accountable through the Home Secretary to Parliament. This latter issue is the main concern of this section and must be seen in terms of a gradual strengthening of central control over the police, to the point at which there may be little substance now in local police accountability. However, the issue of which aspects of policing need to be nationally or regionally controlled and which ought to be under local control has not been clearly debated nor have the areas for national, regional and local control been defined. On the one hand, organised crime and fast transport mean that national and regional policing agencies are needed to pursue and apprehend national and international criminals. On the other hand, there is an urgent and increasingly recognised need for the police to re-establish their links with local communities, in order to secure the co-operation of citizens and community groups in the prevention and detection of the majority of crimes which are locally committed by local criminals (Baldwin and Kinsey, 1982; Scarman, 1981). Hence, on the one hand efficiency may require larger policing areas but on the other, community relations demand the creation of institutions of local contact and accountability. To understand the nature of these problems, we must begin with a brief account of the governance of the police since the Middle Ages.

The development of the police service

The enforcement of law and order in and by local communities has been the basis of policing since Anglo-Saxon times. During the period following the Norman Conquest, the constable as the representative of the village or town was the keeper of the peace, although the whole community had a collective responsibility for apprehending and punishing offenders (Critchley, 1967). From the reign of Richard I onwards, certain knights were appointed to maintain the peace of their areas who were known as the keepers of the peace. This practice was formalised in 1361 by giving them the title of Justice of the Peace (JP). The Justices from that time onward exercised an increasing responsibility for the maintenance of law and order and for a time they became more important than the constable. JPs still have a role in the administration of the police because they make up one-third of the members of local police committees – despite the fact that they are not elected by the public and hence have no claim to democratic legitimacy or to represent anyone other than themselves and their fellow magistrates. However, no attempt has been made to reverse this anachronism, which exists on no other local authority committee. Even the Widdicombe Committee, which came down firmly against the co-option of unelected members onto local authority committees, recommended only that the place of magistrates on Police Committees should be reviewed (Widdicombe, 1986, para. 5:107).

Hence, the administration of justice, together with the maintenance of law and order, was highly localised. JPs became responsible for the appointment of constables and sometimes in larger towns, for that of watchmen as well. In London a varied pattern emerged. In the City of London the Watch of the City was under the control of the Common Council of the City, while in other areas magistrates often organised groups of constables.

The local control of the police is therefore a product of a long tradition in Britain. However, although this system was adequate for the needs of a largely rural society, with the coming of the Industrial Revolution and the movement of the population to the towns, it proved increasingly ineffective. The aftermath of the Napoleonic wars brought increasing civil disturbance and therefore a need for more effective enforcement of law and order which among other things would remove from the army the primary role in dealing with public unrest. The 'Peterloo Massacre' in 1819, when soldiers killed eleven rioters and wounded over 400 more, demonstrated the inappropriateness of using military force against civilian rioters (Briggs, 1959). In consequence, the individual constable was increasingly replaced by a police force. In 1829 the Home Secretary, Sir Robert Peel, secured the passage through

Parliament of the Metropolitan Police Act, hence earning himself immortality in the police nicknames 'bobby' and 'peeler'. His Act created a unified police force in London (except for the City) under the control of two commissioners who were subject to the control of the Home Secretary, hence introducing an element of external supervision of police activities (Bunyon, 1976). In setting up the Metropolitan Police, Peel was influenced by earlier reforms of the Irish constabulary. The Metropolitan Police has remained under the control of the Home Secretary, whereas all other police forces are controlled by the local police authorities established under subsequent legislation. Hence, Parliament is responsible for holding the Metropolitan Police to account, while elsewhere this task has fallen to the councillors who are members of local police committees.

The success of the London experiment led to the establishment of effective police forces throughout the country, although the introduction of 'modern' policing was resisted elsewhere well into the nineteenth century. The Municipal Corporations Act of 1835 required borough councils to establish watch committees composed of not more than one-third of the members of the council and these committees were placed under an obligation to appoint a sufficient number of constables to police the area. The provision of these constables was to be paid for from the local rates and the watch committee was empowered to appoint and dismiss them. However, some municipal councils did not fully implement this requirement, relying on the traditional influences of paternalism, deference and charity to ensure the maintenance of law and order. An Act of 1839 provided for the optional creation of county police forces, which was made compulsory by the County and Borough Police Act of 1856. This also provided central government grants for local police authorities and set up a national police inspectorate (Briggs, 1959, p. 426). The inspectors must report that a police force is efficient before a grant towards its upkeep is made by the Home Secretary, although refusal of the police grant has only been threatened once in recent times, in Derbyshire in 1992. This grant now amounts to half the total cost of the force.

So by the end of the 1850s the policing system as it has existed until the 1990s was substantially in place, although forces have been progressively amalgamated into larger and fewer units from then until the present day. Except for the Metropolitan Police, the Home Secretary had no direct responsibility for policing, which was controlled by local authorities. However, the Home Office exercises regulatory functions and is, of course, responsible for promoting legislation. The possible need for the deployment of the military in support of the civil power was another reason why central government influence over policing was relatively strong. Increasingly too, the central government encouraged the amalgamation of the smaller forces and under the Municipal Corporations Act of 1882 new boroughs with a population of less than 20,000 were prohibited from establishing their own police force. Six years later the Local Government Act of 1888, which established county councils, required borough forces with a population of less than 10,000 to merge with county forces. This Act created county forces under the control of joint standing committees consisting of equal numbers of councillors and magistrates, together with the borough forces controlled by watch committees with no magisterial representation on them. However, these committees had no operational control over the police.

During the Second World War, further amalgamations of police forces were carried out in order to provide efficient policing during the wartime emergency. Some local authorities hoped that after the war they would resume control over their police forces but Chuter Ede, the Home Secretary in the post-war Labour Government, believed that the amalgamations were also needed in peacetime in the interest of efficiency, so he took power to force further amalgamations in the Police Act of 1946. Under this legislation forty-five non-county borough forces were abolished and a number of voluntary amalgamation schemes were agreed. During the passage of the Bill, an amendment was accepted which stated that any council with a population in excess of 100,000 could not be subject to a compulsory amalgamation scheme. So in the post-war period well over 100 separate police forces still existed but further amalgamations took place, culminating in the local government reorganisation of 1972 when the number of police forces in England was reduced to forty-one, excluding the two forces in London. Although the principle of local control over the police was maintained, the effect of the amalgamations, coupled with the introduction of magistrates as one-third of the members of all police authorities, was to render the police increasingly remote from local authority control, especially where the police force was controlled by a joint committee of representatives from several local authorities (Marshall, 1973). Further amalgamations seem likely in the 1990s, reducing the number of forces to around twenty.

The office of constable

Fundamental to any understanding of the relationship between the police and local authorities is the nature of the ancient office of constable. Although a policeman is a local authority employee, he or she is also an officer of the Crown and as such, his accountability to his local authority employers is restricted in a manner unique in local government. As Sir John Anderson wrote (1929, p. 192), 'the policeman is nobody's servant, he executes a public office under the law and it is the law which is the policeman's master.' In 1958 Lord Chesham stated that 'the full responsibility for the enforcement of the law is a matter which is entirely reserved to the chief constable. In the exercise of this responsibility he is answerable to law alone and not to any police authority' (quoted in Marshall, 1965, p. 32). These opinions were tested in law in several cases, the most notable of which was the *Fisher v. Oldham Corporation* case in 1930. Fisher had been mistakenly charged by the police with obtaining money by false pretences. After his release he sued Oldham Corporation for damages, as the employers of the local police force but the court ruled that the local authority was not responsible for the actions of the police because the police officers concerned had been carrying out their duties as officers of the Crown. This was an important judgement because it made clear that in enforcing the law, a police force is not subject to the control of the local police committee because its officers are discharging a duty conferred on them by the Crown (Marshall, 1965, pp. 33–45). The relationship between a chief constable and his local police authority was further defined during the 1950s in a dispute between the Chief Constable of Nottingham, Captain Athelstan Popkess and his watch committee, over police inquiries into the financial activities of the council. When the committee discovered these enquiries they demanded that the chief constable report to them on the matter but Captain Popkess refused, arguing that it was not the business of the local authority to interfere with a police investigation into possible breaches of the law. The watch committee then suspended the chief constable but this decision was reversed by the Home

Secretary on the ground that the chief constable had a duty under the Crown to enforce the law.

These cases demonstrated that, although they are the employers of the police and have a statutory responsibility to ensure that their areas are efficiently policed, the police have a line of accountability to the law which is totally outside the local authority's control, which increases the area of discretion enjoyed by constables far beyond that available to other local authority staff. In consequence, although local police authorities have responsibilities for financing and equipping the police, there is a widespread belief that they have no jurisdiction over operational matters, including the disposition and organisation of the force, as well as the appointment, promotion and dismissal of individual police officers. All of these are the responsibility of the chief constable alone (see Reiner, 1992). This operational autonomy became highly controversial when some police authorities attempted to prevent the deployment of their officers against striking miners during the coal dispute of 1984–1985. They were overruled by the Home Secretary. However, the decision of whether or not to prosecute individuals has now been in part removed from the police to the Crown Prosecution Service, which is under the overall control of the Attorney-General, not the Home Secretary. The police decide whether or not to initiate a prosecution but whether or not it should be pursued and continued are decided by the Crown Prosecution Service. In this respect, therefore, a new line of national accountability has been opened, although this reform has done nothing to enhance the limited powers of local police authorities.

Another restriction on the accountability of the police is that their accountability is to the police committee, not the full council as is the case with all other local authority employees. Hence, councillors who are not members of the police committee are restricted at council meetings to a right to ask the chairman questions about the committee's discharge of its responsibilities. Their only other power is to request the police committee to reconsider a minute: they cannot amend the police committee's minutes or refer them back to the committee. Equally, the police committee can refuse to accede to such a request to reconsider its minutes. There is not even a statutory requirement to present the police committee minutes to the council, although this is habitually done in practice in order to keep councillors informed about the committee's activities. The only respect in which the police committee is not autonomous from the rest of the local authority is finance: hence councillors can if they wish initiate a general debate about the police during the annual budget meeting. In practice, however, there is never much time available for this purpose.

In addition, because of the autonomy granted to chief constables on operational matters, they can refuse to answer questions which in the chief constable's opinion concern operational matters and if the councillor persists, the chief constable can appeal to the Home Secretary to endorse his refusal to answer it. His autonomy as an officer of the Crown also entitles the chief constable to refuse to attend meetings of management teams, policy and resources committees or even full council meetings. The accountability of the chief constable to local councillors is even weaker where the force is a joint one whose police committee includes members from several local authorities, as is the case with the Avon and Somerset, Northumbria, Thames Valley and West Mercia Forces, for example. The chairman can be a member of only one of the contributing councils and in consequence, relatively junior members of the police committee may have to answer questions about its work in the other council chambers.

Since 1984, another form of possible accountability has been added in the form of the local consultative committees established under the Police and Criminal Evidence Act of 1984. However, consultation does not necessarily result in effective accountability because it does not entail that the police are required to act on the views or recommendations of the consultative committees.

Although it is not directly relevant to the subject of this book, we need for completeness to enquire what other forms of accountability the police are subject to – in particular whether their status as officers of the Crown means that they are accountable to Parliament, like the Sovereign's other servants including the civil service and the armed forces. However, the Speaker of the House of Commons has ruled that outside London, 'day to day administration of a county police force or other local authority force lies in the hands of the local councillors' and hence, he rejected attempts to ask parliamentary questions about the activities of provincial police forces (*Hansard*, 1958, col. 1259). The accountability of the police to elected representatives was hence caught in a double bind: the police could not be accountable to Parliament because they were held to be accountable to local councillors, but accountability to councillors was severely restricted because of the status of constables as officers of the Crown. Even in the case of the Metropolitan Police, which has been the direct responsibility of the Home Secretary since its creation in 1829, Parliamentary account-ability has been restricted because successive Home Secretaries have refused to give MPs details of the force's activities.

The accountability of the police to elected representatives has therefore become dangerously attenuated, with the result that people are often not satisfied that allegations of police misconduct have been properly investigated and adequate redress granted. Such suspicions have been aroused by deaths in police custody which were not adequately explained: Liddle Towers and Blair Peach were cases in point here. Public suspicions have been greatly increased by the discovery of police malpractice during investigations into such miscarriages of justice as the 'Birmingham six', the 'Maguire seven' and the 'Guildford four'. The independ-ence of constables protects them from political interference with investigations into corrupt practices by politicians and others but it also means that few safeguards are provided for citizens if the police misuse their extensive powers – or indeed for police officers who are themselves the victims of such abuse (Stalker, 1988). However, the means available for citizens to seek redress where they feel that they have been mistreated by the police have been increased by the establishment of the Police Complaints Authority but this is a national body responsible for investigating complaints originating anywhere in the country. Hence, it may in practice have further attenuated the role of councillors on police com-mittees in taking up complaints against the police.

The Willinck Commission and the 1964 Police Act

These and other matters were investigated by a Royal Commis-sion in the early 1960s, which was itself appointed as a result of public concern about police conduct arising from the case of *Garratt v. Eastmond*. Mr. Garratt was a civil servant who claimed that during the investigation of a motoring offence by the Metropolitan Police, he had been assaulted by Constable East-mond. His attempt to sue for damages ended with an out of court settlement but the Home Secretary announced that no disci-plinary action was to be taken against Constable Eastmond and refused to tell the House of Commons why. The consequence was a motion of censure against the Home Secretary, who accepted that although the case was in itself of small importance, it raised major issues concerning the accountability of the police and the relationship between the police and the public. He said that 'the time has come to have [these issues] examined with the authority and impartiality of an independent inquiry' (*Hansard*, 1959, col. 1196). Hence, a Royal Commission was established in 1960 under the chairmanship of Sir Henry Willinck, to review the constitutional position of the police, including their accountability to local police authorities.

The central issue was whether the responsibility for the police should be removed from local authorities and transferred to the central government, thus creating a national police service. If this were done, it would end a tradition of the local control of policing which, as we have seen, goes back to mediaeval times and beyond, as well as concentrating control over all the state's machinery of coercion in the hands of the central government. Most police officers, including the Association of Chief Police Officers (ACPO) supported the retention of a degree of local control – a view which not surprisingly was supported by the local authority associations. The latter declared that local police forces were essential to the maintenance of democracy and that there would be great dangers in creating 'a Ministry of the Interior on Continental lines'. However, although local authorities pay half of the piper's costs, they do not call the tune because of the Home Secretary's powers over the police (Willinck, *Evidence (Section of Report)*, 1962). Some senior officers argued that efficiency, together with the need to exploit advanced technology, demanded that control over the police should be transferred to national control or at least should be regionalised, in the interests of efficiency. Steps have been taken in this direction, including the establishment of a national police computer and regional crime squads. Hence, in practice, the police are now organised on the basis of a variety of national, regional and local units whose relationships have not been clearly defined.

The issue of the autonomous status of the chief constable was extensively debated: ACPO held to the view that local authorities could not be given the power to direct chief constables on how to enforce the law. The Chief Constable of Birmingham declared that 'The Chief Constable will listen to any opinions that are given but we do deny the right of a police authority to instruct the Chief

Constable as to the way in which his duty should be performed' (ibid). The Association of Municipal Corporations, by contrast, argued that local authorities should be given whatever powers were necessary to ensure that their areas were efficiently policed. In any case, given the Speaker's 1958 ruling, the result of accepting the ACPO view would be that the chief constable would not be able effectively to be held to account by anybody. The evidence submitted to the Willinck Commission was confused and we shall see that the Commission itself fudged the issue.

In view of current debates about the control over the police, it is significant that the arguments for the establishment of a national police force impressed the Willinck Commission but that only one member, Dr A.L. Goodhart, pressed the point to issuing a minority report advocating a national force. The majority instead proposed the strengthening of the Home Secretary's power to ensure the provision of efficient policing throughout the land. He should also compel the further amalgamation of police forces, which reached its climax in the forty-three forces created under the local government reorganisation of 1972.

However, both the Home Secretary who appointed the Willinck Commission, R.A. Butler and his successor, Henry Brooke, made clear their continued commitment to local control over the police. In 1962 Butler told an audience of chief police officers that 'I am quite convinced that it would be wrong for one man or one government to be in charge directly of the whole police force of the country. Our constitution is based on checks and balances' (The Times, 7 June 1962). Henry Brooke declared the following year that 'I am not disposed to accept the Commission's recommendation that I should assume a general statutory responsibility for the efficiency of the police. A Minister should not have responsibility without power' (Hansard, 1963, co. 689). Hence, local authority control over police forces was to survive.

However, in the Police Act 1964, which followed the publication of the Willinck Report a year earlier, the accountability of central and local government for the police was redefined in a manner which did not resolve the issue of to whom the police should be held to account for misbehaviour or negligence. A tripartite system of accountability was established for the police in which the three principal actors were to be the Home Secretary, the local police committee and the chief constable.

The Home Secretary is charged under the Act to act in such a manner 'and to such an extent as appears to him to be best calculated to promote the efficiency of the police'. The Home Secretary could require a chief constable to report to him on any aspect of the policing of a particular area. He can also require a chief constable to retire on grounds of inefficiency. Arguably, therefore, the accountability of the police to Parliament was indirectly increased, since MPs could ask questions of the Home Secretary concerning his exercise of these new responsibilities.

Local police committees were henceforth to consist of two-thirds councillors and one-third magistrates, a composition which survived the general advice of the Widdicombe Committee (1986) against the participation of persons other than elected members in local authority decision-making. Local police committees retained their responsibility for ensuring the efficient policing of their areas but the chief constable's sole responsibility for operational matters was retained, together with his right to ask the Home Secretary to uphold his refusal to answer councillors' questions on matters which were, in his opinion, operational. Indeed, under the 1964 Police Act, he may refuse to answer any question or disclose information if he believes it would be against the public interest to do so or that the information is not necessary for the discharge of the police committee's functions. He can request the Home Secretary to endorse his refusal if police committee members persist with their requests. The Home Secretary's decision is final. Hence, the chief constable is still in important respects effectively accountable to no-one except himself, although the relationship between a chief constable and his police committee chairman may result in more effective accountability to the committee than the Act provides for. The chairman is also responsible for liaising with the remainder of the council, in practice usually the controlling party group, especially in ensuring that the police obtain adequate finance from the council at budget time. Although 51 per cent of the costs of a police force are paid by the Home Office, the other 49 per cent must come from local taxpayers through the local authority's budget. Hence, a chief constable would be foolish to cut himself off from the local political process because he is as dependent as any other chief officer on it when councillors determine their financial priorities. However, councillors are wary of cutting police budgets because by doing so they may be seen to be weakening the forces of law and order.

A particularly contentious issue is the investigation of

complaints against the police. Under the 1964 Act chief constables are required to investigate all complaints made against officers in their forces. The deputy chief constable is the officer within each force who is responsible for the investigation of complaints and the record of his actions is subject to annual inspection by the Inspectors of Constabulary. All such reports must be sent to the Director of Public Prosecutions unless the chief constable is satisfied that no criminal act has been committed and the local police authority must be informed about complaints – this is usually done in the chief constable's annual report. A senior police officer from another force is always brought in to investigate serious complaints.

After many years of demands for the creation of a police ombudsman, which was stimulated in particular by a number of widely publicised deaths in police custody in the 1970s, the Police Complaints Board was established in 1976, which subsequently became the Police Complaints Authority. Its members are appointed by the Home Secretary, so the Authority is a national body with no responsibility to local authorities nor any formal relationship with them, although it may submit reports to local police committees. The police investigate complaints themselves on behalf of the Authority and report to its members. Usually, a single member of the Police Complaints Authority is given the task of monitoring the investigation of each complaint. The lack of an independent investigation force for complaints against the police has been repeatedly criticised but the creation of such an independent investigatory body has always been resisted by the police. However, we have noted that they were in part unsuccessful in resisting the removal of their control over the decision to prosecute and continue with a prosecution; they lost the latter power to a separate Crown Prosecutions Service.

A further controversy concerning the accountability of the police arose after the Brixton riots in 1981, which had been sparked off by insensitive police tactics, such as frequent street questioning and searches of black youths. In particular, a search and arrest operation known as 'Swamp '81' and the use of the Special Patrol Group in the area provoked public anger which spilled over into rioting. The Government asked Lord Scarman to conduct an inquiry into the events leading up to the riots. He concluded that changes in policing methods were urgently needed to restore relations between the Metropolitan Police and black communities like that in Brixton. He recommended more training, as well as the establishment of local advisory committees consisting of community representatives and policemen to discuss local policing issues (Scarman, 1981). The establishment of such advisory committees has since become widespread and was included in the 1984 Police and Criminal Evidence (PACE) Act but doubts still exist about both the effectiveness of local accountability and the conduct of the police. The relations between the police and working-class communities were again called into doubt by outbreaks of violence between police and pickets during the miners' strike of 1984–1985, as well as further racial incidents in a number of communities since 1985. Senior police officers now appear to be increasingly ready to recognise that the traditional policy of isolating the police from urban communities is counterproductive; that they need to restore close relationships between police officers and local communities, which were increasingly lost through the introduction of 'panda' cars and the removal of police officers to special housing units in the 1960s. The question has to be asked how far these were the result of the creation of larger and hence more remote local police force areas. These events were followed by insensitive, sometimes unduly violent confrontations with picket lines and racial minorities in the 1980s, especially as paramilitary methods of policing seemed to develop, with large numbers of police dressed in intimidating helmets and protective clothing confronting pickets or demonstrators. One former chief constable, John Alderson, has long advocated the restoration of close links between the police and local communities and his views now appear to be winning wider acceptance within the police service. Awareness of the danger of racialism within police forces is also increasing, with the Commissioner of the Metropolitan Police, Paul Condon, who was appointed in 1993, stressing the importance of eliminating racialist attitudes within the force early in his tenure of office.

However, local authorities as such appear to be making little contribution to the restoration of relationships between police and local communities: perhaps they cannot do so because the county councils, which are now the police authorities, are too large to be able to relate effectively to small communities such as villages, streets and housing estates. In any case, doubts about the effectiveness of local police authorities were further increased by the failure of some police authorities to influence police tactics during

the miners' strike, when the police were subject to national control
in combating the strikers through the National Reporting Centre
which was set up under the Chairman of ACPO to co-ordinate the
police response to the strike.

The management of the police: local government reorganisation and after

The Willinck Commission resolved the Constitutional status
of the police, although it did not provide for more effective
local accountability. Under the 1972 Local Government Act the
number of forces was reduced to its present forty-three, although
the number of combined forces where control was vested in more
than one local authority was reduced. County councils were
made the sole local authorities responsible for policing, although
this power was transferred to joint boards of district councillors
in the former metropolitan county council areas after the abolition of the metropolitan county councils in 1986. Police committees are charged to 'secure the maintenance of an adequate
and efficient police force for the area', an obligation which is
enforced by the annual inspections of Her Majesty's Inspectors
of Constabulary.

In view of the increased role given to the Home Secretary in
1964, it is of at least passing interest to note that he severely
constrained the new local authorities in their appointments of
chief constables after the new local government system came into
existence in 1974. Where new forces were created, the local
authorities concerned were allowed to choose their chief constables only from among the chief constables of the forces which
had previously existed in their areas: in at least one case, all the
eligible officers but one withdrew before the appointment interview, so that the police committee concerned was faced with
Hobson's choice. The Home Secretary also controls other senior
appointments, for example, usually vetoing the promotion of
officers to the top three ranks from within their own police forces.

The modern police committee could be said to be responsible
for providing the tools with which the police carry out their duties,
while the chief constable is responsible for recruitment, discipline,
promotion and operations. The committee does have the responsibility for appointing the chief constable, his deputy and assistant
chief constables but in making these appointments they are

subject to close Home Office guidance. The Home Office must be sent the shortlist and will indicate which candidates the Home Secretary is prepared to support. In the past, it has been suggested that Home Secretaries have used this power to ensure the promotion to the topmost ranks of a particular kind of officer, especially those who have taken the Senior Command Course at the Bramshill Police College. The Home Secretary is most unlikely to approve the promotion of candidates for chief constable or deputy chief constable who are already serving in the force concerned, in order to prevent unduly parochial attitudes and practices developing within forces.

The extent of local councillors' influence, let alone control over the police will be still further attenuated by proposals announced by the former Home Secretary, Kenneth Clarke, in March 1993. He has suggested that councillors should be reduced to holding only half the seats on police committees: eight out of sixteen members. Of the other eight, three would be magistrates and the remaining five would be appointed by the Home Secretary from among people whom he deems to have relevant expertise or experience. Such persons would be likely to include businessmen who can advise on increasing the efficiency of police forces. Furthermore, the Home Secretary would appoint the police committee chairman, rather than the police committee electing him or her. The Home Secretary has argued that only one person in ten even knows that councillors have a role in the government of the police and that it would be more efficient to transfer control to management committees of businessmen. However, the principle of retaining local forces as opposed to a national police force seems likely to be retained, although there are very clear indications that forces are likely to be amalgamated and hence police force areas will be made still larger.

The fundamental question for local government has to be whether local government's responsibility for the police should be retained or not, in the context of a careful analysis of which aspects of policing are best organised nationally, regionally and locally. Local policing has long been regarded as an important safeguard against tyranny; on the other hand, to give local politicians operational control over the police might open the way to corrupt influence over their efforts to prevent and detect crime. However, if local authority control over the police is to be removed, care must be taken to ensure that their accountability to Parliament is unambiguously guaranteed and that means for dealing with complaints against them are further strengthened.

There is also an urgent need to develop closer links between the police and local communities. The Home Secretary has advocated achieving this by altering the relationship between the head-quarters of police forces and local police stations. Headquarters should reduce the importance of their line management and discipline roles, becoming co-ordinators and supporters of local police activity rather than commanders of local policing (*The Guardian*, 24 March 1993). The creation and maintenance of local consultative committees should also be further encouraged as a means of maintaining contact between police officers and local communities, although their effectiveness varies considerably.

For local authorities themselves, the police constitute a marginal element in their management because of the extent of the chief constable's autonomy, which means that he cannot be compelled to participate in authority-wide management, including manage-ment team meetings. Furthermore, the autonomy of the police committee from the rest of the council renders control over its activities impossible for council leaders or party groups, except in the restricted circumstances of the budgetary process and the annual budget meeting of the council. On the other hand, one has to question whether 650 already overloaded Members of Parlia-ment can effectively guarantee that the police can be held to account for their use of resources, their efficiency and effectiveness, as well as their mistakes and misdeeds. Indeed, the Home Sec-retary has in a sense recognised this by his proposal in March 1993 to establish a police authority for London because the account-ability of the Metropolitan Police to the Home Secretary alone is inadequate to secure the effective accountability of that force (*The Guardian*, 24 March 1993). However, the issue of national, regional and local structures and control have yet to be adequately resolved and may need to be discussed in the context of a wider debate about local and regional government, which will be addressed in the final chapter.

THE FIRE SERVICE

Local authorities are also responsible for another uniformed, disciplined service: the fire brigades. Again, central control is particularly strong. Since 1972, county councils have been responsible for the fire service, which is responsible for the prevention of fires and their extinction when they occur. The allocation of the fire service to the county councils was the culmination of a trend towards the amalgamation of brigades into a smaller number of larger units in the interest of securing consistent standards of fire cover throughout the country.

During the Second World War, 1,440 local fire brigades were amalgamated into a national fire service but the Home Secretary, Herbert Morrison, promised the local authorities that this function would be returned to them after the war (Donoughue and Jones, 1973). However, when the service was restored to local government control in 1947 the former 1,400 local fire authorities were reduced to 141 and a further reduction to 62 occurred through local government reorganisation in 1972. When the abolition of the GLC and metropolitan county councils was proposed in 1983, many within the fire service were concerned that if responsibility was to be transferred to the metropolitan district councils, the trend towards fewer and larger local fire authorities would be reversed, which would allow parochial concerns over the siting of fire stations to take precedence over efficiency.

Because of the perceived necessity of ensuring that standards of fire cover are consistent throughout the country, central control over the fire service, like that over the police, is relatively strong. Fire brigades are subject to annual inspection. Standards of fire cover are prescribed by the Home Office: the Fire Brigades Union 'would be horrified at the thought that local authorities should ever be able to determine their own standards of cover: in the Union's view this inevitably would lead to a drastic reduction in standards' (Rhodes, 1987, p. 322). The appointment of the chief fire officer must be approved by the Home Secretary.

However, in a number of other respects, the fire service is subject to less central control. County councils do not have to appoint a separate committee to oversee the fire brigade and this duty may be combined with others, such as waste disposal, emergency planning and consumer protection, under the control of a public protection committee. More significant is the absence of any specific grant towards the fire service. The fire service is supported by the central government through the revenue support grant and the fire chief must therefore compete for resources against the other departments which provide the council's services. However, councillors are well aware that if a major fire disaster occurred because they had given insufficient funds to the local fire brigade, the political consequences for them would be severe. Nonetheless, the Fire Brigades Union is sufficiently dubious about the willingness of councillors to provide sufficient resources to provide effective fire cover that it has expressed a consistent preference for central control over the fire service, for nearly twenty years. A third difference is that whereas the siting of police stations is considered an operational matter to be determined by the chief constable alone, subject only to obtaining planning permission, councillors decide where fire stations should be built, which can lead to parochial competition among them for the location of a fire station in their wards, which may sometimes produce locations which are not consistent with maximum efficiency. On the other hand, the Home Office exercises extensive control over equipment, including fire engines and fire hydrants, in order to ensure that equipment can be used anywhere if a major fire breaks out and the local brigade has to be reinforced by fire engines from other areas. Hence, 'Committees have relatively little discretion when deciding on the provision of . . . equipment if the recommendation has come from the Central Fire Brigades Advisory Council' (Puffitt, 1979). On this committee sit representatives of the Home Office and the fire service unions as well as those of the local authority associations, so local authorities are in a minority.

The fire brigade, like the police, can only be integrated with the rest of a local authority's functions and staff to a limited extent because it is a uniformed service with its own loyalties, rules and traditions. Firemen's loyalties are primarily to the service, their colleagues and their superior officers, not to the local authority as such. Only the most senior officers will be involved at all extensively in relations with other departments, especially when they are bidding for resources. They will tend to resist attempts to involve their service in corporate local authority activities such as central workshops and repair depots, on the grounds that the standard of reliability they need is so high that they must have control over their own workshops and mechanics. In any case, the equipment and operation of the fire service is subject to strong Home Office control, as we have seen. However, whereas chief constables are almost invariably successful in resisting attempts to incorporate their activities with those of other parts of the local authority, chief fire officers may have to submit to a requirement to use central maintenance or workshop facilities rather than providing their own. Nonetheless, the chief fire officer is likely to be numbered among the doughtier opponents of corporate management and is assisted in this resistance by the extent of Home Office control over his service. He is likely to favour a 'service ideology' of commitment to the management of the fire brigade as an autonomous and distinct entity, rather than accepting the 'management values' which are inherent in the efforts of chief executives and other 'topocrat' officers to control the activities of all the local authority's departments (Stewart, 1983). Finally, like the police, arguments that the fire service should be nationally controlled in the interests of its efficiency are stronger than for most of the other services provided by local authorities.

EMERGENCY PLANNING

Section 138 of the Local Government Act 1972 authorises local authorities to spend money in order to plan for any emergency or disaster. In general, they have two main responsibilities: to prepare for action in case of an attack by a foreign power and to prepare plans for dealing with civil emergencies. Some of these powers date from the legislation passed before the Second World War to ensure that the country could cope with the effects of heavy bombing. Thus, in 1937, the Air Raid Precautions Act required local authorities to prepare schemes to protect their local populations in the event of an attack. The Civil Defence Act 1939 extended these provisions and during the Second World War local authorities played a vital role in combating the effects of bombing raids on the cities, although they were deprived temporarily of their control of the fire service by Morrison's decision to set up a national fire service for the duration of the war.

After the war ended, local government regained its fire service powers in 1947 and as the international climate deteriorated, bringing with it a growing possibility of a nuclear war, civil defence once more became an important local authority function. Under the Civil Defence Act of 1948 local authorities continued to act as civil defence authorities and since then, they have been able to claim from the Government 75 per cent of their expenditure for civil defence purposes.

At the present time, therefore, local councils have a responsibility to plan for emergencies and many of them appoint emergency planning officers. Although the degree of such advance planning varies enormously throughout the country, most authorities have prepared plans for dealing with a nuclear attack. The county councils have the most important role; their emergency planning teams would act as the co-ordinating agents in the event of an attack (P.G. Richards, 1979). During the 1980s, however, as the Peace Movement gained in strength, many Labour-controlled local authorities became increasingly reluctant to make plans for civil defence during a nuclear war or to take part in exercises designed to test their capabilities in the event of war, because they supported the Labour Party's non-nuclear defence policy. In consequence, the Home Secretary took steps to compel such authorities to co-operate in civil defence provision and exercises. Hence, again, the response to expressions of local policies has been an increasing determination by the central government to compel them to comply with the Government's instructions, regardless of the views of councillors or their electors. However, the need for emergency planning to deal with civil emergencies has been repeatedly indicated by such events as the Flixborough explosion on South Humberside in 1974, which posed a potentially serious pollution risk. Many similar accidents more recently have reinforced the need for effective emergency planning. Some have revealed its absence, with tragic consequences.

CONCLUSIONS

By far the most controversial and difficult issue raised by the uniformed and emergency services operated by local authorities is police accountability. It seems probable that local authorities' role in the control of the police will be further attenuated in the 1990s, with councillors becoming a minority on police committees. Nonetheless, public accountability is essential to ensure that the very extensive powers necessarily possessed by the police are not misused, although it is obviously undesirable for the details of their operational activities and procedures to be disclosed in open debate. It is also important to ensure that people who feel they have been mistreated by the police or have suffered from abuses of police powers, should have effective channels for ensuring that their complaints are thoroughly investigated by persons whose independence from the police is not in doubt. If local accountability is to be further reduced, therefore, a stronger police ombudsman or complaints authority, together with clearer accountability to Parliament, are urgently needed.

In terms of local authority management, the integration of the police and the fire brigade into a local authority's overall management structures and processes will continue to be particularly difficult. Chief constables may refuse to attend meetings of chief officers' groups, policy and resources committees and the like and will be supported in their refusal to do so by the Home Office. Chief fire officers do not enjoy the same degree of protection but are also likely to try and maintain the maximum possible independence from the rest of the authority which employs them and to resist controls intended to secure the most efficient possible use of money and manpower.

In another way too, the management of these services is likely to become increasingly divergent from that of the rest of the local authorities of which they form part, because they are likely to be only relatively marginally affected by market-orientated reforms such as compulsory competitive tendering. The police and the fire service are concerned above all with the maintenance of public order and safety, hence politicians both central and local are unlikely to wish to be seen to impose reforms which may jeopardise the standards to which these services are provided – the main reason for their extensive supervision by the Home Office. It would be a brave politician who would insist on reforms which might subsequently be blamed for an incident which resulted in major loss of life or damage to property. Also, the nature of the services themselves, with their paramilitary discipline and high degree of professional solidarity, will enable them to resist such changes if they are proposed either by local councillors or by ministers. The close relations between ministers, senior officers and the relevant trade unions render it unlikely that a Home Secretary or a local council will unduly disturb the manner in which the police and the fire service carry out their functions.

The final issue concerning these services is the most fundamental of all: the ability and willingness of councillors to make policy decisions about them, especially concerning the allocation of resources to them. The Chief Constable and the chief fire officer enjoy particularly strong support from their sponsoring central department, the Home Office, which also exercises a high degree of control over the operation of police forces and fire brigades. The chief constable's hand is further strengthened by the 50 per cent police grant paid by the Home Office, which enables him to argue that only half the cost of his service falls to be met by the local authority. Finally, few councillors would wish to appear in public to be reducing the level of fire cover or weakening the forces of law and order, even if it appears to them that the use of funds for other purposes would better protect public safety. Youth clubs to keep youngsters off the streets may more effectively reduce crime and vandalism than the purchase of panda cars, but councillors who advocate such a shift of resources will quickly be attacked by local news media and the public for reducing the forces of law and order.

Nonetheless, such choices ought to be discussed and made. Preventative social work or youth clubs reduce juvenile crime more effectively than extra spending on police equipment. Conversely, official reports have made it clear that reduced spending on the youth service in North Tyneside, which led to the closure of local youth clubs or restrictions on their staffing and opening hours, was one of the main causes of the riots on the Meadowell Estate in North Shields in 1991. Equally, effective checking by consumer protection officers of the safety of electrical equipment such as heaters will reduce fire hazards, possibly more than employing a few extra fire prevention officers. The impediments to open debate in these fields are considerable but it should nonetheless take place in terms which secure the acceptance of and participation in such debates by the police, the fire service and the public.

Chapter 7

The management of resources

The management of resources has always been a matter of vigorous and even acrimonious dispute both within and outside local government. In 1975, the then Prime Minister, Harold Wilson, declared that some of the new local authorities established by the 1972 reorganisation had 'more chiefs than Indians'. In 1979 Mrs Thatcher made it clear that extravagance and inefficiency in individual councils would be attacked by her administration. Tales of local government bumbledom abound in the press and at countless public bars. As Britain's economic performance has deteriorated and resources have become scarcer, local authorities have been compelled to try and make better use of their resources and to be seen to be doing so. The pressure to increase efficiency has been increased by the almost continuous financial pressure that successive Governments have inflicted on local authorities since 1976. Since then, only in 1978–1979 have local authorities not faced demands for expenditure reductions.

On a more positive note, many new means to improve the efficiency of resource use have become available to local authorities. These have included operational research, work study, organisation and methods techniques, revolutionary improvements in information and communications technologies and new methods of budgeting and financial control. Thus both the pressures imposed on local authorities and the opportunities available to them have combined to produce major changes in their approaches to managing their resources. Furthermore, a range of new professions associated with the management of resources has come into existence since the 1950s, including operations research officers, corporate planners, statisticians and a host of others. Their efforts have been added to those of the more traditional resource management tasks, including internal audit, budgeting and land and property management. Most of the personnel function has been developed in local government since the appearance of the Mallaby Report in 1967.

FINANCE

The treasurer has always been one of the most important officers employed by local authorities, responsible as he or she is for collecting the authority's income, advising on what expenditure can be undertaken, as well as monitoring the efficient and proper use of the money dispensed to finance the council's services and projects. The role of the local authority accountant has changed very considerably, with the development of new methods and techniques of financial management, coupled with the increasingly stringent financial climate within which local authorities have had to operate. Financial pressure has been almost completely unremitting since 1976, when Denis Healey was obliged to demand reductions in public expenditure, including that of local authorities, in return for a loan from the International Monetary Fund (Dell, 1991). The training of local authority accountants, for which the syllabus is set by the Chartered Institute of Public Finance and Accountancy (CIPFA) now includes systems analysis, policy analysis, cost–benefit analysis and much else besides the traditional accountancy disciplines. The modern local government accountant is increasingly expected to play a range of managerial roles. The treasurer controls a budget which may run into hundreds of millions of pounds. As a principal member of the council's management team he or she makes important contributions to major policy decisions and the preparation of future plans, since almost nothing can be undertaken unless the money is available to pay for it.

Accountants traditionally had three functions in local authority management: budgeting, auditing and accounting. These roles remain but the budgetary process in particular has changed under the twin spurs of new methods and financial stringency. These functions will be discussed in turn in the remainder of this section.

Budgeting

Budgeting has always been the treasurer's most important contribution to the policy-making processes of local authorities because the treasurer and his or her department must calculate the demands for expenditure being made on the authority and the resources that are available to meet those demands. This process culminates in February or March each year when the council must meet to approve its budget and set the level of its local tax for the coming financial year.

Local authority budgeting is a process of choice as to how best to allocate a finite amount of resources among competing demands for expenditure on services. It is hence unlike budgeting in the private sector because extra demands cannot be met by ordering more of the good or service being demanded. Rather, the amount of demand that can be met is determined by the extent of the resources available. Those who are responsible for preparing a council's budget must therefore consider an equation involving the authority's income and expenditure. On the income side the factors to be considered are the amount of Government grant the authority is likely to receive, the amount the authority can raise from balances and income charges and the amount it can raise through local taxes without losing the next local elections or provoking protests or even a taxpayers' revolt. On the expenditure side, the council must consider the services it must by law provide: here, the only major issue it can determine is where efficiency can be improved, thereby releasing resources for other purposes. Then, the extent to which the council wishes to provide discretionary services and for what, must be determined. In considering these issues, councillors will be pressed by a multitude of trade unions and other pressure groups all demanding increased spending on the services to which they attach the most importance.

The balancing of this equation is influenced by both external and internal factors. Most important among the external factors is the central government, in the form of the Ministry which is responsible for 'sponsoring' local government. In England this is the Department of the Environment. In Scotland, Wales and Northern Ireland it is the relevant 'territorial' Department: the Scottish, Welsh and Northern Ireland Offices. Their approach to seeking control over local authority budgets varies significantly: the approach of the DoE has been shown to be more confrontational than that of the three 'territorial' ministries (Elcock and Jordan (eds), 1987: Elcock, Jordan and Midwinter, 1989; Midwinter, Keating and Mitchell, 1991). The influence of the other external actors – political parties, pressure groups and local business people – is marginal, despite the obligation imposed on local authorities to consult representatives of the latter during the preparation of their budgets. The local electorate are the ghost at all councillors' feasts and sometimes they may visit the consequences of increases in local taxes on the councillors who voted for them. Michael Parkinson (1985) demonstrated that when Liverpool City Council was controlled by a succession of minority administrations, a large increase in the rate resulted in a loss of seats for the party which had proposed it. Councillors generally believe that their actions will influence their popularity with the electorate and hence their chances of being re-elected. They will not, therefore, increase local taxes beyond the level which they believe the electorate will accept.

Government and Parliament have also set the rules within which local authorities have to prepare their budgets. These include the *ultra vires* rule, which means that councillors who vote for illegal expenditures may be surcharged and disqualified from office. They may also be similarly treated if they delay setting a budget for too long after the beginning of the financial year – as councillors in Liverpool and Lambeth learnt to their cost in 1986. Labour councillors in Sheffield came near to suffering the same fate as a result of their delay in setting a budget that year – which could have cut short the Parliamentary career of that council's former Leader, David Blunkett (Elcock and Jordan (eds), 1987). The other rules of the game are the statutory obligations imposed on local authorities to provide many services, which absorb between 80 and 90 per cent of their budgets; a requirement not to budget for a deficit (an obligation from which the Chancellor of the Exchequer is exempt) and a requirement not to budget for excessive balances: any balance above that which is adjudged by the district auditor to be 'reasonable and prudent' can be disallowed and the council obliged to return it to local taxpayers in the form of a reduction in local taxation (see Hepworth, 1984).

However, the main influences on local authority budgets are to be found within the local authority itself, in the form of the conflict between the two groups of actors described by Wildavsky (1979) in his classic study as the 'advocates' and the 'guardians'. The 'Advocates' are the spending departments and the committees to which they report, who want to increase their service provision and hence their expenditure. Furthermore, they will be under pressure from their local policy communities, including trade unions, pressure groups and clients, to provide more and better services and hence spend more money. Opposed to them are those officers and councillors who must take overall responsibility for ensuring that the budgeted expenditure is within the limits of the resources which are reasonably likely to be available in the coming financial year. These 'guardians' include the treasurer and his or her colleagues, the chief executive officer, the leader of the council (who will almost always be the chairman of the policy and resources committee) and the chairman of the finance committee or sub-committee. These latter officers and members must take an overall view of the authority's needs and circumstances, hence they may be designated 'topocrats', responsible for the authority's affairs as a whole, who will be opposed by the 'technocrats' in the spending departments who wish to spend more money on providing more and better services within their own professional fields. Given the habitual departmental fragmentation of local authorities (see Chapter 9 below), which is reinforced by the professional specialisation of most of their staff, this tussle between 'Advocates' and 'Guardians', or between departments and the core executive, is likely to be tough and lengthy, with much of the advantage lying on the side of the 'Advocates' because of the professional concern of staff to provide the best possible services, coupled with the demands of clients and customers for more and better local services.

Traditionally, the 'Advocates' have also had the advantage of initiating the budgetary process in local government because the preparation of local authority budgets tends to be demand-led, as illustrated by Table 7.1.

The process begins with the preparation of estimates by the spending departments. Only after these estimates have been collated does it become apparent that they must be reduced in order to contain the demands departments wish to make on resources within the bounds of the likely availability of resources.

This pressure is increased by the tendency of departments to include all possible items in their estimates because if they are not included and money subsequently becomes available, it may not be possible to implement them because they were excluded from the initial budget. Hence there is no council approval to spend money on them and this would need to be sought, thus delaying their execution. Also, chief officers and committee chairmen need

Table 7.1 Loamshire County Council: financial planning cycle

Time of year	Event	Comments
May–September	Committees consider their revenue needs for next three years.	Preparation of reports for committees describing present activities and future projects and assessing the best means of work towards the achievement of the committee's objectives. These reports present in total an overall 'authority profile' of present activities and future plans.
	Finance sub-committee makes preliminary assessment of resources available.	Preliminary assessment of resources likely to be available in the coming financial year. Must be provisional in the extreme because major national decisions about resources will not be made for several months yet, especially the block grant settlement. This is declared around the turn of the year after negotiations between the Government and the local authority associations but nowadays authorities learn of their grant allocations very late in their budgetary cycles or even after they have been completed.
July–September	Policy and resources committee considers the needs statements of other committees, determines broad strategy and likely rate of growth in coming year in the light of the finance sub-committee's preliminary assessment of resources.	The first opportunity for an overall review of the authority's achievements and prospects, an opportunity often not fully taken because of the demands on the policy committee but, if members wish, at this point all activities and policies can be reviewed and revised.
September–October	Finance department assembles new growth commitments. Departments prepare draft capital programmes.	Information is rendered precise and assembled for next stage. The consequences of all capital projects for capital and revenue expenditure are projected forward for three years. A seven-year projection of requirements for sites is required because of the long delays which tend to occur in getting planning permission and site acquisition.

October	Policy and resources committee determines global revenue allocations and priorities for capital programme. (*Note*: Informal indications are available of the likely outcome of the block grant negotiations.)	The first major political decision is now made: the overall rate of growth in expenditure, at constant prices, to be allowed and its allocation between committees in the light of the committees' needs and the council's policy priorities.
	Committees consider capital estimates 'without financial commitment at this stage'.	Committees present their proposals for capital schemes to finance and policy committees.
November–December	Committees prepare detailed revenue estimates for the coming year, explaining their commitments and proposals for new growth within the targets set for them by policy and resources committee, with the option of claiming extra funds from the policy reserve established as part of the growth-setting exercise in October.	Committees must decide what to cut out of their commitments or new growth proposals in the light of the 'ceilings' on their expenditure imposed by the growth rate set by policy committee. (It is far easier to cut growth items than existing commitments.)
January	Detailed estimates must be considered against available income by finance and policy committees and these committees recommend the rate precept for the coming year. (Note that in November the block grant settlement should have been announced, so this is the first point at which the resources available can be accurately assessed.)	The second major political decision must now be taken: how high to set the rate precept. The impact of new growth on the ratepayers may be reduced if balances can be drawn on to meet part of the new expenditure. In election years it is likely that reserves will be drawn on to the maximum possible extent for this purpose.
February	Full council sets the rate precept.	A major set-piece political debate but all the decisions have been taken before.

to be able to give some ground during negotiations over the budget with the treasurer and the finance committee, so items will be included which can be surrendered during this process without depriving the department of important or essential expenditure: some items in the estimates are therefore 'fairy gold', for which no-one seriously expects that money will be made available. Once the estimates are collated, a cutting exercise will be conducted through the winter, in order to produce a level of expenditure which will not provoke an excessive local tax rise. This process may entail putting pressure on departments and committees to make cuts, imposing a percentage cut on all of them, requiring the treasurer to impose a cuts regime or demanding that departments analyse their programmes to establish where cuts can least harmfully be made (Hepworth, 1984; Greenwood *et al.*, n.d.). However, all such procedures are essentially incremental because continuing or 'base' expenditure is unlikely to be at all thoroughly scrutinised: it will be assumed that this expenditure continues to be necessary, especially since much of it will be for the discharge of statutory obligations. Budget scrutiny will therefore be concentrated on new or 'growth' items and discretionary activities.

One major area of uncertainty in this process is the amount of grant which is likely to be received from the central government. The announcement tends to be made by the DoE or 'territorial' ministry very late in the budgetary year – around and possibly after Christmas. Furthermore, the Conservative Governments which have been in office since 1979 have frequently changed the rules governing grant distribution and local government finance more generally. In consequence, local authorities have tended to budget for balances which will protect them against sudden changes in central government policy, which the Audit Commission (1984) estimated had cost local ratepayers £1.2 billion between 1979 and 1983. The Audit Commission criticised the Government for creating this uncertainty, hence forcing local authorities to levy extra local taxation: this report therefore earned the Commission the headline in *The Times*, 'Watchdog Bites Master'.

However, as fiscal pressure has increased, the tendency has been for the early stages of the budgetary process to be reversed, with leading members and senior officers meeting to determine a budgetary strategy on the basis of a preliminary judgement of what resources are likely to be available in the next financial year, within which the spending departments and committees are

required to prepare their estimates. In consequence, the importance of central control over the budgetary process by a 'Guardian'
group has increased in recent years (Elcock and Jordan (eds), 1987;
Elcock, Jordan and Midwinter, 1989). However, such strategies do
not always eliminate the need for speedy reductions in estimates
between the New Year and the council's annual budget meeting,
especially when a late central government grant announcement
produces an unexpectedly low rate of grant (see Barlow, 1987).

Arthur Midwinter (1988; Elcock, Jordan and Midwinter, 1989)
identified three such types of strategy, which he described as
'compliance', 'shadow-boxing' and 'brinkmanship' strategies.
'Compliance' strategies, where local authorities accept that they
must prepare their budgets within the constraints of central
government guidelines, are the most common. Some authorities
willingly accept the Government's demands for retrenchment,
either because they are members of the same party or because
there is a tradition of fiscal prudence in the authority (Sewel and
Dyer, 1987). Many councils have adopted a 'standstill' strategy.
Here, the authority's leading members and officers agree that the
committees' estimates must be prepared on the basis that no
growth in expenditure (in real terms) is to be permitted in the next
financial year. Hence, if a spending department and its committee wish to incur expenditure on a new activity or service, they
must identify items which can be cut out of the budget or on which
expenditure can be reduced, in order that they can afford the new
spending. In practice, the result is usually creeping growth in
expenditure because the cuts offered by spending committees are
not sufficient to pay for their new items. However, the amounts
involved are relatively small and are accommodated in the end by
drawing on balances, making small increases in local taxation or
virement from other budget heads.

Authorities which engage in 'shadow-boxing' strategies engage
in tactics to reduce the impact of Government constraints on
spending on their own service levels, tax rates and employees.
In the early 1980s, 'creative accountancy' became a popular
approach to avoiding having to make cuts in council services and
employment. This involved a range of financial deals which often
involved foreign banks, many of which were legislated against in
progressive Acts dealing with local government finance. However, as quickly as the Government plugged one loophole, local
authorities would discover others (Parkinson, 1986). Third, some

authorities attempted to put pressure on the Government to relax the spending regime by giving them more grant or making other concessions, through 'brinkmanship' strategies which involved setting the budget and rate level as late as possible. However, councillors in Liverpool and Lambeth were surcharged for their authorities' delay in setting a budget in 1986, because the authorities lost revenue during the delay (Parkinson, 1987). Councillors in Sheffield narrowly avoided similar action (Haigh and Morris, 1987). Hence the risk entailed in adopting a 'brinkmanship' strategy is that councillors may fall over the edge into illegality, so becoming liable to surcharge (which almost always leads to personal bankruptcy) and disqualification from public office.

We can now explore some more specific policy and management issues to which the budgetary process gives rise, as well as noting some of the attempts that have been made to improve local authority budgeting over the last twenty years or so. The process as described above is inherently incremental. Adjustments will be made at the margins and continuing expenditures will not be scrutinised at all carefully, especially if they are the result of the authority's implementation of its statutory duties. Scrutiny will be concentrated on new or 'growth' items or on the discretionary services which the council is not obliged to provide. The 'base' or 'committed' budget will hence escape examination, unless ways of increasing the efficiency with which statutory obligations are carried out are sought in order to reduce the consequences for the authority of fiscal restraint. However, much ink and effort has been expended on ways in which this incremental process might be improved.

Attempts to improve the budgetary process have focused on two issues: the desirability of planning further ahead than the immediately coming budget year and the value of scrutinising the 'base' or 'committed' budget more carefully. The first objective was reflected in the attempted introduction of planning, programming, budgeting systems into the UK, with the Plowden Report on the Control of Public Expenditure which advocated forward planning of public expenditure by central government. Decisions made to spend money today result in commitments in ensuing budget years, which can be predicted and projected forward to indicate the extent to which freedom of manoeuvre will be restricted in the future by expenditure committed now. Such a procedure was developed by the public expenditure survey (PES) system in central government, which was introduced in 1963. PES entailed a five-year forward planning system, which was reduced to three years in 1980 (Heclo and Wildavsky, 1974; Gray and Jenkins, 1985). However, the development of the survey has not reduced the tendency of Whitehall's budgetary process to be incremental; indeed one observer declared that 'the Treasury's conversion of five-year expenditure planning into an even more formidable bulwark of inert incrementalism is breathtaking' (J.E.S Hayward, 1974, p. 291). Many local authorities experimented with financial planning systems in the early 1970s, including Mersey-side and Humberside County Councils, both, of whom attempted to plan their expenditure for three years ahead. However, the frequent changes in the local government grant regime which were made in the early 1980s killed off most attempts at such financial planning; one survey of local authority budgets in the mid-1980s detected only one authority among seventeen that was attempting financial planning (Elcock and Jordan (eds), 1987).

The second and related attempt to improve the management of resources has been to press budgeters into examining their 'base' or 'committed' budgets more closely, in order to save money which could then be used to provide new services or reduce local taxation. Here the technique often advocated is zero-based budget-ing (ZBB), which requires activity managers to prepare reports justifying their services and the expenditure on them. However, the consequence of doing this is likely to be to generate an information overload for leading politicians and senior officers: an attempt by a small Scottish district council to introduce ZBB resulted in the production of a 600-page document, which few busy councillors or senior officers could find time to read. The main beneficiaries, therefore, would be the activity managers themselves, as long as they were able to benefit from the reports they had prepared (Charlton and Martlew, 1987). However, in the early 1990s Cheshire County Council has developed a more workable form of ZBB, which is called the Policy and Base Budget Reviews. This process reduces the danger of information overload by concentrating on reviewing a limited range of the council's activities. It uses small review teams which are a combination of reviewers from both inside and outside the services involved, so that the 'insiders' can explain the service to the 'outsiders.' Hence also the roles of 'Advocates' and 'Guardians' are retained within the review teams (Roberts and Scholes, 1993).

Implicit in much of this is a tendency to centralise control over the budgetary process, which traditionally has been demand-driven by the 'advocates': the service departments and committees. Royston Greenwood (1984; see also Elcock and Jordan (eds), 1987; Elcock, Jordan and Midwinter, 1989) identified a tendency for the overall control over the budget to be assumed by small and informal groups of leading councillors and senior officers. These groups include the leader of the council and the chairman of the finance sub-committee, together with the chief executive officer and the treasurer or director of finance. The opposition's principal finance spokesperson is often included too. These groups play a major role in setting budget strategies. In addition, Greenwood argues that during the process, the informal group is likely to have to play one or both of two roles which he describes as the 'Spanish Inquisition' and the 'sweat shop'. The former will operate during the autumn, when it is likely to interview the service committee chairmen and their chief officers, either two by two or in a larger meeting, in order to identify possible spending reductions and more generally exert pressure on them to reduce their estimates. The 'sweat shop' operates shortly before the budget meeting of the council, to impose last-minute spending reductions in order that expenditure can be made to equal income without having to raise local taxation excessively. Chris Game gives a vivid description of the 'sweat shop' in operation in Birmingham City Council which illustrates the less than rational processes which may operate at this stage:

> After weeks of attempted prioritisation and careful calculation, some of the most critical allocation decisions were actually taken quite literally at the eleventh hour in a 'short, sharp round-the-table exercise': 'Right, we'll have a million and a half off Education, half a million off Social Services, so much off Consumer Protection and so on – that's how it was finally done'. As one leading member recalled, it was 'all a bit bloody frayed'.
>
> (Game, 1987, p. 64)

However hard councillors and officers try to review their budgets carefully and in good time, unexpected problems, usually in the form of an unexpectedly low Revenue Support Grant, often produce episodes like this one in Birmingham.

The final outcomes of local authority budgetary processes always consist of reductions in spending beyond the levels which the 'Advocates' desire. However, even after seventeen years of almost unremitting financial stringency, few local authorities have been forced to make major service cuts or impose compulsory redundancies on their staff. The reason is that they are able to deploy a wide range of tactics to avoid imposing service cuts and redundancies. Harold Wolman (1984) identified this phenomenon in a cross-national study of local authority budgetary processes: there is a ladder of measures which local authorities may take to deal with financial stringency: only the final rungs of that ladder entail service cuts and redundancies. Thus, Wolman argues that local authorities 'behave as organisations concerned with maintaining their equilibrium relationship with their external and internal environments' (Wolman, 1984, p. 261). Hence, they will buy time, increase their local revenues and seek to reduce spending in ways which do not affect service levels. Such expedients include reducing administrative costs, reducing wages or contracting services out to the private or voluntary sectors because they can provide them more cheaply. Local authorities will cut their capital budgets before their revenue budgets because this can be done without cutting services or dismissing staff, although it may hurt the local building trade. Only if all these expedients fail will they reduce their services and make staff redundant.

Prepared on the basis of recent research on local authority budgeting, Table 7.2 indicates that local authorities will resort to a wide variety of expedients before they reduce their services or dismiss staff.

This analysis indicates the range of measures that are available to local authorities in avoiding damaging their services and hence their clients, as well as having to reduce their workforces. In the Public Administration Committee's study of local authority budgets in 1985–1986, not a single authority was identified which had been compelled to impose service cuts and redundancies (Elcock and Jordan (eds), 1987). In March 1993 a study of local authority budgets in the North of England revealed that over 90 per cent of all the respondent authorities were able to achieve over 93 per cent of their 'standstill' budgets despite a particularly severe financial regime imposed by the Department of the Environment. Most were planning to spend at significantly above their standard spending assessments but although some 1,800 job losses were anticipated, few if any authorities were planning compulsory redundancies: 'many authorities in the North will

Table 7.2 Approaches to avoiding cuts

Defensive	Buy time: postpone non-essential services: all departmental estimates contain 'fairy gold' items which no-one seriously expects to get through the process.
	'Sore thumbs': offer up service cuts that are likely to be politically unacceptable, so that the policy and finance committees will allocate more funds to avoid these cuts.
	Increase charges for those services which are charged for, including admission fees, transport fares, admission tickets and library fines.
	Make efficiency savings by demanding less use of secretaries, photocopiers, telephones, etc.
	Reduce capital spending: this will result in local builders becoming redundant but not the council's own staff.
Creative defence	Sell council assets, including surplus land and properties.
	Use private contractors or voluntary organisations to provide services at costs lower than the council can provide them itself.
	'Grantmanship': maximise income from grants from the Government, the European Community or other sources.
	'Creative accountancy': defer pressure by forward borrowing.
Management change	Introduce PPBS and ZBB to force managers to scrutinise the 'base' budget more closely.
	Seek efficiency savings throughout the authority by reforming work practices, reducing administrative overheads.
	Develop performance measurement and performance indicators to encourage greater efficiency.
If all else fails . . .	Impose service reductions and voluntary redundancies
	Impose service reductions and compulsory redundancies.

only entertain compulsory redundancy as a last resort. Every effort will be made to absorb job losses by way of natural wastage, voluntary redundancy and redeployment' (Harrop, Rose and Cousins, 1993, p. 15). One change noted in this survey was an increase in capital spending but this was the result of a Government decision to permit local authorities to spend more of their revenues from council house and other sales than had previously been permitted. Local authorities were thus quick to take advantage of any relaxation in the stringency of the financial climate.

Again, a survey of 1993 budgets mounted by the *Guardian* (30 March 1993) found that the impact even of the severe financial regime imposed on the local authorities responsible for education and social services was very variable. Table 7.3 shows that some authorities were still able to expand their spending on social services and education. Others were able to maintain standstill budgets but the majority had felt compelled to impose reductions. It also indicates some common target areas for reductions, demonstrating that discretionary services tend to suffer especially badly under financial pressure.

This table also demonstrates that many of the tactics listed in Table 7.2 are still available to most local authorities to permit them to avoid making cuts in their most essential services. It demonstrates furthermore that no authority owned up to making staff redundant either voluntarily or with compulsion. However, most had had to cut posts from their establishments with the consequence that more teachers, social workers and other local

Table 7.3 Selected trends in local authority education and social services spending budgets, 1993–1994

Service	Social services	Education
Growth	19	14
Standstill	11	8
Cuts	78	92
Voluntary redundancy	–	–
Compulsory redundancy	–	–
Closures of homes, etc.	22	
Increase user charges	22	
Cut discretionary awards		33
Cut administration and central services		44

Source: The Guardian, 30 March 1993, p. 6

authority staff seemed likley to join the 35,000 whose jobs were axed in 1992–1993 (the *Guardian*, 30 March 1993, p. 6).

Local government budgeting is thus still essentially incremental and the impact of financial stringency varies but a wide range of expedients and techniques have been adopted in order to minimise the effect on the services, clients and employees of the financial pressure local authorities have had to endure since 1976 and especially since 1979. They have not been compelled either fundamentally to change the way in which they go about preparing their budgets or the levels of services they provide. However, to achieve the latter they have had to become increasingly ingenious, including finding new avenues of escape from the Government's incessant demands for cuts when loopholes are closed by legislation.

Auditing

Although the budgetary process is the most important contribution which the finance department makes to local authority policymaking, other developments have also changed the traditional role of the local government accountant. Auditing has been significantly changed by the establishment of the Audit Commission in 1982. The finance department still undertakes internal audits within the authority and prepares the annual reports and accounts but the remit of auditors has changed from one which was principally concerned with fiscal accountability – that is, ensuring that the council's funds have been spent in accordance with the law, the policies of the council and without misuse or corruption – to seeking ways of improving the council's efficiency and effectiveness. This includes ensuring that it makes the best possible use of its resources to produce the most service for the resource available, as well as ensuring that those resources are used to achieve the authority's policy objectives as far as is possible.

The Audit Commission has encouraged this development of the auditors role in several ways. First, it publishes handbooks of good management practice, both in general terms and in the context of particular services. Hence the Commission encourages local authorities to learn from one another's experience and management innovations. Second, it publishes league tables which show the amounts individual authorities spend on their services per head of their populations. A high level of spending need not be an indicator of inefficiency but it should prompt councillors and auditors to enquire whether there is a valid reason for high spending or whether inefficiency is responsible.

The Audit Commission also represents the interests of local government to Whitehall and elsewhere. The report which indicated that the vagaries of central government policy had cost ratepayers £1.2 billion through no fault of local authorities themselves, is a case in point. Its work is now widely accepted within local government as a valuable aid to increasing efficiency and improving the quality of services.

Financial analysis

Other tasks in which local authority accountants may become involved is the assessment of alternative policy proposals through cost–benefit analysis. This is now a well established but still controversial means for deciding whether to undertake new projects or maintain existing services. Cost–benefit analysis (CBA) is applied welfare economics. The costs and benefits relating to a proposal must be established as precisely as possible and computed to produce a rate of return (or cost if costs exceed benefits) (Spiers 1974). This assessment must cover social and other factors as well as the financial ones, although the former may be difficult to quantify. Thus, for example, identifying all the costs and benefits arising from, say, a bypass road can be impossible. It benefits motorists, bus passengers and truck drivers, all of whom will arrive at their destinations more quickly: these benefits can easily be costed. The costs of acquiring the land, building and maintaining the road can also be assessed fairly precisely. However, other costs may not be detected when the analysis is prepared, for instance demands from nearby residents for grants to soundproof their houses or for nuisance caused by fumes and vibration, which become apparent only after the road has been opened to traffic. Equally, the benefits accruing from safer traffic are hard to establish with any certainty. The values allotted to particular items may be highly controversial: the value of a church with a Norman tower which would have had to be demolished to make way for London's third airport was assessed at £51,000 by the Roskill Commission: a figure which Tony Aldous (1972) described as 'a particularly derisory price-tag'. It is clearly extremely difficult to put a monetary tag on such an item about which all could agree. However, if CBA is to be any use to policy-makers, such price tags have to be established. Sometimes, however, the exercise may be relatively easy, as when a local authority established that a major street lighting renewal scheme would produce a rate of return of 23 per cent because of the energy saving it would generate.

Even after all these difficulties have been overcome, the question of what rate of return justifies proceeding with the project still has to be decided. The economist's answer will be to relate this to current interest rates – a practical solution where money must be borrowed to finance the project. However, a required rate of return of 10 per cent may seem unduly high to the project's enthusiasts but too low to its opponents, whatever interest rates may be at the time. Hence, CBA, like budgeting, leads the local government accountant far from columns of figures and into debates about policy decisions where concrete and quantifiable factors are inextricably bound up with values and subjective judgements. The accountant must therefore play a role in advising on the value or otherwise of proposals for capital and current spending emanating from the service departments, on what services and projects can be afforded, how much the authority needs to raise in local taxation and whether services can be financed by means other than raising taxation to undesirable or unacceptable levels. Hence the director of finance and his or her staff must be at the centre of many of the council's most important policy processes, advise on controversial issues and play a major part in developing the council's overall approach to its functions and responsibilities. The days when they could remain absorbed in ledgers and the law are long past.

LAND

The second major resource used by local authorities is often forgotten in books on local government: land and property. Local authorities are landowners on a very large scale. They buy land for their own purposes: to build houses, schools, libraries and roads, for example. For many of these purposes, moreover, they have the power to acquire land compulsorily, after a procedure which usually includes the holding of one or more public inquiries before a minister confirms a local authority compulsory purchase order and the value set on the land concerned. However, not all the projects proposed by local authorities come to fruition and some land and property becomes redundant, for instance when village primary schools are closed because there are no longer sufficient children in the village to support them. Furthermore, since 1980, local authorities have been put under increasing pressure to dispose of land and property holdings which are vacant and for which they have no immediate use: a requirement to do this was included in the Local Government, Planning and Land Act of 1980.

Local authority estates officers and valuers are therefore involved in a continuous process of buying and selling land and property. The volume of such transactions is very considerable. They are also responsible for the management of the council's land and properties, for instance fixing rents for council-owned properties which are let to employees of the council or to outside individuals or organisations. They manage council-owned allotments or smallholdings and estates. Most local authorities have established land or estates committees or sub-committees which are responsible to the council for overseeing the work of their estates and valuation departments. Some local authorities own airports, which pose their own problems of estate management and can be both expensive and controversial assets for a local authority to maintain and operate. In the 1980s and 1990s local authorities have come under considerable pressure to dispose of their airports to private companies but many have resisted this pressure, especially during the property slump of the late 1980s and early 1990s, which would have reduced the receipts from the sale of an airport. However, the operation of the airport may be contracted out to a private company.

The professional officers who are responsible for the purchase, management and disposal of local authorities' land and property are distinct from the majority of local government officers in several ways. First, many of their activities are indistinguishable from those of their professional colleagues in private practice. A local authority must normally buy and sell land and property on the open market. Even where compulsory purchase orders are used, the land or property's value must be assessed in relation to market prices in order to determine the amount of the compensation to be paid to the owner of the site or building concerned. A local authority's estates and valuation officers need therefore to maintain continuous contact with what is happening to the land

and property market in the authority's area, so that they can make advantageous purchases and sales on behalf of their employers. In keeping in touch with the private market, a local authority's valuer must be familiar with the quality of the land and properties in the area and with local estimates of their values. In consequence, especially in large authorities, an individual valuer will concentrate on a particular, possibly quite small, area within the local authority's territory and will monitor land and property sales in it. Such men and women not unnaturally see themselves as providing a professional service to the other departments of the authority and feel that they are rather isolated from the rest of the authority's activities. Much the same can be said about estate management functions such as running small-holdings and allotments, maintaining and assessing rents for service properties like school houses and caretakers' accom-modation. For all these reasons the local government valuation service has tended to stand somewhat apart from other com-mittees and departments and not to become deeply involved in corporate management. The similarity of their work to that of private practitioners also means that contracting out land and property work to the private sector may be relatively easy and is likely to become more common as compulsory competitive tendering is extended to this activity.

Two functions in particular which fall within the estates officer's purview have important political and social consequences for the local authority people and area. The first is the management of smallholdings and allotments. At present day land values and with farmers' needs for expensive machinery and other capital equipment, the tenancy of a local-authority-owned smallholding has become almost the only way in which a young person can hope to become established as a farmer in his own right. Long past are the days when Joseph Chamberlain's 'three acres and a cow' seemed an economically desirable agricultural proposition. A reasonably plentiful supply of smallholdings is therefore essential if young people in the countryside are to continue to be able to set themselves up as farmers, yet smallholdings land is chronically susceptible to being taken over by other departments of the local authority for their own purposes. It is always easier to commence a new project quickly if the land required is already in the ownership of the council. Also, the sale of such land may be attractive when revenue needs urgently to be raised to counter central government grant reductions or the imposition of a severe capping limit.

Again, rapid rises in food prices have increased the demand for allotments in urban and suburban areas but as with small-holdings, the pressure from other departments such as highways, housing, education and refuse disposal tends to reduce the area of land which local authorities have available for allotments. Small-holdings and allotments are attractive because the land is already in the authority's ownership. Hence, not only are the costs of acquisition likely to be reasonable but long delays in the acquisition process are less likely, especially if the land is being purchased for controversial and possibly unsightly projects. The financial pressures of the 1970s and 1980s also render the sale of such assets as smallholdings and allotments to increase the council's income; an increasingly desirable activity, especially from the point of view of the 'guardians' who are hard pressed to make the authority's budget balance. Hence smallholdings and allotments committees and holders must fight hard to prevent their land holdings being slowly whittled away.

A second type of landholding which presents particular problems is municipal airports. The establishment and development of an airport is often considered desirable for attracting new industries to the local authority area but airports are seldom profitable and may require considerable subsidies. Indeed, the establishment and development of an airport may be too expensive for a single authority to undertake, hence the airport may be jointly owned by a consortium of several authorities and managed by a joint committee, as is the case with Newcastle Airport, for example. The specialist staff required for air traffic control must be hired either from the Civil Aviation Authority or from private firms and they are expensive. Facilities must also be provided for Customs and Excise and security staff. Increasingly stringent safety regulations imposed by the Civil Aviation Authority must be observed, often at considerable expense, for example, in providing more and better fire appliances. Finally, the landholding needed for an airport is itself a large investment and if the land were sold, the council would gain a considerable sum of money to spend on other services or to invest at a good rate of interest. All in all, therefore, a municipal airport can seem to be a very expensive luxury, especially when the public expenditure climate is hostile. Sometimes, an airport may be sacrificed to some other goal. For example, Sunderland Borough Council surrendered its airport for redevelopment so that the Nissan car factory would be attracted to that city. Less dramatically, some of the landholding may be suitable for an industrial estate but this will entail investment in the construction of roads and the provision of other services such as energy and water supplies. There are also strong pressures from the Government to privatise municipal airports. Selling the airport to a private sector organisation will also produce a substantial capital windfall for the authority. Hence, the chief officer and his committee chairman who are responsible for an airport will have to fight hard in official and political discussions of resource allocation to ensure that the airport gets the resources it needs. They cannot, therefore, afford to become too cut off from contact with officers in other departments and the senior members of the council.

Valuation and estate management was, for a long time, a relatively stable and conventional professional corner of local government which came under relatively little pressure from corporate management techniques. Its importance was temporarily increased very considerably by the passage of the Community Land Act 1975, which conferred powers on local authorities to buy land which was earmarked in structure and local plans for development and then lease it to developers, so ensuring that the council rather than the developer gained the increment in value which accrued from the development of the land. While it was in force, the Community Land Act was a stimulus for estates officers to develop much closer links with town and country planners because the process was intended to be 'planning led'; decisions by planning committees to zone land for development would initiate its purchase by the council's estates department before it was leased back to private developers. However, the Act was repealed in 1980 by the Thatcher Government before it had had any considerable impact. The powers for local authorities compulsorily to assemble land for their own functions was retained, but they have also come under great pressure to dispose of land which they are not using, under a clause in the 1980 Local Government, Planning and Land Act (which repealed the Community Land Act) which empowers the Secretary of State for the Environment to compile a register of such landholdings and direct local authorities to dispose of them. Not surprisingly, the Conservative Governments of the 1980s and 1990s have sought to restore the free market in land, although local authorities still have considerable powers to acquire land and property for their own purposes.

PERSONNEL

The management of personnel in local government has been subject to as much, if not more pressure to change than that of finance or land. Like most public sector organisations, local authorities are labour-intensive; some 60 per cent of their expenditure goes on the wages, salaries, superannuation and other payments made to or on behalf of their employees. Local government has been severely criticised in recent times for the allegedly excessive rate at which the number of people employed in it has grown. There was a particularly vociferous chorus of complaints about this in the years that followed local government reorganisation, with the result that successive Governments have attempted to impose controls on local authority staff numbers: a national 'manpower watch' was introduced in the 1970s. The financial stringencies of recent years have combined with growing anxieties about seemingly inflated local authority staff numbers to persuade local authorities to make increasing efforts to make better use of their existing staff, in order to reduce demands for extra posts. The pressure imposed by compulsory competitive tendering to reduce labour costs in order to retain service contracts within the local authority have also produced major changes in personnel management in local government (Fenwick, Shaw and Foreman, 1993).

Since 1950, methods of improving personnel management and establishment control have expanded greatly. Work study and organisation and methods techniques have developed rapidly. Computers have made the task of collecting, storing and analysing personnel records easier and quicker, a development which alarmed some trade union leaders because of the fear of job losses, as well as possible threats to privacy. In 1984 the Data Protection Act both improved the legal protection of confidentiality and gave data subjects the right to see information held about themselves on computers and correct it where it is inaccurate (Elcock, 1986).

The development of these and other new management techniques led the Fulton Committee to urge the speedy development of systematic personnel management in the civil service (Fulton,

1968). Similarly, the Bains Committee (1972) urged local authorities to recognise that:

> The human problems of management in local government are in no way different from those in industry or the civil service. The resources devoted to the solution and more important the prevention of those problems in local government are in our view generally inadequate.
>
> (Bains, 1972, para. 6:14, p. 67)

Local government had not, in the Bains Committee's view, made adequate use of the techniques available for improving its efficiency in the use of personnel. However, concern about personnel management is relatively new in local government. In the mid-1960s, the Mallaby Committee was charged with investigating the staffing of local government and its report (1967) was hardly a recipe for a radical change of approach to personnel management. In the chapter devoted to this subject, the committee made frequent references to the previous inquiry into local government staffing carried out by the Hadow Committee in 1934 and it did little more than endorse the recommendations of the earlier committee. Thus the Hadow Committee had recommended that local authorities should create establishment committees responsible for personnel matters, including controlling the size of the authority's departments and vetting requests for new posts. This was establishments work as traditionally understood in the public services: a concern to restrain the size of departments and ensure that new posts are created only when they are absolutely necessary (see Chapman, 1988, Chapter 2 for an account of traditional establishments work in the civil service). The establishments committee should be advised by the authority's clerk, a member of whose staff should take responsibility for personnel matters. This approach was largely supported by the Mallaby Committee twenty-three years later. Its main concern was that although most local authorities had adopted the Hadow Committee's recommendations on this matter, 'both the duties of these officers and the terms of reference of these committees vary considerably' (Mallaby Committee, 1967, para, 429, p. 138). The standard of personnel management could be improved by encouraging all authorities to adopt the structures and practices of the best, not by radical change which would produce a broader approach to personnel management or encourage the rapid adoption of the new techniques then becoming available. Five years later, the Bains Committee, by contrast, argued that existing methods were inadequate and took the view that 'by comparison both with industry and with other areas of the public service, local government appears to lag behind in its recognition and development of the personnel management function' (Bains, 1972, para. 6:3, p. 63). The approach enunciated by Hadow and endorsed by Mallaby was no longer good enough. Since then, many aspects of personnel management have been potentially or actually revolutionised by the development of human resource management (HRM).

The Bains Committee wanted a change from the negative administrative 'policeman' role of the establishments committee and officer, to a more creative one. They had been concerned principally with the administration of wages and salaries, industrial relations and disciplinary problems, as well as recruitment and appointments procedures. Another long-standing responsibility was for training, although much of this was done through staff attending courses of study for the entrance examinations of professional institutes. Above all, establishments officers and committees were expected to scrutinise the requests of the authority's other committees and departments for extra staff, preventing their growth where possible (Mallaby, 1967, p. 137). The Bains Committee, by contrast, argued that personnel managers should also be involved in manpower planning: they should assess the authority's future personnel needs, then recruit and train the staff to meet those needs. They should also deal with career development and job enrichment, evaluation and analysis, staff appraisal and training. The latter should no longer consist principally of ensuring that staff were sent on the appropriate professional courses and sat the appropriate professional examinations. It should also develop a broader consciousness among staff of the range of the local authority's activities, so as to reduce the blinkering effect of the professional training which is the traditional approach to a senior local government post. Thus, the Bains Committee noted with approbation an industrial concern's definition of personnel management as being:

- to promote the effectiveness of human resources both in the short and long term;
- to create and maintain a climate in which changes which are to the advantage of the company can be achieved.

Local authorities should be trying to improve job quality, train members and senior officers in selection procedures and interviewing techniques, plan staff careers and encourage secondments to other local authorities and elsewhere to widen their outlook and increase their knowledge. Above all, the Bains Committee criticised local government for concentrating too much on the 'demand' side of personnel management: the controlling of establishments and giving too little attention to the 'supply' side: recruitment, training and career planning.

During the 1980s this change of role has been greatly reinforced by the development of human resource management. This has four main features. First, the functions of recruitment, training, appraisal and rewards should be integrated in a proactive approach to the management of staff. Second, employees' commitment to the organisation's goals should be increased. Third, the task of doing this should be devolved to line managers throughout the organisation and lastly, collective relations between employers and workers should be supplemented or replaced by the development of more individual relationships between workers and their employers (Farnham, 1993, pp. 108–109). The focus therefore shifts from ensuring the maximum economy of staffing to developing the individual employee's talents, abilities and motivation: a revolutionary change in expectations which has occurred over a relatively short period.

However, the role of the personnel manager in local government is reduced by comparison with colleagues in the private sector, because many personnel matters are outside the control of the individual local authority, partly because of the national expectation that used to prevail that public sector organisations should be 'model' employers, who religiously observe the letter of the law in such matters as health and safety at work, or equal opportunities. Also, the salary scales for officers, the wages of clerical and manual staff and the conditions of service for all employees are negotiated nationally between representatives of the local authority associations and the trades unions whose members are employed by local authorities, through a series of Whitley Councils. These national agreements are enforced and interpreted by regional councils which ensure that one authority does not adopt staff gradings or payments which embarrass others in the region by generating trade union pressure for more generous treatment by all authorities. The local government service is thus in part national and in part local. Its members are employed by individual local authorities but their salaries and conditions of service are mainly nationally determined and variations among similar authorities are marginal. Posts may be differently graded or set at different points on incremental scales. Bonus payments for clerical and manual workers vary but the bulk of each employee's income is determined by the national salary and wage negotiations. National bodies were established during the 1960s to co-ordinate recruitment, training and management services. These included the Local Authorities' Management Services Advisory Committee (LAMSAC), the Local Authorities' Conditions of Service Advisory Board (LACSAB) and the Local Government Training Board (LGTB) but most of their functions have now been absorbed by a single Local Government Management Board (LGMB). The extent of national supervision and control over local authority pay, conditions of service and training inhibits the introduction of many personnel management techniques developed in the private sector, where the individual company has considerable or even complete autonomy in setting its wage rates, conditions of service, training programmes and other aspects of its personnel management. However, the LGMB also provides a stimulus to improving management by disseminating information about successful practices in individual authorities and about new techniques – a role which is also performed by the Audit Commission.

A second major issue is the uncertain status of the personnel officer within local authorities. Both the Mallaby and Bains Committees urged that an authority's committees and chief officers should be prepared to accept the advice of the personnel officer with the same readiness as they accept that of the treasurer within his or her professional competence, despite the difference between the long-standing and prestigious accountancy profession and the newer and still uncertain profession of personnel management. Many of the latter's methods and tools are still in the process of development and are of uncertain effect. The professional qualification of membership of the Institute of Personnel Management (IPM) has won general if not universal acceptance in industry and was accepted in 1971 as the appropriate qualification for personnel officers in local government. However, as recently as 1978, personnel officers 'held a variety of more or less relevant qualifications' (Poole, 1978, p. 136) and their status is still not securely established.

The personnel officer's rank within local authorities is also problematical. He or she may or may not have chief officer status and may or may not have direct access to the chief executive. Equally, personnel is commonly the responsibility of a sub-committee of the policy and resources committee, rather than that of a full committee, although the chairman is likely to have direct access to the council's leading politicians (Bains, 1972, *passim*).

The 1974 reorganisation, together with the prompting of the Bains Committee and LAMSAC, brought about advances but serious problems about the status and influence of personnel officers remain. They tend to be unpopular with the other chief officers because they feel that they are perfectly capable of managing their staff themselves: Personnel is in short an un-necessary impediment to busy professional people anxious to be about their business, which they feel they are quite competent to handle themselves. This attitude tends to be especially pro-nounced in social services departments, where many of the staff are field-workers who must by the nature of their work have considerable autonomy. Resistance is even stronger in education departments and police forces, which have long been accustomed to managing their own personnel affairs largely independent of the rest of their local authorities. Hence, they are particularly resentful of the attempts of personnel managers and other preachers of corporate management to interfere in their affairs. Only the treasurer's men and women are at all readily accepted as having a right to intervene, because their role as the guardians of the probity of the local authority's spending is accepted but they are not loved.

In his review of the local government service in the late 1970s, Kenneth Poole says that 'the new local authorities have taken personnel management more seriously than their predecessors and because of their larger size have been able . . . to employ whole-time personnel staff'. Many personnel officers had achieved chief officer status. (Poole, 1978, pp. 137–138) However, a study by the Institute of Local Government Studies (INLOGOV) at the University of Birmingham found personnel units within local authorities which were subsumed within other departments (Green-wood *et al.*, n.d., pp. 157ff). They found that 'there is a degree of uncertainty about what the structural position of personnel should be' and that 'Personnel officers are not normally full chief officers' (*ibid.*, p. 161). The personnel officer still is not assured of a status equivalent to that of the treasurer or the director of administration. These problems are exacerbated by the relative newness of the personnel function and personnel officers' lack of the informal contacts within other departments that form an important part of treasurers' and clerks' communication networks (*ibid.*, p. 174). However, this problem may be overcome if the chairmanship of the personnel committee or sub-committee is entrusted to a leading politician (Elcock, 1975), although a mere sub-committee of the policy and resources committee, as recommended by the Bains Committee, is unlikely to attract such a person. The personnel department may also lack adequate access to the authority's mainframe computer if this is controlled by the finance department, as is usually the case.

The functions performed by personnel officers have changed considerably in recent years. They are best considered individually, although they may not be performed by personnel staff in all authorities. It is helpful to consider them in terms of Greenwood *et al.*'s classification of them as 'core' functions exercised by most if not all personnel departments, which would have been found in establishments departments before reorganisation. 'Non-core' functions may be carried out elsewhere and 'peripheral' functions are allocated to personnel departments for no very clear reason (Greenwood *et al.*, n.d., pp. 161–162).

The 'core' functions are recruitment, training, management services and establishment control. Recruitment is carried out through advertisement followed by shortlisting and interview. However, those carrying out the final selection may be professional colleagues of the interviewees and may show favouritism, so that the detached presence of a personnel officer at the interview may offer a valuable safeguard. For more senior posts, councillors may also be present, although there have also been cases of members showing partiality during interviews for the appointment and promotion of members of their authorities' staff. As a result of a recommendation of the Widdicombe Committee (1986, para. 6:163) that councillors should be excluded from appointing staff below the grade of principal officer, many English local authorities have excluded councillors from making appointments below the top two or three tiers of departmental hierarchies. Since chief officers, their deputies and assistant chief officers must be expected to work frequently with councillors, the involvement of members in making appointments at these levels is accepted as both desirable and necessary but they are not needed for appointments lower down the departmental hierarchies, although the involvement of councillors in all appointments was formerly traditional in parts of the North of England, for example. It is still common in Wales. The personnel department may arrange training in interviewing techniques for members and senior officers. (see Poole, 1978, pp. 150–152)

On issue which has become increasingly prominent in recruitment and career development is equal opportunities. Legislation to reduce and if possible eliminate discrimination on grounds of gender or race has combined with increasing support, especially among Labour councillors, for campaigns to recruit and promote more women and blacks, to cause most local authorities to announce in recruitment advertisements that they are 'equal opportunities employers'. Many authorities have appointed equal opportunities officers to ensure that women and members of racial minorities receive fair treatment during the recruitment and career development processes. The importance of this issue for local authorities is increased by the traditional and still common expectation that, like other public service organisations, they should act as 'model' employers, adhering strictly to the law and offering examples of the best employment practices (see Farnham, 1993, pp. 104–107). Equal opportunities, like union recognition, the agreement of disputes procedures and strict observance of health and safety at work legislation, are all areas where local authorities and other public service organisations have been expected to set a good example to the private sector.

The training organised by the personnel department commonly involves making staff aware of the work of the authority as a whole, thus reducing their professional isolation, mainly through the provision of induction courses when officers join the authority. Staff will also be encouraged to improve their qualifications, especially where general administrative staff are recruited without professional qualifications. Such staff may be funded to attend day-release courses for BTEC Higher National Certificates, Certificates and Diplomas in Management Studies or other similar qualifications offered by universities and colleges. They may study for membership of the Institute of Chartered Secretaries and Administrators (ICSA). Specialist management institutes such as INLOGOV, the School for Advanced Urban Studies (SAUS) at Bristol University and other specialist institutes at the Universities of Bradford, Kent and elsewhere offer training courses for more senior local government staff (Farnham, 1993, pp. 161–162). Departments may also need assistance in organising training for their staff for professional qualifications, although they are more likely to be able to arrange these courses for their own staff without the intervention of the personnel department. One personnel officer told INLOGOV researchers that 'Departments tell Personnel what training they require. The personnel department try and assess and tell the departments what training they ought to have. There must be a marriage of minds' (Greenwood *et al.*, n.d., p. 163; see also Poole, 1978, Chapter 8). Local authorities' commitment to training has always varied widely and has frequently been reduced by budget cuts in recent years, with the result that many training courses in universities and colleges which have relied on local authorities for recruitment have seen their student numbers reduced. Some have been forced to close.

Management services techniques are also developed and provided by personnel departments, although only two such techniques have been widely adopted in local government. These are work study (the measurement of tasks in order to devise means of getting them carried out more rapidly and efficiently, usually linked to bonus schemes) and organisation and methods (O & M); the giving of advice on the management and control of organisations, together with their procedures. Work study is applied chiefly to clerical and manual workers, while O & M involves more senior staff in the assessment of lines of responsibility and accountability. Other techniques such as systems analysis, job enrichment and operational research have not been widely adopted in local government.

The Bains Committee recommended that management services should be separated from the personnel function and given a separate identity (1972, para. 6:17–6:19, p. 68) but this advice was largely ignored (Greenwood *et al.*, n.d., pp. 163–164). However, reorganisation produced heavy demand for O & M and work study as new departmental structures were established and as bonus schemes inherited from the old authorities have had to be unified and rationalised. The increasingly harsh financial climate of the last two decades increased the attractiveness of techniques which can produce savings in manpower and money (ibid., p. 164).

The last 'core' function is establishments work. Although pay scales are determined nationally, there are many aspects of pay and conditions of service which need to be determined by individual local authorities. Posts need to be graded, bonus schemes prepared and negotiated with unions and precise hours of work, including 'flexitime' schemes need to be established. These last have the social benefit of reducing pressure on roads and public transport at rush hours by spreading out the times when large numbers of local authority staff arrive at and leave Town and County Hall, but they have to be arranged and monitored. Then there is the traditional 'policeman' role of vetting requests from departments and committees for additional staff, the task which more than any other produces friction between the personnel department and the others. If he or she is to be effective in this role, the personnel officer needs the firm support of leading councillors and the chief executive.

The most important 'non-core' function of personnel departments is industrial relations, which Greenwood and his colleagues identify as 'non-core' solely on the ground that 'it is not a function for which there is a specialist staff in the (personnel) department' (Greenwood *et al*; n.d., p. 162). Industrial relations has, however, become a very important issue in local government, for several reasons. First, there is the considerable amount of legislation affecting industrial relations which has been passed in recent times. The matters covered include trade union recognition and the right of workers to join or refuse to join unions; health, safety and welfare at work, unfair dismissal and many others, including prohibitions against gender or racial discrimination. Hence, the personnel officer and his or her staff must be heavily involved in local consultation and negotiations with the trade unions. Meetings of the joint consultative committee, which consists of representatives of the authority and the unions, may take up 'much of the personnel officer's time' (Poole, 1978, p. 141). In addition, he or she must advise on and become involved in negotiating settlements of local industrial disputes, grading appeals and disciplinary hearings. The personnel officer must assist in and advise on the development of a coherent industrial policy which is in accordance with councillors' wishes and which other departments will follow – all within the confines of the national legislation and Whitley Council negotiations. The personnel officer's ability to win the confidence of his or her fellow officers, as well as that of the unions and councillors, is of crucial importance.

It has become the more so as industrial relations have tended to become more conflictual. Union membership among local authority employees has increased greatly over the last thirty years. As local government unions have seen the security of employment, wages, conditions of services and in some cases the professional status of their members challenged, militancy has increased. On most estimates, over three-quarters of local authority employees are members of unions (Laffin, 1989, p. 45). However, we have seen that most negotiations have taken place nationally, particularly through the Whitley Councils. Challenges to wage levels arising from the Government's incomes policies in the 1960s and 1970s provoked increasing militancy, culminating in the 'Winter of discontent' in 1978–1979, when many groups of local authority and other workers staged industrial action to resist a Government incomes policy.

The increasing financial pressures imposed upon local authorities, especially since 1979, sometimes coupled with greater ideological commitment on the part of union officers and members, have altered the climate of industrial relations in local government very considerably. Laffin (1989) has argued that 'The new politics of austerity involve serious problems of policy change. The implementation of retrenchment policies encounters strong opposition from all levels of staff and their unions' (p. 35). He argues that traditional strategies of co-operation, conciliation and the co-option of elected members – especially Labour councillors – to the side of the unions, have sometimes given way to increasing confrontation. Sometimes this has occurred in strange circumstances. In 1986 Liverpool City Council declared its entire workforce redundant as part of its campaign against the Government's spending restraints but the unions refused to accept this move as a defence of their interests, despite Labour councillors' assertions that it was. The unions demanded and secured the withdrawal of the redundancy notices (Parkinson, 1987, pp. 72–73). Generally, the former consensual industrial relations that prevailed in local government have given way to uncertainty and sometimes conflict. For management, 'policies of retrenchment are usually associated with the less consensual management strategies of conciliation and confrontation' (Laffin, 1989, p. 174). For the unions, the problem is 'finding a middle way between too much confrontation and too much collaboration' (ibid., p. 177). In the middle of these tensions the personnel officer and his or her staff must try to maintain industrial peace.

The pressure has been further increased by the introduction of compulsory competitive tendering because it confronts unions and managers alike with a dilemma between enforcing and accepting reductions in wages and conditions of service in order to win contracts, or accepting the loss of work to private firms, together with the resultant redundancies. A study of managers in the North-east of England in the late 1980s indicated that managers and unions had tended to combine, in a region where most local authorities are Labour-controlled, to renegotiate terms and conditions of service so that tenders would be won by the local authorities' own direct service organisations (Elcock, Fenwick and Harrop, 1988). A later study indicated a range of responses, from hostility and fear, through pragmatism and neutrality, to positive enthusiasm for tendering (Fenwick, Shaw and Foreman, 1993, p. 7). Unions are commonly involved in the process of competitive tendering to a more or less limited extent, although sometimes they are excluded altogether and are confronted with management decisions in which they had had no involvement. At the other extreme, union officers might be involved in preparing the agenda for tendering (ibid., pp. 14–15). All in all, the effect of CCT has been to increase the uncertainty and tension between unions and managers, in consequence rendering the conduct of industrial relations an increasingly delicate task, in which personnel officers must be centrally involved.

However, industrial relations has also been influenced more positively, at least in some respects, by the development of human resource management (HRM) as an approach to personnel management. This entails regarding workers and staff as a resource of which the best possible use must be made and includes more careful attention to recruitment and career planning. In this process, the personnel management and industrial relations approaches of the private sector are being increasingly adopted in public services: 'Public service and private sector employment practices . . . are increasingly converging but with the private sector providing the dominant model to be followed' (Farnham, 1993, p. 124). Thus, performance-related pay may be introduced in order to stimulate better performance, although the extent to which this is possible in local government is limited by the continued prevalence of national, rather than local pay bargaining. However, a concerted effort is being made throughout the public services to reduce the importance of national bargaining and increase scope for local negotiations (Farnham, 1993).

Second, the enthusiasm of workers to achieve the organisation's goals must be stimulated: again this is somewhat problematical in local authorities which have a very wide range of functions and tasks to perform, hence it is difficult to set a few, clear objectives with which all staff can identify. A related feature is an attempt to move away from collective bargaining towards dealing with and motivating individual workers, through such devices as appraisal and performance-related payment as well as employment on temporary contracts, as opposed to tenured employment until retirement. Also, a concerted attack has been mounted on national pay bargaining structures, although the impact of this on local government, with its Whitley Council system, has been limited. Also, individual staff appraisal is becoming more prevalent: most teachers at all levels of the education service are now subject to some form of individual appraisal, for example. From the point of view of personnel officers, however, the most radical change involves the devolution of the management of staff from central personnel departments to line managers. Hence, HRM is likely to weaken further the already uncertain position of the personnel function in local government.

The other 'non-core' and 'peripheral' functions of local government personnel officers can be mentioned briefly. They include advising on employee welfare, including the application of health and safety legislation; the provision of catering services for staff and workers and sometimes a role in the provision of computers. Personnel officers may also advise the authority on manpower planning and budgeting.

Hence, the personnel officer in a modern local authority is potentially an important figure: one of the 'topocrats' or 'guardians' (Wildavsky, 1979) – officers responsible for the overall management of the authority and for enabling its members and employees to cope with the management changes in is under pressure to make. However, the status of the personnel officer has long been uncertain. He or she has to share many functions with other senior officers, especially the treasurer – indeed, the professional syllabus of CIPFA includes training in management techniques. Also, the professional status of the personnel management function is still more uncertain in local government than that of finance and other management professions. A further loss of influence may result from the devolution of the management of staff to line managers under HRM strategies. Nonetheless, the personnel manager has an important role to play in assisting local authorities to make the best use of their human resources and to cope with financial pressures, as well as those being generated by the extension of CCT to an increasingly wide range of services.

CONCLUSION

The rapidly changing context within which resource managers in local authorities must operate, together with continual financial pressure, has forced change on all the professions whose main function is ensuring that local authorities use their resources efficiently in order to carry out the functions entrusted to them by Parliament. In finance, the tendency is towards centralising control over the budget in order to cope with financial stringency. In personnel management, however, greater decentralisation may be the order of the day because under HRM, line managers are regarded as being best placed to know how to make the best use of staff. However, the need for central departments and officers with the skills and ability to ensure that local authorities can cope with the changing demands made upon them will continue and probably increase.

Part IV

Planning, management and co-ordination

Chapter 8

Planning: the reduction of uncertainty

Introduction

Planning is at once a necessary and a controversial local government activity, whether it is discussed in the specific context of town and country planning (see Cullingworth, 1967) or in the more general context of the development of corporate planning (Eddison, 1973) and the development of business strategies for local authorities as a whole (Bryson, 1988a and 1988b). In this chapter we therefore discuss planning in terms of town and country planning, other areas of management and the preparation of wider corporate plans by local authorities.

Planning is necessary both because local authorities need to develop coherent views about the direction and manner in which they are going to develop their services and because they are legally required to undertake a wide range of planning functions, especially in the management of the physical environment, the provision of many facilities and the development of transport networks. Local authorities thus need to develop corporate planning processes as well as forming committees and departments to discharge their town and country planning responsibilities.

On the other hand, planning is a controversial activity. Planners may become arrogant high priesthoods or the plans they prepare may be seen as unrealistic and therefore irrelevant (Wildavsky, 1973). Planning involves intervention in the social and economic activities of citizens, which may not be regarded as legitimate, especially by proponents of free-market liberalism. The dominance of the national government by free-market liberals in the mid-1980s resulted in the emasculation of the town and country planning system in that period and threatened some town and country planning functions with total abolition (Thornley, 1990). It is therefore important to begin by attempting to rise above these political controversies, through stating a series of propositions about planning as a part of local authorities' policy-making and management processes.

Above all, planning is concerned with the reduction of uncertainty. John Friend and Neil Jessop (1969) declared that:

> Any process of choice will become a process of planning (or strategic choice) if the selection of current actions is made only after a formulation of possible solutions over a wider field of decision relating to certain anticipated as well as current situations.
>
> (Friend and Jessop, 1969, p. 110)

Reducing uncertainty includes, for example, defining in what locations particular developments are likely to be accepted by the local planning authority. This will both provide guidance for prospective developers as to which sites to select for new factories, shopping malls, housing estates and so on and will also indicate where transport links and public utilities are likely to be required to support industrial, commercial or housing developments.

However, in certain contexts uncertainty may be regarded either as inevitable or desirable. For the traditional conservative, who believes with the late Michael Oakeshott that

> In political activity, men sail a boundless and bottomless sea; there is neither harbour for refuge nor floor for anchorage, neither starting place nor appointed destination. The enterprise is to keep afloat on an even keel; the sea is both friend and enemy; and the seamanship consists in using the resources of a traditional manner of behaviour in order to make a friend of every hostile occasion.
>
> (Oakeshott, 1962, p. 127)

Setting a goal and establishing a series of stages through which to progress towards it is an illegitimate activity because one can and should do no more than hope to survive for another day (see also Sisson, 1959; 1991).

The other set of ideological assumptions which negates the need or legitimacy of strategic planning is free-market liberalism. Here it is the reduction of uncertainty which is illegitimate because the success of a competitive market depends on entrepreneurs competing away their excess profits because they do not know what prices their competitors are setting or how efficient they are. Hence, not merely should no attempt to be made to reduce uncertainty; it is to be regarded as beneficial because the spur of uncertainty causes entrepreneurs to increase their efficiency, reduce their profit margins and, therefore, reduce their prices.

However, unless one subscribes to one of these two views, the reduction of uncertainty becomes a desirable managerial goal. John Friend and a succession of collaborators have developed a methodology which proposes ways to reduce uncertainty over time (Friend and Jessop, 1969; Friend, Power and Yewlett, 1977; Friend and Hickling, 1987). They suggest that planning should proceed by reducing uncertainty in three dimensions, as illustrated in Figure 8.1. The reduction of uncertainty about the environment (UE) entails carrying out research and investigations. The reduction of uncertainty about values (UV) entails the consultation of policy-makers, notably elected politicians – councillors and ministers. The reduction of uncertainty about related organisations should lead to improving communication and co-ordination links with them. In this context, the planning organisation may develop a 'reticulist' function. 'Reticulist' individuals or organisations have the appropriate communication and negotiating skills to encourage communication among all those involved in or affected by strategic plans being prepared by themselves or others (Friend, Power and Yewlett, 1977). By engaging in all these three forms of uncertainty

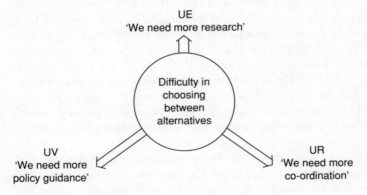

Figure 8.1 Uncertainty and decision-making
Source: J.K. Friend and W.N. Jessop, *Local Government and Strategic Choice*, London, Tavistock, 1969, p. 95

reduction, the cloud of uncertainty will be reduced over time and the likelihood of achieving policies which are both well grounded in accurate information and acceptable to those who must carry them out will be increased.

From this approach to the reduction of uncertainty, several further features of planning follow. The first is that the process of preparing plans may be at least as important as the final outcome in the form of a plan document. Thus, Tony Eddison boldly declared that 'planning is more important than plans' (Eddison, 1973, p. 177). What is required is to identify key tasks and standards of performance, investigate them and propose policies for dealing with them. These policies are then implemented and their effects reviewed (ibid). The planning process is therefore essentially a cyclical process in which the local authority will learn and respond to both the demands made from its external environment and to its own experience in preparing, implementing and reviewing its plans. In consequence, policies should improve through the acquisition of greater knowledge and experience.

Second, plans consist of a series of general statements about how the local authority proposes to deal with the issues facing it. Within these general statements, councillors and officers will be able to deal with the individual cases and more routine decisions coming before them, in the expectation that their actions will be both consistent and in conformity with the values and policies set in the plans.

Third, planning is essentially concerned with the longer term: it compels policy-makers and managers to look beyond their immediate preoccupations, in order that they may be able to ascertain and determine the longer-term consequences of their activities. However, the length of this forward view will depend on the nature of the service involved. Where major investments are required, as in highway development, a twenty-year plan period may be needed. However, three years may be long enough for personal services like social work (Elcock, Fenwick and Harrop, 1988).

Lastly, strategic plans set the context for the taking of individual and routine decisions by incremental processes. It is impossible to plan for all eventualities, or to carry out a full uncertainty-reduction exercise for dealing with each routine decision or individual case. Therefore, many local authority policy-makers and managers have accepted the 'mixed scanning' approach advocated by Amitai Etzioni (1968). This entails carrying out an initial survey of the main issues, problems and crises facing the local authority. This enables planners to identify the key issues which need the study and analysis indicated by the processes of reducing uncertainty, in order to make 'contextuating' decisions – policy guidelines which can then be used in the taking of incremental decisions about routine matters or individual cases. If routine decisions begin to produce protests, injustices or in other ways undesirable results, this may indicate the development of 'policy stress' and the need to take a new 'contextuating' decision in order to develop policies whose outcomes will be more satisfactory and acceptable. Where no 'contextuating' policy statement exists, policy stress indicates the need to prepare one.

In local government, the development of planning methodologies was initially concentrated in the town and country planning function but they have become increasingly widely accepted in the development of corporate plans and business strategies for local authorities as a whole. John Bryson has argued that strategic planning in public service organisations is:

> a disciplined effort to produce fundamental decisions and actions that shape and guide what an organisation is, what it does and how it does it.
>
> (Bryson, 1988, p.11)

The need for strategic planning therefore stems both from statutory obligations and from the necessity of organisational coherence to ensure that the values of policy-makers are executed as efficiently as possible – unless, of course, the policy-makers concerned are either traditional conservatives or free-market liberals, in which case they are likely to reject or dismantle strategic plans and the processes developed for preparing them.

We will therefore next trace the development of the discipline of town and country planning because this is the longest established form of planning in local government, in which many of the issues and methodologies discussed so far have been developed. We can then go on to reflect on wider issues of corporate and strategic planning in local government. Town and country planning includes both the preparation of strategic plans at several levels and the taking of decisions in individual cases – planning applications – within the context of those plans.

The origins and development of town and country planning

The role of town and country planners has changed vastly over the last century or so but one consistent theme has been a sensed need to intervene to protect and improve the physical environment. Its origins can be traced back to the nineteenth century, when concern about the 'condition of England question' was expressed in the Victorian belief that if the surroundings of the working people could be improved, their productivity would increase and their health, cleanliness and even their morals would become better. Their children could then rise to the professions and the middle classes. From such attitudes sprang the garden city movement, which was the beginning of town and country planning as we know it. The idea of replacing old, worn out city centres with new garden cities was expounded by Ebeneezer Howard and Patrick Geddes. Enlightened industrialists put their precepts into practice: the Cadbury family founded Bournville in 1878, Lever established Port Sunlight in 1887 and Joseph Rowntree urged urban renewal as a result of his studies of the conditions of the poor towards the end of the century. He put his ideas into practice in York from the 1890s onwards (Allison, 1975, Chapter 3). All these initiatives led ultimately to the passage through Parliament of the Town and Country Planning Act 1909, which empowered local authorities to prepare schemes for the development of new housing areas. It was only a partial reform which left the problems of older towns and cities untouched. Nonetheless, by 1915 seventy-four local authorities had produced 108 schemes which controlled the development of 198,000 acres of land (ibid., p. 41).

Between the two world wars the planning system was steadily broadened and improved but new problems such as ribbon development were causing concern and in any case rural areas were left almost completely uncontrolled by planning legislation. In 1942 the Scott Committee on land utilisation in rural areas warned that the design of agricultural buildings ought to be controlled and that some land should be 'zoned' as not available for development to prevent the loss of farmland to housing and other forms of development. Hence, the town and country planning system needed to become more comprehensive in the towns and to be extended to cover the countryside (Allison, 1975, pp. 44ff). The post-war Labour Government therefore passed the 1947 Town and Country Planning Act, which created the planning system and profession of modern times. This Act 'embodied the principle that all development rights belong to the State' (Government pamphlet quoted in Allison, 1973, p. 55). Local planning authorities (then county and county borough councils) were required to prepare plans for the comprehensive control of land use, including development plans consisting of a report of survey, followed by a written statement of the policies to be followed in considering the area's future development and to what use land in the area should be put. However, even planning applications which conformed with these policies could be rejected if, for example, the design of the proposed buildings was poor or the development would be unduly obtrusive. Hence, the discretion given to local planning authorities was considerable.

These development plans were to be accompanied by programme maps showing the stages by which the authority was proposed to implement the development plan and, where necessary, more detailed plans such as town maps would be prepared. The entire exercise was intended to cover a period of twenty years from the development plan's preparation and the plans were to be reviewed at least once every five years. The development plan had to be approved by the appropriate minister* after a detailed assessment of it by the ministry and the holding of a public inquiry (Cullingworth, 1967; Allison, 1973: Sharpe, 1975).

The 1947 Act also established the modern development control procedure, under which local planning authorities are empowered to refuse planning applications or impose on applicants 'such conditions as they think fit' but an applicant may appeal to the minister against a refusal of planning permission. Local authorities may also revoke planning permissions but in this case the developer is entitled to compensation, which may prove prohibitively expensive for the local authority. However, a developer who proceeds without planning permission or defies a refusal of planning permission may be ordered to demolish all buildings or other works and restore the site to its original condition. However, all these powers require the minister's consent, so that the minister

* Footnote: Successively the Ministry of Town and Country Planning, the Minister of Local Government and Planning, the Minister of Housing and Local Government and (since 1970) the Secretary of State for the Environment. In Scotland, Wales and Northern Ireland the various roles outlined here are formally the responsibility of the appropriate 'territorial' Secretary of State.

acts as a check on unreasonable or unjustifiable acts by local planning authorities (Cullingworth, 1967, pp. 82ff).

In determining appeals against refusals of planning permission, the minister may decide the issue on the basis of written submissions from the applicant and the local planning authority, or may order the holding of a public inquiry into the application. The outcome is formally determined by the minister but, since 1977, most appeals coming before public inquiries have been determined by the inspector who conducts the inquiry. Occasionally, the minister exercises his power to 'call in' a planning application for his or her own determination – this is done where major developments which affect the national interest or nationwide public policies are concerned. Nuclear power and similar installations have been frequent cases in point and have resulted in some lengthy public inquiries at which major national controversies have been aired, such as the desirability of nuclear power generation and the need for more airport capacity in the South-east of England.

Hence, local planning authorities do not have complete control over the development of their areas, although they can reasonably expect that a development or structure plan which has been approved by the minister will be upheld in planning appeals unless there are major reasons for not doing so; these may, however, include a change of minister, with the new incumbent bringing new values to bear on the planning appeals process (see Elcock, 1985a). Furthermore, the minister is empowered to make a General Development Order which removes some activities from planning control. This has always included agricultural buildings despite the Scott Committee's recommendation that they should be subject to planning control. In the 1980s development in enterprise zones was largely removed from planning control.

One major reason for developing planning control was the impact first of the railways and then of the motor car on patterns of settlement and industrial development. As travelling became easier and safer, people could live further from their workplaces. Furthermore, industrial developments increasingly occurred on the edges of towns and cities, close to major roads. In consequence, the activities of local planning authorities aroused a great deal of local and national controversy, with the result that the process proved to be both slow and cumbersome. An enormous amount of information about existing land uses had to be collected before the preparation of development plans could begin. The process of ministerial certification of plans was long drawn out because of resistance to proposals that would restrict development. Furthermore, many activities had to be allowed to continue because they had begun before the Town and Country Planning Act came into force. Even if the developments were unsightly and did not fit in with the new plans, compensating their owners for ceasing their activities was usually prohibitively expensive.

The process was further impeded by a shortage of professional town and country planners in the 1940s and 1950s. Furthermore, they had difficulty in establishing their professional identity and status because they were often on the staff of the county's architect, surveyor or engineer rather than in a separate planning department. Local authorities did not always establish separate planning committees either, so the planners had to compete with other professions for attention and resources. However, by the time of local government reorganisation in the early 1970s, both the development control system and the planning profession were fairly well established. The profession is governed by the Royal Town and Country Planning Institute (RTPI), although amateurs still become involved in planning through the Town and Country Planning Association (TCPA), which anyone can join. The planning profession is thus peculiarly open.

However, planning had taken a long time to gain momentum and in consequence, twenty years after the passage of the 1947 Act many plans were still incomplete. Others were out of date and no longer matched contemporary realities. In any case, there was a good deal of concern about the complexities of the planning system and the rigidity of development plans and town maps where they existed (Gower Davies, 1972). The Greater London Development Plan's development dragged on for many years, with the result that it became out of date before it was completed, especially as public opinion became more supportive of conservation and more opposed to large-scale redevelopment and grandiose roadbuilding schemes.

Consequently, by the 1960s there was a widespread feeling that a review of the 1947 Act was long overdue. The planning process was subject to four major criticisms. First, whatever the planners proposed, they could do little to make it happen. Land in depressed areas can be zoned for industrial use and provided with roads, mains services and even ready-built factories but if industrialists cannot be induced to use the sites, they will remain empty and become derelict. The area's unemployed workers will leave for more prosperous places or stay in the dole queues. Again, the granting of planning permission for houses does not ensure of itself that they will be built.

The second major criticism was that there was little or no provision for strategic planning, whereby town maps and other plans could be co-ordinated. Neighbouring towns and cities compete for industrial development and provide an excess of industrial land between them. Resources can be wasted by building too many houses of the wrong type in the wrong place. Again, houses have been built where sewers or other essential services are inadequate or cannot be made available. In order to improve co-ordination among local planning authorities, a new approach to strategic land-use planning was also required, a demand which was given an additional impetus by the estab-lishment in 1965 of the regional economic planning councils, although these were abolished in 1979.

Third, criticism abounded of the inflexibility of local authority plans, especially town maps as well as of the time taken to consider planning applications, the costs involved in preparing them and if planning permission was refused, the further time and expense involved in fighting an appeal.

Lastly, the appeal system itself was unsatisfactory because there was no appeal against a local planning authority's decision to grant planning permission despite objections. Also, local planning authorities often did not explain their policies and reasons for refusing (or for that matter granting) planning permissions to applicants, neighbours or even at planning appeal inquiries. The reports of the inspectors who conducted these inquiries were not published until after the passage of the Tribunals and Inquiries Act of 1958. Section 12 of this Act, which has been rigorously enforced by the courts imposes a duty on inspectors and ministers to give the reasons for their recommendations and decisions in planning appeal cases (Elcock, 1969).

Another long-standing issue is planning blight: the reduction in the value of properties because they are on the line of proposed road routes or close to developments which will render their surroundings less pleasant. Such blight can last for years, reducing property values and making properties difficult or impossible to sell. However, since 1959, people thus affected can serve a Blight

Notice on the planning authority concerned requiring them to purchase the land or property involved. Nonetheless, planning blight is widely regarded as an unfair imposition on property owners (Cullingworth, 1967, p. 87).

Structure planning

In 1965, therefore, the Minister of Housing and Local Government, Richard Crossman, established a Planning Advisory Group consisting of town clerks, treasurers and planning officers, with a remit to review the working of the planning system (Crossman, 1975). The group reported in 1966 and its recommendations were enacted in the 1968 Town and Country Planning Act. This Act introduced a new overall plan, the structure plan, which was to be a set of general proposals for the development of counties and county boroughs over a fifteen- to twenty-year period. These structure plans must be approved by the appropriate minister after an examination in public and were to be reviewed every five years. Within the context of structure plans, local and action area plans are prepared. These are not subject to ministerial approval although they are required to be in accordance with the provisions of the structure plan. This division became increasingly important because the new system only came fully into force after the local government reorganisation of 1972–1974, when structure plans became the responsibility of county councils and local planning that of district councils. Planning applications are then to be determined within the context of structure and local plans. A clear separation was built into the system, therefore, between strategic land-use planning on the one hand and the preparation of local plans on the other. Most development control functions were also vested in the district councils and most of the counties' development control functions were transferred to the district councils in 1980, so sharpening this division still further.

Structure plans began to display several of the features of the planning methodology we began with. First, it was made clear from the beginning that structure plans were to be used to increase communication and co-ordination among the national, regional and local authorities which are responsible for the control and development of the environment. In its *Development Plans Manual*, published in 1971, the Department of the Environment laid down seven main functions for a structure plan. These were:

1 Interpreting national and regional policies.
2 Establishing aims, policies and general proposals.
3 Providing a framework for the preparation of local plans.
4 Indicating action areas.
5 Providing guidance for development control.
6 Providing a basis for co-ordinating decisions (primarily in lieu of action area plans).
7 Bringing main planning issues before the minister and the public. (Department of the Environment, 1971, para. 3:10)

Structure plans were therefore intended above all else to be vehicles for reducing uncertainty and enhancing national, regional and local co-ordination. It was soon made clear too that structure plans should also follow a 'mixed scanning' approach, dealing only with major issues affecting the county rather than forming attempts at the old style of comprehensive master planning. In 1974 the Department of the Environment issued a circular which declared that:

> In preparing their structure plans, authorities should . . . concentrate on those issues which are of key structural importance to the area concerned and their interrelationships . . . Issues which are not of structural importance should not normally be dealt with.
>
>   (Department of the Environment, 1974, para. 5)

A little later the DoE said that 'Planning . . . is a continuous process which is not completed when a plan is produced' and that the assumptions underlying structure plans must be continuously checked to see whether they are still valid (ibid., para. 27). They are to be 'rolled forward' every three to five years to embrace a further period of time thus maintaining their status as a fifteen- or twenty-year look forward into the county's future. Hence the view that the process is at least as important as the plan itself because it encourages a continuous process of collective learning was officially endorsed. David Smith (1974) studied fifteen of the first thirty structure plans issued and found that:

> Each plan-making process tended to display one of two main characteristics – a dependence upon the formation of an optimum and unifying land-use strategy or identification and resolution of spatial and non-spatial social and economic problems through a series of planning policies.
>
>   (Smith, 1974. p. 26)

Again, the themes of offering unifying policies to reduce uncertainty and concentration on a limited range of key issues emerged in his study.

A case study: The Humberside Structure Plan

Humberside County Council was one of the first in the country to submit its structure plan to the Secretary of State for approval. In consequence, it was one of the very few authorities to produce a second plan before structure planning went into eclipse in the mid-1980s. The reason was that it adopted a 'key issue' approach in which issues were identified by discussion among planning committee members, consultation with the public and an increasing range of groups and organisations – some 1,800 of them were involved in the preparation of the structure plan. The six key issues thus identified were then tackled using the procedure outlined in Figure 8.2.

Draft policies and options were prepared and submitted for consultation, after which the planning committee would select an option for adoption as a draft structure plan policy. At this stage it was sent out for a further consultation exercise but it was also available as a council resolution for the making of decisions about planning applications by both the districts and the county council itself, so it could be tested through experience. After all this had been done, the consultation draft structure plan was prepared and in turn circulated for comments, after which the final version was prepared for submission to the Secretary of State early in 1977. The examination in public was held that autumn and the plan was accepted by the Secretary of State in 1979 (see Elcock, 1985a). A second structure plan was prepared using a similar learning and consultation process, which was submitted to the Secretary of State early in 1985. New key issues were inserted and some older ones withdrawn, especially because of the need to acknowledge the changed national ideological background as a major influence. For example, attempts to restrict the development of out-of-town shopping centres ran so contrary to the policies of the Thatcher administrations that a structure plan policy imposing such a restriction was deleted, although it had already been destroyed by a series of decisions on planning appeals by the Secretary of State for the Environment upholding a series of such developments (Elcock, 1985a). By this time,

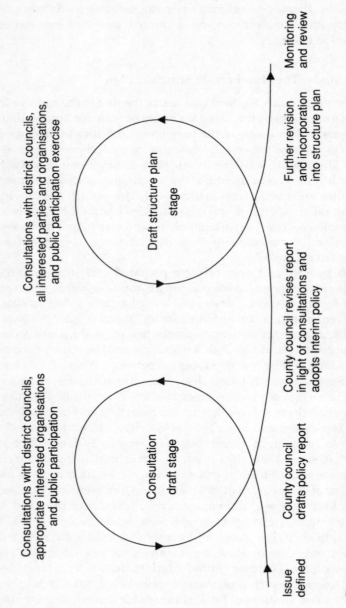

Consultations with district councils, appropriate interested organisations and public participation

Consultations with district councils, all interested parties and organisations, and public participation exercise

Issue defined

Consultation draft stage

County council drafts policy report

County council revises report in light of consultations and adopts Interim policy

Draft structure plan stage

Further revision and incorporation into structure plan

Monitoring and review

Figure 8.2 Humberside county structure plan policy formulation process

however, structure planning was severely in eclipse and threatened with abolition.

Transport planning

In the late 1960s, local authorities also acquired new and extensive powers and duties in transport planning, with the passage of the Transport Act of 1968, the intention of which was to procure the development of integrated passenger transport systems in order to reduce the impact of traffic in towns – an issue of increasing concern which had been examined in the Buchanan Report (1963), which had produced proposals for the wholesale demolition of town and city centres to make room for the motor car – proposals which were increasingly unacceptable. In consequence, the 1968 Act was passed to promote integrated transport systems to encourage people to make more use of railways, buses and other forms of public transport rather than using cars, especially on radial journeys to and from town and city centres. The need was to reverse the vicious cycle under which passengers were deserting the railways and buses, with the result that fares went up and services were reduced or withdrawn.

The 1968 Transport Act initially established passenger transport authorities to operate and co-ordinate public transport in the major conurbations, and control over these authorities was vested in the metropolitan county councils and the Greater London Council in 1972. They were required to secure efficient and integrated transport services and to prepare annual transport policy and programme documents, which constituted both a strategic plan for the development of integrated passenger transport systems and bids for central government resources to do so, in the form of a transport supplementary grant. These authorities promoted some imaginative schemes, notably the Tyne and Wear Metro light rail system and the South Yorkshire County Council's decision to hold public transport fares indefinitely at their 1975 levels in order to encourage an increasing switch of passengers from cars to public transport. The council's argument was that the transport subsidies involved cost far less than the new road developments which otherwise would have been required. However, such policies were vigorously attacked after 1979 and the local authorities which controlled the passenger transport authorities were abolished in 1986. In consequence, links between local

authorities, in particular their planning committees and departments, were considerably loosened. Although the passenger
transport authorities still exist, they are required to provide
transport services on a commercial basis and in competition with
private operators.

In the non-metropolitan or 'shire' counties, public transport
services were controlled either by the district councils or private
operators but the county councils are still required to prepare
transport policies and programme documents. Here, the county
council's ability to promote integrated transport services always
depended much more on their ability to persuade operators to co-
operate, with the inducement of subsidies. In both types of county
council, however, much of the work of preparing transport
policies and programmes was vested in the planning department
– rightly because many of their provisions would be closely
related to those of the structure plan. However, nowadays most
transport services are provided commercially and the transport
policies and programme documents have become in the main a
means for local authorities to bid for central government grants for
road-building and maintenance.

Transportation planning and structure planning affect and
should influence policies and services well beyond the remit
of the planning department and its committee. Planners and
highway engineers work closely together but many planning
decisions have implications far beyond those which mainly
concern the planning department itself. Decisions about the
location of industrial developments affect the refuse collection and disposal services, the highways engineers and many
others. Decisions about new housing developments have implications for education, libraries and social services, among
others. Hence, planning departments need to be involved both
in co-ordinating the activities of the council's own services and
in encouraging communication and co-ordination with other
public and private service organisations. An important aspect of
planning is therefore the need to get a large number of formally
independent organisations to work with one another. Corporate
managers in local authorities and inter-organisational co-
operation must therefore take account of the planning functions
of local authorities in preparing their own strategic or business
plans. We shall return to this point in the last section of this
chapter.

Public participation

A third development in the 1960s which has had an enduring impact on the development of town and country planning was an increasing demand for public participation in planning decisions, as well as many others. In 1969 the Skeffington Report, *People and Planning*, recommended that the more routine appeal decisions should be made by the inspector conducting the public local inquiry instead of being referred to the minister for decision. It urged planning authorities to explain more fully the reasons for their planning decisions and requirements for a variety of participation procedures were built into the planning process after the publication of the Skeffington Report. Hence, in the preparation of their structure plans, county councils are obliged to conduct a series of such exercises and these must be reported as part of the structure plan which is submitted to the Secretary of State for the Environment for approval. The Secretary of State must approve this account of the participation process before proceeding to the detailed examination of the structure plan itself. The examination in public gives a further opportunity for the public to make their views known on the issues selected by the Secretary of State for discussion. Public participation exercises are also carried out during the selection of new road routes, which have sometimes led to considerable disorder at highway route inquiries (Levin, 1979).

In carrying out their development control function of dealing with planning applications, local authorities are required to advertise them in the press and by notices near the site of the proposed development. Lists of applications may be sent to parish councils and residents' groups and may also be displayed in libraries and other public buildings. Adjoining owners are notified. Usually this process generates little interest but sometimes the announcement of planning applications provokes angry public meetings and demonstrations. Even if active unpleasantness does not break out, dealing with considerable numbers of objections and protests is expensive and time-consuming. Above all, much of this protest is generated by what has come to be known as the NIMBY ('not in my back yard') syndrome: residents or property occupiers resist developments which may be required in the public interest but which they believe will damage their environment or reduce the value of their properties. Gypsy sites, sewage works and hostels for the mentally ill or young offenders are frequent causes of such protests. Stan Proctor (*The Guardian*, 29 July 1980) described public participation as a 'current fetish' which 'has now degenerated into "private protest" in a myriad of ways'. Planning committee members must be determined that objections which are inspired by nothing more than a desire to push a proposed development away from their particular locality should almost invariably be ignored, otherwise development and the provision of public services become impossible.

In any case, opportunities for public participation in planning processes have been greatly reduced in the 1980s (Thornley, 1990). Structure plans are no longer being prepared. Many development control functions in the cities have been removed from local authorities and transferred to urban development corporations, who determine developments in the interests of business developers, rather than local communities. In the 1990s the establishment of an urban regeneration agency threatens to remove still further development control powers from local authorities, hence depriving not only the local authorities of their functions but also their citizens of opportunities to participate in decision-making. However, local authorities have been compelled to open their proceedings to public scrutiny, especially by the Public Bodies (Admission to Meetings) Act of 1985, which severely restricts their ability to exclude the public and the press from council and committee meetings: this may now only be done for specific reasons relating to the necessary confidentiality of commercial dealings or personnel matters.

Effective public participation has required planning officers to develop new skills, including marketing skills, in order to try and encourage an often apathetic public to pay attention to their proposals and comment on them, as well as developing effective communications with local and national pressure groups, industry and other public authorities who are affected by local authorities' plans and the planning applications coming before planning committees. Occasionally, by contrast, public order is threatened at meetings and demonstrations which may involve planning officers and committee members in exciting, sometimes potentially dangerous confrontations with angry members of the public. Sometimes they may, indeed, have to seek the protection of the police: not a desirable aspect of the development of public participation.

Some other planning issues

Local plans and development control

The other major responsibilities of planning committees and planning officers are still largely similar to those established by the 1947 Act. However, one important change was the division of the planning function between the county and district councils in 1974, which also had the effect of increasing the number of planning committees and departments in local government, because previously planning had been the responsibility of only the larger tier of local authorities: the county and county borough councils.

In particular, development control was divided between the two tiers of authority, with county councils being given responsibility for mineral workings and some other major schemes, while district councils deal with the vast majority of planning applications. The county councils' development control powers were further reduced by the Local Government, Planning and Land Act of 1980. The district councils also prepare most local plans, in accordance with a programme – the development plan scheme – which has to be agreed among the county council and the district councils within the county. Its main function is to plan the use of specialist planning staff, especially at the county council level.

Also, planning applications must normally be determined within the context of the policies laid down in the county council's structure plan and any other plans prepared by the county or district councils. However, since the abolition of the GLC and the metropolitan county councils, the metropolitan district councils have been charged with producing their own unitary development plans to replace the structure plans prepared by the former metropolitan county councils. These unitary development plans are being prepared in the context of central government policies which favour industrial and commercial development and which are set out in regional strategic guidance, without which councils cannot proceed with their unitary development plans. The scope of these plans is also restricted by the lack of control the metropolitan district councils possess over developments promoted in their areas by urban development corporations. Above all, however, the preparation of these plans is hampered by the small geographical size of most metropolitan boroughs, which means that the preparation of the plans requires co-ordination and agreement among contiguous borough councils. This is often hard to obtain and requires lengthy negotiations. Hence, the small size of the metropolitan boroughs, together with their often artificial boundaries, makes this a rich source of inter-authority conflict and few unitary development plans have yet appeared.

One form of local planning which may briefly be noted here is the subject plan, which deals with a particular local issue. A good example is intensive livestock units, which are not only unsightly and smelly but also generate traffic problems as bulk supplies of foodstuffs and other materials are delivered to them and the animals are taken from them to market. This produces problems for the highways authority, the authorities responsible for refuse collection and disposal, the regional water company and others, so in some areas subject plans have been developed to control intensive livestock units. For instance, this problem became acute in the Holderness district of Humberside in the 1970s because of the rapid expansion of intensive pig-rearing units there, which produced the headline 'More Pigs than People' in the local newspaper. The county and district councils therefore prepared an agreed subject plan to restrict the growth of intensive units and control their location, despite the limited powers available to planning authorities to control agricultural buildings. This was one case of a common planning dilemma: of having to balance modern industrial, transport and other demands against those of urban and rural conservation.

Both the two-tier planning system which prevails in the 'shire' counties and the unitary planning system in the metropolitan boroughs are thus sources of inter-organisational conflict, which make the systems cumbersome and difficult to operate. Disagreements between county and district councils over planning applications have on occasion given rise to considerable tensions between them. Sometimes one local authority has embarked on a policy of active and public opposition to another's policies and often one council can either thwart another council's intentions altogether or at least make their achievement a difficult, tiresome and time-consuming process. In 1976 Stan Proctor commented that 'the planning duties of counties and districts are closely inter-related and there is ample scope for duplication of effort and wasteful use of resources' (Proctor, 1976, p. 100). When ill-will is added to poor communications and a lack of co-ordination, unwillingness to co-operate and political opposition, delay and time-wasting are likely to increase rapidly. Such conflict can develop over the county councils' powers as highway authorities to issue directions requiring a district council to reject a planning application on highways or traffic grounds. The district council may or may not accept the direction as reasonable. Many county councils have delegated this power to the appropriate chief officer and its exercise seems to be a very effective method of making enemies of the members and officers of district councils. There may, therefore, seem to be good arguments for developing unitary structures across the whole country but what may be seen on the one hand as the tiresome time-wasting inherent in the two-tier system, may from another point of view be a valuable set of checks and balances which enhance democratic account-ability and inhibit abuses of power by planning committees and chief officers who often have considerable development control powers delegated to them.

Gypsy sites

The need for differing perspectives on planning issues can be illustrated by a particularly contentious issue with which many planning authorities have had to wrestle: the provision of sites for travelling people, commonly (if often erroneously) referred to as gypsies. Their problems became acute largely because of the planning legislation itself. The presence of gypsies is often resented by local house-dwellers and since 1947 it has been necessary to obtain planning permission in order to establish a caravan site, even on land owned by travelling people themselves. Such applications are almost invariably fiercely resisted and planning permission is therefore very difficult to obtain – a problem which has been made worse by changes in the gypsies' means of livelihood. The mechan-isation of agriculture has eliminated much of the seasonal harvest-ing work on which gypsies used to rely and the advent of the spin-dryer has reduced the demand for clothes pegs, the manufacture of which is another traditional gypsy industry. In consequence, gypsies have increasingly resorted to the collection and sorting of scrap metal in order to make a living. This activity, although socially useful, is unsightly, messy and in other ways unpleasant, which makes district councils yet more unwilling to grant planning applications for gypsy sites (Adams *et al.*, 1975a and 1975b).

In 1968 the Government attempted to alleviate the problem by passing the Caravan Sites Act, which obliges local authorities to provide sites for people of nomadic habit who reside in or resort to their areas, and the county councils acquired this legal duty under the 1972 Local Government Act. The county councils carry out strategic studies of regular movements of gypsies and the present location of encampments, preparatory to proposing the establishment of sites in locations where the travellers are likely to use them. The district councils must then comment on these proposals and must also grant licences for the operation of the sites once they have been established. Hence, it is difficult, if not impossible, for county councils to establish sites without the consent of the district councils. The duty to provide sites for travellers is defined in very broad terms. No ethnic group is singled out for attention and hence the argument often advanced that a particular group of caravan dwellers are 'not real gypsies', is irrelevant. However, this point has become still more contentious in the 1990s with the growth in the numbers of 'new age travellers' who travel from one festival site to another. In any case, in the 1970s a research project demonstrated that gypsies are 'not simply a social group but a cohesive ethnic group with membership based primarily on descent. They are not, as has sometimes been thought, the drop-outs from house-dwelling society' (Adams *et al.*, 1975a, p. 138). The definition in the Act which entitles travellers to the provision of a site is also wide – it embraces residents and those who resort to the area. The 1968 Act also provided that local authorities which make adequate provision for gypsies might be granted designation and thus acquire the right to exclude further travellers from their areas. This provision has been hard to implement because of opposition to designation from gypsy pressure groups (Adams *et al.*, 1975a and 1975b; Vernon, 1976). Initially, designation was only offered to whole counties but it is now available for district areas, which gives the district councils more incentive to grant planning applications for caravan sites. However, implementation of the Caravan Sites Act has been painfully slow and less than half Britain's gypsies have somewhere they can legally live.

The central problem is that although county councils have acquired the obligation to provide gypsy sites, planning permissions must either be obtained from district councils or their agreement to county council applications for deemed planning permission must be sought. Dissatisfied district councils can appeal to the Secretary of State for the Environment to reverse a county council's planning permission for a gypsy site. The district council must also grant a site licence and provide services such as refuse collection to the site once it has been opened. The result is that the efforts of county councils to provide sites are obstructed by district councils, often for years, in a process in which the county council must carefully lobby for support in fulfilling a legal obligation which it has the duty but not the powers to implement: it is rather like competing in a three-legged race because the county and district councils are indissolubly tied together but are constantly under pressure to diverge – district councillors must take note of local residents' objections on pain of likely defeat at the next local elections, whereas county councillors can afford to take a more strategic view of the issue because few county councillors' re-election prospects are likely to be affected by the establishment of a gypsy site in a particular ward. However, provided that it is unobtrusively located and properly managed, a gypsy site, once established, soon becomes an accepted part of the local landscape. In short, the provision of gypsy sites is a classic example of the difficulty of taking decisive action in a two-tier local government system in which one authority can block or delay the implementation of another's policies (Elcock, 1979). The desirability of checks and balances needs to be weighed against the need to solve urgent problems like those of travelling families only a quarter of whom had any place where they can legally live at the time the Caravan Sites Act was passed. However, in 1992 the Department of the Environment proposed the repeal of the Caravan Sites Act because of the increasing difficulty in controlling and finding sites for the 'new age travellers'. The statutory obligation imposed on local authorities by the Act is their only shelter from public hostility towards the provision of gypsy sites. If that shelter is removed, there will be no chance of provision being made for gypsies to live legally, let alone acquire a reasonable standard of life because no local politician will risk the unpopularity that providing sites will provoke from local residents, not least as a result of the 'NIMBY' syndrome.

Economic development

Planning authorities, especially in the poorer areas of the country, are responsible for attracting new industries to their areas and promoting the expansion of existing industries. Again, the economic development function is carried out by both county and district councils. It involves chiefly providing information about the area to potential industrial investors and developers and advising them about what Government, European Community and other assistance is available to them in the local authority's area. Until recently, no formal powers existed in this field, although they are now provided under the Local Government Act of 1989; previously economic development activities had to be funded from the amount provided for under Section 172 of the 1972 Local Government Act, which permits local authorities to undertake such activities as appear to councillors to be beneficial to some or all of the inhabitants of their areas. This amount was initially set at a 2-pence rate, but the principle has been preserved under the Community Charge and Council Tax regimes.

In the 1980s especially, this activity was expanded by the establishment by many local authorities of enterprise boards or enterprise agencies in their areas, which were set up to promote industrial development, invest in enterprises, create small workshops and science parks (see King and Pierre, 1990). The GLC and metropolitan county councils were particularly energetic in establishing such agencies, which have mostly survived their founders' abolition (Cochrane and Clarke, 1990; Harding, 1990; King and Pierre, 1990). Sometimes such economic development strategies were seen as part of a wider attempt to develop socialist economic policies in local authorities and as such, became highly contentious (Lansley, Goss and Wolman, 1989, pp. 83ff). Nonetheless, economic development is now accepted as a legitimate local authority concern as indicated by its endorsement in the 1989 Act. Local authorities also press for the extension of assisted area status to their areas, the establishment of enterprise zones in them and the extension of European Community economic assistance to their areas: a notable example in recent years has been RECHAR, the European Commission's programme to assist in the redevelopment of declining coalfield communities. However, economic development activities are inhibited by the anti-intervention stance of the central government since 1979 and overt resistance to Government policy in this field has now largely ceased.

Planning and the Thatcher regime

The eclipse of planning: the 1980s

The arrival of the Thatcher administration in 1979 at first changed planning only relatively marginally. Planning controls over some developments were withdrawn and we have seen that the development control function was largely removed from the county councils. However, in the 1980s and especially after Nicholas Ridley became Secretary of State for the Environment in 1986, the planning system was systematically attacked. Structure planning in particular went into eclipse and almost disappeared altogether: the strategic dimension of planning came in for particularly severe attack as a result of the Government's support of free markets and its antipathy towards government intervention in industrial or economic activities which, it felt, should be regulated solely by market forces.

First, although some county councils, including Humberside, submitted second structure plans (Elcock, 1985a), the Department of the Environment made it increasingly clear that it no longer regarded the preparation of such plans as a matter of importance. The scope of structure planning was reduced in the early 1980s, especially through the 1985 White Paper, *Lifting the Burden* (DoE, 1986) which aimed to reduce the impediments to business development imposed by the planning system. It also reduced the opportunities available for public participation in the planning process, in the interest of securing speedier decisions about plans and planning applications for developers (Thornley, 1990, pp. 124ff.). When the decision was taken to abolish the GLC and the metropolitan county councils in 1983, one of the reasons advanced in the White Paper, *Streamlining the Cities* (DoE, 1983) was that these authorities had been created during 'a fashion for strategic planning, whose time has now passed' (ibid.). Flynn *et al.* (1985, p. 1) commented that 'there was now a climate which did not require the strategic role with which those authorities were charged when they were established'.

The removal of the GLC and metropolitan county councils was soon followed by a proposal from Nicholas Ridley as Secretary of

State for the Environment, to abolish structure planning entirely and replace it with a more modest system of county reports (DoE, 1986). Although the abolition of structure plans was not in the end proceeded with, they continued to be accorded a low priority by all concerned, both in central and local government. Many county planning departments disappeared, being merged with other departments concerned with highways or other related subjects.

At another level, the influence of planners in local authorities was reduced by the creation of the Urban Development Corporations (UDCs) in many of the major cities during the 1980s. Some UDCs, notably the London Docklands Development Corporation, have rejected local authority views on the development of their areas, while others have sought to establish partnerships with local authorities. However, we have seen that one effect of both UDCs and Enterprise Zones has been to remove considerable tracts of land from local authority control altogether.

Strategic management and business planning: an apotheosis for planning?

By the end of the 1980s, however, the concepts involved in planning – both in the town and country planning system itself and more widely in local authorities' corporate planning and management systems – were becoming more significant once again because an increasing number of local authorities realised that strategic management could assist them to cope with the increasingly severe problems – especially of financial pressure – which they were facing. Many local authority managers responded initially to the climate of uncertainty created by frequent legislative change by abandoning much of their strategic planning activity: the manager who declared that 'planning is impossible' (Elcock, Fenwick and Harrop, 1988, p. 22) would have found many sympathisers, not least among town and country planners who had seen many of their functions and powers either removed or downgraded. However, especially after the third Conservative election victory in 1987, many local councillors and even more senior managers in local government could no longer cope by making incremental spending reductions and hoping to survive in an increasingly stormy sea of central government stringency and pressure group protests. As one treasurer put it, the possibility that the cavalry would come over the hill in the form of a

Government more sympathetic than Mrs Thatcher's to public spending, disappeared after the 1987 election (Elcock, Fenwick and Harrop, 1988). They accepted the need to prepare for spending reductions either by preparing new strategic plans or by dusting off old ones. Newcastle upon Tyne City Council, for example, prepared the first of a series of medium term plans directed towards bringing its services and spending in line with the resources that were likely to be made available to the council under the Conservative Government.

This change came about partly because many of the concepts of strategic planning which had been developed in the 1960s and 1970s, reappeared in the later 1980s in textbooks on strategic management in business and government (Bryson, 1988; Johnson and Scholes, 1988). In particular, the existence of strategic management in business organisations made it more legitimate in local authorities because one of the central themes of the 'new public sector management' (Hood, 1991) was the importance of learning from business practice.

One central concept of such works on business planning and strategic management, which they share with the work of Friend and Jessop and others in the 1960s and 1970s, is the significance of the organisation's relationship with its environment. The development of SWOT (strengths, weaknesses, opportunities, threats) analysis was significant here because the identification of an organisation's internal strengths and weaknesses must, according to this analysis, go hand in hand with an examination of the external opportunities and threats facing it. Similarly, PEST analysis involves the study of political, economic, social and technological changes to identify both the problems to which the organisation must respond and the opportunities they offer to it.

One aspect of strategic management is therefore to determine what internal changes the organisation needs to make in order to respond to the external pressures upon it. This can be illustrated in Figure 8.3, which indicates on the basis of a study of large public service organisations in the North-east of England how they regarded themselves and their relationships with their external environments. The analysis could be used to indicate what changes they needed to make in order to improve both their internal performance and their relationship with their environments. Hence:

Relationship to environment	Managerial stance	
	Proactive	Reactive
Outward-looking	A	B
Inward-looking	C	D

Figure 8.3 Four types of managerial stance in relation to the environment

Type A organisations, which are both proactive and outward-looking, carry out consumer research and marketing. They are likely to subscribe to the public service orientation (Stewart, 1986) and to be sensitive to community needs and demands. They will probably be structurally decentralised and will try to anticipate future problems, thus developing some form of strategic management.

Type B organisations, which are reactive and outward-looking, will need to cope with emergencies as they arise. Some local authority services, notably police forces and fire services, must be largely reactive because they must cope with the emergencies which are reported to them but they can also be outward-looking, for example, undertaking crime- or fire-prevention work. These organisations will seek to reduce the impact of spending cuts on the quality of their services as far as possible.

Type C organisations, which are proactive and inward-looking, are likely to respond to problems, whether they are caused by the external environment or internally, by restructuring themselves. They need to reassure and motivate their staff and will probably develop close links with trade unions in order to secure their co-operation with organisational changes. They will generally seek to generate a consensus within the organisation to secure support for changes.

Type D organisations are reactive and inward-looking. They will constrain their budgets within externally set resource limits and will tend not to undertake much strategic planning or management. They will seek to preserve their services and the employment of their staff, monitoring staffing levels and seeking to avoid redundancies (based on Elcock, Fenwick and Harrop, 1988, pp. 23–23; see also Greenwood, 1987).

It is important to emphasise that there is no moral or other virtue in being in any one box of this matrix rather than any other, because the organisation's location will be determined by both the nature of its functions and its management style, both of which may be appropriate to its functions. However, the matrix enables managers to pose two questions. The first is whether their organisation is in the correct box. If the answer to this question is negative, then managers need, second, to identify the appropriate box and plan how they are going to move towards it, perhaps by a series of stages as advocated by John Bryson (1988). However, the demands for more responsiveness to customers, which have been intensified since the appearance of the Citizen's Charter in 1991, suggest a need to become both more proactive and more outward-looking.

A second revival was a renewed interest in securing a consensus both within local authorities and among those with whom they deal as customers and clients about what the local authority is trying to achieve. Such statements of objectives are often contained in mission statements or corporate plans. The preparation of annual business plans is required in a wide variety of public service organisations, such as the executive agencies established in Government departments under *The Next steps* programme. Local authorities and individual local authority services likewise are increasingly preparing mission statements and corporate business plans. Thus, Northumbria Police Force declared in its strategic plan, published in October 1992, that the plan:

> is a guide which will allow all members of Northumbria Police, the Police Authority, Home Office and the general public to know what the force is trying to achieve. Most important of all, it provides a blueprint which enables people to understand how their individual contributions will best support the overall aims of the force. It will help everyone to pull together and focus their energies in such a way as to make the maximum impact upon the potential problems which are likely to be encountered.
>
> (Northumbria Police, 1992)

This statement of objectives is addressed both to those working in the police force and to those who must relate to it as citizens in order to achieve an improvement in the prevention and detection of crime.

Similarly, Newcastle upon Tyne City Council declared in its medium-term plan for 1993–1994 to 1995–1996 first that the council is:

> committed to the principles of local democracy, i.e. local democratic control over the provision of local services, the ability to represent the interests of the local community in all contexts, regional and national, the ability to respond to the needs of the local population.
>
> (Newcastle City Council: Chief Executive's Department, 1993, Para. 2:1)

The council goes on to declare that its 'business is the welfare of local residents', secured through its own services, services purchased from other providers, grant aid to voluntary agencies and collaboration with such other organisations as the local health authorities and universities (ibid., Para. 2:2)

In both these cases, the statement of objectives is aimed both at the organisation's own staff and at those who must relate to it as suppliers, clients or collaborators. This emphasis on relations with outside organisations has become much more important as structures of local governance have become increasingly fragmented during the 1980s. We shall return to this issue in Chapter 10.

However, it may be difficult to develop a sufficient consensus, both internally and externally, to permit the acceptance of such statements of objectives by all those who work for or relate to the local authority. In local government this is especially difficult because of the political struggle which must take place within the council chamber, although equally the vigour of this struggle is a major aspect of the promotion of local democracy. Nonetheless, there is also a danger that, in an attempt to procure consensus, the statement of goals may be too anodyne to provide effective guidance for staff or collaborators.

In a rapidly changing environment, strategic planners and managers have a delicate balance to strike between being sufficiently able to adapt to change in order to respond to changing circumstances, pressures and demands while at the same time not changing their plans so frequently that they become useless for their basic function of reducing uncertainty. This is particularly difficult in a country which is governed to a greater or lesser extent in accordance with a free-market ideology which demands uncertainty in order that public authorities, like entrepreneurs, shall be exposed to competition.

The final problem with which strategic planners and managers alike have to come to terms is how they can avoid either being regarded as an arrogant high priesthood (Wildavsky, 1973) because they are attempting to prescribe what their colleagues in the local authority should do, or alternatively being regarded as irrelevant because their plans are too abstract to be related to the real world. Town and country planners have often been accused of being arrogant and autocratic; Jon Gower Davies (1972) wrote in the early 1970s of a 'planners' ideology' under which housing areas were being bulldozed and replaced regardless of the wishes of local residents. 'The planners' are regularly accused of making dictatorial or inappropriate decisions in local newspapers up and down the land. On the other hand, there is a need for local authorities to have the capacity to think about their longer-term policy goals as well as dealing with the day-to-day problems which beset them. Hence, many local authorities have established central policy units to prepare corporate plans and policies. Clearly, these units must relate closely to their authority's planning departments because the latter will hold a great deal of information about the demographic and physical structure and environment of the area. The planning committee and department will also have been involved in the preparation of local plans of the various kinds discussed earlier. However, central policy units may fall into one of three traps. They may come to be regarded as irrelevant 'ivory towers' which do little to assist busy councillors and service professionals to meet the needs of the authority's citizens. They may, by contrast, be regarded as arrogant high priests if they appear to lay down the law about how the local authority should proceed, especially if there is no strong consensus about its goals. Finally, and very commonly, central policy units may become absorbed in advising on how to deal with immediate crises, playing a 'fire-fighting' role which runs counter to Wildavsky's advice that their value is that 'by getting out of the fire-house environment of day-to-day administration, policy analysis seeks knowledge and opportunities for dealing with an uncertain future' (Wildavsky, 1969, p. 190). This is an excellent definition of the planner's role, whether as town and country planner or strategic manager.

The strategic planner, on the basis of the analysis presented in this chapter, has three main functions. The first is to reduce uncertainty about the future, for him or herself, the local authority for which he or she works and for other actors within the local community. The second is therefore to develop communication networks by developing and encouraging better communication and co-ordination among departments and organisations, hence playing the 'reticulist' role discussed in Chapter 10 (Friend, Power and Yewlett, 1977). The final task is to assemble a consensus behind the authority's corporate, statutory and other plans so as to secure their effective implementation. These goals are, however, difficult to achieve and give rise to wider issues of corporate planning and management, to which we turn in the next chapter. The issue of inter-organisational co-operation is addresssed in Chapter 10.

Chapter 9

The rise and rise of public management

INTRODUCTION: PRESSURES FOR CHANGE

Local authorities have three main functions: the provision of services for citizens, the management of their resources of money, land and people and planning to reduce uncertainty about the future. The traditional pattern of administration and decision-making in the various activities which make up these three functions was a series of departments each reporting to a separate committee of councillors and relating their work only occasionally to that of the authority's other departments. Equally, the only point at which the committees' decisions were brought together and related one to another was when all the minutes of the committees were brought to the full council meeting for final approval. Only at that stage could committee decisions be examined to see whether they conflicted with the decisions of another committee; whether the overall use of resources by committees met the priorities which councillors wished should be followed and whether their decisions formed part of a coherent plan for the authority's future activity. This traditional pattern of decision-making and administration took similar forms throughout the country (Greenwood and Stewart (eds), 1974). Rather like the mass-produced statues of Queen Victoria which can be found somewhere in most English city centres, until the 1960s most local authorities throughout the country had similar political and administrative procedures and structures, which in turn suffered from the same weaknesses.

These traditional procedures and organisational structures have come to be regarded as inadequate for three main reasons. The first was the need to establish more co-ordinated service provision and resource use, as well as more coherent policies. This resulted in the development of corporate management during the 1960s and its adoption, to a greater or lesser extent, by most local authorities after the local government reorganisations of the 1970s. The principal objective of corporate management was to improve co-ordination and efficiency by establishing a stronger core executive at the centre of local authorities to control the activities of councillors on committees and officials in departments. The aim was, therefore, to increase the number and power of 'topocrats' – councillors and officers responsible for managing the affairs of the local authority as an entity – relative to that of the specialist 'technocrats' who have traditionally dominated the management of local authorities through their control of the departments through which their services are provided.

The second was the increasing concern of local authorities to improve their relationships with the users of their services in the 1980s, following the public disillusionment with public services and their providers which helped bring Margaret Thatcher to power in 1979 (Elcock (ed.), 1982). This concern with 'getting closer to the customer' (Hague, 1989; Gyford, 1991) led in turn to the development of the public service orientation (Stewart, 1986; Ranson and Stewart, 1989). The third was the development of the 'new public sector management' in the 1980s and 1990s, with its stress on management values, especially the 'three Es': economy, efficiency and effectiveness (Hood, 1991). The development of public management has also been heavily influenced by the policies of the Thatcher and Major administrations, which have included reducing the role of the state and the proportion of the gross national product spent on state services, exposing public services to market forces through competitive tendering and privatisation and seeking to ensure greater responsiveness to consumers, especially since the promulgation of the Citizen's Charter in 1991, with its pre-occupation of treating the recipients of public services in a manner similar to that accorded to the customers of a private business (Connelly, 1993).

The consequence for local authority management of all these thrusts for change has been the development of many diverse management structures and styles, with the result that no longer can one assume that the same administrative procedures and management structures exist in local authorities throughout the land. Local government management is now a large and exciting field of study, with a great variety of variations in management structures and processes among individual councils, from which other authorities can learn. This learning processes is promoted by the Audit Commission, the Local Government Management Board and a series of centres for local government management education, training and research in various parts of the country. In this chapter we shall discuss the pressures which have led to successive developments in local authority management and the ways in which local authorities have responded to them.

Throughout local authority management structures and processes, a basic conflict can be detected between what John Stewart (1983) called professional ideologies and management values (pp. 102–105). The former develop because local authority professionals are:

> trained not only in certain skills but also to hold a particular set of beliefs, to make certain assumptions and to hold certain values. Professional training inculcates professional standards and builds up professional knowledge. In a developed profession the skills , values, assumptions and beliefs are linked to constitute an ideology which powerfully influences action.
>
> (Stewart, 1983, p. 102)

The development of such ideologies is influenced, as we saw in Chapter 5, by the historical development of the service concerned, the statutes which govern its provision and the extent to which the profession is practised outside local government.

Increasingly, however, such ideologies come into conflict with management values. Managers are 'concerned with the uniform application of the policies of the authority, rather than with the requirements of individual cases.' In consequence, they will:

> tend at times to be critical of the 'narrow' professionalism of some of their staff. They will emphasise their own necessary concern with the many cases and not merely with one case – and hence for a wider, implicitly a management perspective.
>
> (Stewart, 1983, p. 104)

It is with the impact of the increasing importance of management values in relation to professional ideologies that the next section is concerned.

The corporate gospel: towards the federal authority

In the 1960s, the need for better managerial co-ordination within local authorities produced increasing pressures for new management structures and processes, the effects of which came to be known collectively as corporate management and corporate planning. The first of these pressures was increasing evidence that local authorities were providing services in ways which conflicted with those provided by other departments of the same authority, as well as with those of other agencies operating in the same field (Donnison, 1962). This problem was intensified with the increasing desire to enable the elderly, the mentally ill and handicapped, the disabled and other disadvantaged people to live in their own homes in the community, rather than being cared for in institutions. In order to ensure that the right living conditions, educational provision, financial support and treatment regimes were provided, co-ordination was needed both within the local authorities responsible for the provision of personal social services and with local health-care agencies, which since at least the end of the Second World War have been chiefly controlled by authorities independent of local government; indeed since 1972 local authorities have controlled very few health-care functions. Co-ordination is also required in the 'shire' areas between the social services departments of county councils and the housing departments of district councils. Co-ordination was improved by the creation of 'generic' social services as a result of the Seebohm Report but it is still often inadequate. Where child deaths or injuries have occurred through parental ill-treatment or abuse, official reports have almost invariably found that failures of communication and co-ordination both within local authorities and between them and other agencies, were in part to blame. If teachers, social workers or hospital staff had reported observing a child's bruises, unhappiness, listlessness or emaciation to a central point, systematic and repeated ill-treatment and abuse might have been detected and effective action taken to protect the child before a tragedy occurred (Colwell 1974). Equally, over-zealous conduct by individual professionals – the cause of the unjustified removal of children from their parents' homes by paediatricians in Cleveland – might have been checked by others (Butler-Sloss, 1988).

In the 1960s too, attempts at regional planning for economic development and transport co-ordination produced new demands for improved communication and co-ordination, both within local authorities and between them and other agencies. The establishment of national and regional economic development bodies in the 1960s, together with the passage of the 1968 Transport Act, generated such demands.

A second source of pressure for the better co-ordination of incoherent service provision, was an increasing concern about whether local authorities were using their resources efficiently. This concern was reinforced by the increasing availability and recognition of new techniques that offered opportunities to increase local authorities' efficiency, especially in the management of personnel. These included organisation and methods, work study and other personnel techniques, as well as PPBS and ZBB in the finance field, all of which were discussed in Chapter 7. Both the search for efficiency and the new techniques available implied a need for stronger central control by a local authority's policy-makers and managers if efficiency gains were to be achieved. Further pressure for increased central control stemmed from the possibility of reducing the costs of local authority supplies by establishing central purchasing units which could negotiate advantageous bulk purchasing prices with suppliers, as well as central workshops which could be more fully employed maintaining the authority's vehicles and other machinery than was the case with separate departmental workshops. Lastly, the advent of the mainframe computer required centralisation because these were so expensive and their capacity for the storage, analysis and presentation of information was so great that they could only be employed efficiently within local authorities on a centralised basis. To have several departments running computers would be hopelessly uneconomic in terms of both the expense involved and the level of use of each machine relative to its capacity.

Ironically, since 1970, further developments in information and communications technologies have been a spur, by contrast, to decentralisation because micro-computers or terminals linked to networks enable local staff to have information at their fingertips. The relatively junior staff serving the public can therefore obtain the information they need to reach decisions on individual cases without the need for management chains of communication and control, thus sometimes developing the 'polo effect' – an organisation with a hole at the middle (Booth and Pitt 1985). However, in the early 1960s, the arrival on the local government scene of the mainframe computer was one of several pressures towards better co-ordination and stronger central control within local authorities.

In consequence, the 1960s and 1970s saw the development of what Greenwood and Stewart (eds) (1974) called the federal structure. This was the basis of the set of managerial changes, largely to the structures of local government, which are collectively described as corporate management. Their central thrust has been the development of stronger mechanisms of control at the centre of local authorities, in order to improve co-ordination and the efficiency of resource use.

Corporate management's development came from several sources, including a series of management consultants' reports. Thus, Hull and Liverpool City Councils called in McKinsey and Co., Inc. and Stockport employed Boozey Allen and Hamilton, Inc., to review their management structures. The reports of these consultants were heavily influenced by the practices of large business organisations, especially in America and their recommendations were not always completely accepted by the local authorities who commissioned them (Greenwood and Stewart (eds), 1974). Nonetheless, through discussing the consultants' reports the members and officers of these authorities became familiar with the concepts of corporate management and planning, as well as with PPBS and ZBB.

The development of corporate management was also given official encouragement, especially through the Maud Committee's report on the management of local government (1967) and the Bains Report on management structures for the new local authorities established by the 1972 Local Government Act (Bains, 1972). The Maud Committee's report advocated radical changes in the management structures and processes of local authorities, most of which proved too much for most councillors and officers to stomach. These included the creation of a management board of between five and nine members to co-ordinate policy and review committee decisions; with this went a proposal to confine members to considering general issues of strategy, leaving detailed administration to the officers. Thus the Committee declared that:

> While it is clear that the overall development and control of services should be the responsibility of members, in our view the day-to-day administration of services, the decisions in case-work, the routine process of inspection and control

should normally be the function of the paid officers and not of the members.

(Maud Committee, Volume 1, 1967, para. 146)

Since for the majority of councillors ward casework forms their principal motivation for council service, this proposal was not likely to win general acceptance. It has, nonetheless, been re-iterated many times since. Thus, in a handbook prepared for the Local Government Training Board in 1988, Barratt and Downs advise that councillors can best control their authorities by

concentrating in the full council on giving clear, operationally meaningful overall *directions* and delegating power to carry out those *directions* to more appropriate levels of decision-making. These *directions* will be about what they want the council to achieve and about how they want the achievements to be achieved.

(Barratt and Downs, 1988, p. 34, their italics)

Councillors are, however, unwilling to be confined to such general policy-making roles. The Maud Committee also recommended strengthening the role of the clerk as an overall co-ordinator of policy and management.

The Bains Committee displayed greater political realism. It replaced the management board with a larger policy and re-sources committee, recommended the appointment of a chief executive officer and proposed streamlined committee structures which would reduce the number of main committees an authority appointed to around half a dozen (Bains, 1972). The Bains Report had considerably more practical influence than the Maud Com-mittee, although few if any authorities accepted its prescriptions in full. We will explore the Bains Committee's recommendations in more detail in the context of the specific management changes made in local governemnt after 1972.

Some local authorities had developed their own new structures at the same time as the Maud and Bains Reports were being prepared. Newcastle upon Tyne City Council engaged a prin-cipal city officer in 1965 to co-ordinate policy and service pro-vision (Elliott, 1971). Again, after the Conservatives gained control over Leeds City Council in 1967, they reduced the number of its committees from twenty-six to eleven, delegated routine decisions to officers by changing the council's Standing Orders and created a 'troika' consisting of the Town Clerk, the City Treasurer and the City Engineer to co-ordinate the council's departments' work. At member level all committee minutes were submitted to the Finance and Planning Committee before their submission to the full council. This committee could therefore check that the other committees' activities were consistent with one another and with council policy, as well as ensuring that the committees' demands could be met from the resources available to the authority. Bradford City Council also developed a streamlined committee structure at this time (Bains, 1972, Appendix G).

Many of these ideas were brought together in a book which might be described as the manifesto for corporate management, J.D. Stewart's *Management in Local Government: A Viewpoint*, published in 1971. This was followed by a series of publications from the Institute of Local Government Studies at Birmingham University advocating corporate management. Other units based at universities, as well as the Local Authorities Management Services and Computer Committee (LAMSAC) followed suit. The climax of all this activity was the appointment of the Bains Committee by the Department of the Environment to advise local authorities on their management structures.

The 'governmental' local authority

Another major reason for the development of corporate management was a change in local authorities' own perception of their role, which led to the development of what Greenwood and Stewart (eds) (1974) call the 'governmental' local authority. Traditionally, local authorities had regarded themselves as being responsible primarily for the discharge of the functions and the provision of the services entrusted to them through statutes by Parliament. However, in the 1960s, increasingly they were urged to take a wider view of their role and to regard themselves as responsible for the general well-being of the communities they serve, as well as discharging their statutory duties. Thus McKinsey and Co., Inc. urged Liverpool City Council that 'the job of any city government is to create an environment in which the citizens can live and work comfortably in health and safety'. The Royal Commission on Local Government in England (1969) stated that local authorities have 'an all-round responsibility for the safety, health and well-being, both material and cultural, of people in different localities' (both quoted in Greenwood and Stewart (eds), 1974, p. 2). This view not only implies the development of far more complex networks of communication between the local authority's own committees and departments but also that its members and officers should seek to influence and co-ordinate the activities of such other organisations as Government departments, large industrial companies and the other public service agencies operating in their areas. They need also to involve providers of entertainment, sporting and cultural activities.

The adoption of a 'governmental' approach entails the creation of a strong central organ within the local authority which is able to give a lead not only to the authority's own members and officers but also to others outside it. It also demands coherent policy-making and forward planning (Dror, 1973, 1975; B.C. Smith, 1976), a need further strengthened by the acceptance of planning as a continuous process of learning and adjustment, as discussed in Chapter 8, in which both the council and other agencies need to become involved.

The 'governmental' approach can be illustrated by the growth of industrial or economic development activities by local authorities. Local authorities, especially in areas with declining industries and high levels of unemployment, have become increasingly involved in efforts to persuade domestic and foreign industrialists to undertake new investment in their areas, sometimes forming enterprise boards or similar agencies for this purpose. This became a significant and sometimes controversial area of local authority activity in the 1980s. Local authorities also play an important role in preparing submissions to the European Community for grants from the Regional Development Fund, the Social Fund and other EC structural funds, for their areas. In the North-east of England they have combined to co-ordinate their activities on a regional basis through a committee of European Community Development Officers.

The impact of such developments has been further to strengthen the drive towards more central control and co-ordination within local authorities. In particular, the policy and resources committee, its chairman (usually the leader of the council) and the chief executive officer, become the focus for co-ordinating policy developments and communicating with other agencies.

Corporate management: the principal features

By the early 1970s a considerable number of initiatives had therefore been proposed, by official committees, individual local authorities, management consultants and academics. After re-organisation they were developed in a variety of ways by the local authorities established then. Rather than discuss the recommendations of the various reports in detail, we can explore the principal features of corporate management and make some assessment of the impact of each of them on the management of individual local authorities and of local government generally.

i Policy committees

The first major recommendation was that local authorities should establish a committee of councillors responsible for the overall co-ordination of policy, as well as the management of resources. The Maud Committee's (1967) small management board found little favour but the subsequent proposal by the Bains Committee that local authorities should establish policy and resources committees won general acceptance after 1972. However, the Bains Committee left two issues unresolved. The first was the size of the committee; the second was whether it should consist only of representatives of the ruling party, thus functioning as a local government equivalent of the Cabinet, or whether it should include councillors from all the interests represented on the full council. The one-party policy committee was always relatively rare and has now been prohibited because since 1989, all decision-making committees must be composed of representatives of the parties in proportion to their numbers in the full council.

Policy and resources committees tend to be relatively large, commonly consisting of between a quarter and a third of the members of the full council. They often include all the committee chairmen. It is usually impossible to exclude some chairmen because they, their committee colleagues and their departments will resent thus being given a second-class status. However, this means that relatively few policy and resources committees can concentrate on matters of general policy because they will inevitably be drawn into committee problems, inter-committee disputes and relatively minor issues. Significantly, a study by Greenwood *et al.* (n.d.) found that few policy committees were the principal policy-making *locus* which 'will produce its own ideas, send things back to service committees, direct them in their behaviour' (Greenwood *et al.* n.d., p. 194). Rather, many policy committees come late on the scene, receiving and commenting on the other committees' minutes and sometimes being absorbed mainly in resource management. Some such committees become dress rehearsals for the set-piece battles between the leader of the council and the leader of the opposition at the subsequent meeting of the full council, with policy decisions being taken in party executive meetings before the policy and resources committee meets.

ii *The chief executive officer*

Most local authorities now possess a chief executive officer, although a few never established the post and some others have dispensed with it, sometimes in circumstances of controversy. He or she will also be responsible for forming a management team of chief officers to co-ordinate management and the policy advice tendered by officers to the members. The Bains Committee recommended that the chief executive should not also have responsibility for a department but increasingly chief executives have accepted departmental responsibilities, partly in order to save a chief officer's salary and partly to improve their own security of tenure because they can be seen to have practical involvement in one of the main managerial responsibilities of the authority (see Lomer, 1977; Barberis and Skelton, 1987; Norton, 1991, pp. 159ff). Also, without a department, the chief executive will have only a small staff who may be unable to keep him or her in touch with the activities of the authority's departments.

Initially almost all chief executive officers were lawyers, because many of them had been the clerks of the local authorities which had existed before reorganisation but this hegemony has steadily declined, so that Alan Norton (1991) found that chief executives had been recruited from a range of professional backgrounds, as Table 9.1 shows.

The effectiveness of a chief executive officer depends above all on the relationship he or she establishes with the leader of the council. A failure in this relationship may well result in the dismissal of the chief executive', for example, when the party in control changes, as occurred in Birmingham City Council in 1976 (Haynes, 1980). On

Table 9.1 Main professional backgrounds of chief executive officers, 1990

Profession (and related activities)	% of chief executives
Law	46.5
Accountancy/finance	19.5
Secretary/administration	9.5
Planning	5.4
Architecture	0.2
Engineering	5.0

Source: Adapted from Norton, 1991, Table 10–1, p. 152)

other occasions, friction between the chief executive and the political leadership has led to the former's dismissal, as occurred in Humberside County Council in 1982. On the other hand, in some 'hung' councils the chief executive has played a vital role in bringing together the leaders of the party groups in order to negotiate ways of ensuring that the council's business can be carried on despite the impossibility of one party forming an administration or even passing a decision through the council unless it obtains the co-operation of another party (see Barlow, 1987; Clements, 1987; Leach and Stewart, 1988; Widdicombe, 1986). The Widdicombe Committee (1986) recommended that the position of chief executives should be protected by the imposition of a statutory requirement on local authorities to appoint one but this recommendation has not been implemented by the Government.

iii Streamlined committee structures

The traditional committee structure was criticised by the apostles of corporate management because there were too many committees, too little co-ordination between them and they became too preoccupied with matters of detail. In consequence, most local authorities have reduced the number of their committees and increased the scope of each committee's remit. However, the recommendation made by the Maud Committee that committees should be 'deliberative and representative bodies' making recommendations to the policy committee or management board has not found general acceptance for the reasons outlined earlier. The Bains Committee's view that service committees should be replaced by programme committees has also not been generally acceptable. In any case, the statutory requirement to establish several service committees, for example for education, police and housing, has further inhibited radical reform of the committee structure. Another obstacle is the ambition of prominent councillors to hold committee chairmanships or vice-chairmanships: such offices may need to be created to ensure their loyalty and this may entail the creation of more committees than the minimum necessary for the effective management of the council's business (see Elcock, 1975 for an example).

iv Resource sub-committees

Most local authorities have accepted the Bains Committee's recommendation that sub-committees of the policy and resources committee should be responsible for the management of the authority's resources of money, land and personnel, although the number and status of such sub-committees varies. Most have also appointed performance review sub-committees, with a remit to advise the policy and resources committee on the efficiency and effectiveness of the council's use of its resources in the achievement of its policy objectives. Performance review was generally of marginal importance in the 1970s but has gained considerably in importance under the pressures of the 1980s, to which we return later (see Jordan, 1987; Midwinter and Monaghan, 1993, Chapter 5).

v Fewer departments

Again, statutory requirements have inhibited the combination of departments into fewer, larger units whose activities are easier to co-ordinate but, in general, there are fewer departments than existed before 1972. Libraries, parks, theatres, concert halls, recreation centres and the like are controlled by leisure services committees instead of by separate committees for each type of leisure facility, as was commonly the case before 1972. The fire brigade, consumer protection services and emergency planning are combined under public protection committees. Again, in accordance with the recommendation of the Bains Report, planning and highways functions, as well as those for the planning and provision of public transport, are commonly controlled by planning and transportation committees. Although the titles of these committees vary between authorities, these combinations of functions under single multi-purpose committees are common.

vi Central Policy Units

The final result of the demand for more co-operation and co-ordination in the development and implementation of local authority policies has been the development of central policy or research units by many local authorities, with a remit to develop new policies for the authority and co-ordinate departmental policies through corporate planning and new budgetary processes. Thus, output budgeting requires that the annual budget should present not only the costs of existing programmes and proposals but also what the authority is achieving with the money it is spending. It must above all present to councillors the implications of a range of alternative policy choices. A great deal more than figures in columns is needed if members, especially leading members, are to be able to choose from among policy options which have different-price tags attached to them and which offer differing possible outcomes. Officers and members must work together to prepare decisions which they are prepared to defend in unison against public hostility.

However, members and officers alike tend to become absorbed in the pressures of immediate demands and crises and thus they have too little time to think about general policy or review the achievement and impact of previously set objectives. Aaron Wildavsky recognised that policy-makers must have or provide for themselves the opportunity to escape from these daily pressures: 'by getting out of the fire-house environment of day-to-day administration, policy analysis seeks knowledge and opportunities for dealing with an uncertain future' (Wildavsky, 1969, p. 190). The analyst's role is essentially creative: he or she must collect information and suggest what objectives should be adopted in the light of that information, together with the ideological demands of members. The analyst must also be free and able to challenge established professional orthodoxies. Hence Yehezkel Dror advised local authorities to establish special units for policy analysis whose members can think systematically about the present state of affairs and consider desirable future developments:

Optimal policy-making requires systematic thinking that is based on knowledge and oriented towards innovation on medium and long range policy issues. Not enough of such thinking can generally take place in action-oriented organisations because of both the pressure of acute problems and the way that a pragmatic organisational climate, based on experience and oriented towards executing policies, depresses innovation.

(Dror, 1973, pp. 260–1)

To apply this to local authorities, officers in the ordinary service departments and councillors sitting on the service committees are unlikely to have the time to innovate because of the day-to-day pressures they are under from the public, interest groups, other members, other departments and so forth. Because they become deeply involved in coping with these pressures, they lose (if they ever had it) the desire to innovate. Hence, many local authorities have created policy and research units to obtain information about population and other trends, the council's physical, economic and social environment, developments in other local authorities and to obtain such other information as they think is relevant. On the basis of this research, they are expected to prepare policy proposals which may challenge the service committees' established policies and the provision of established services by departments. Their role is above all to challenge prevailing orthodoxies within the authority and to offer proposals for its future development.

A study of local authorities in the North-east of England, for example, demonstrated that almost all the authorities in this region had established central policy or research units to undertake this function and their existence is common elsewhere. The roles that they play are, however, more variable. Some are able to develop new policies and predictions for the future as proposed by the policy analysts but others find themselves used mainly in a 'fire-fighting' role to find ways out of immediate crises (Elcock, Fenwick and Harrop, 1988; G.M. Norris, 1989). Indeed, in central government, the central policy review staff moved away from giving overall strategic advice to the Cabinet, and after the mid-1970s they concentrated mainly on advising the Cabinet on how to deal with specific issues or resolve immediate crises (Blackstone and Plowden, 1988). The reverse danger is that if it concentrates on preparing strategic policy advice, the central policy unit may become an ivory tower, isolated from the day-to-day activities of

the authority and therefore offering unrealistic advice and proposals. Indeed, the Bains Committee was doubtful about the
wisdom of establishing separate corporate planning units for fear
that they would become excessively isolated from 'the reality of
what is actually happening on the ground' (Bains, 1972, para. 7:28,
p. 84). Dror, by contrast, argued that 'usually, new units are
necessary' but that care must be taken to integrate them with
existing departments. He went on to say that:

> The connection of such units with actual policy-making is a very
> complex political and bureaucratic operation, the success of
> which cannot be taken for granted. Changes in the training of
> senior officials, new advisory services for the council, formal-
> isation of deliberative patterns by the chairmen and even
> courses for senior politicians – these are among the possibly
> needed innovations in the local policy-making system if one
> wants actually to use policy analysis broadly and deeply.
>
> (Dror, 1975)

The implications and demands of policy analysis must be understood and accepted throughout the system if a 'think tank' is not to
become isolated and resented by members and officers who are
immersed in running services. It must also keep in touch with
universities and other bodies who may have contributions to
make to the council's policy-making.

The composition of central policy units may also be problematical because local government officers may be reluctant to
deviate from their established professional careers in order to
serve in them and thus for a time lose their involvement in their
professional activities and networks. Outsiders of the right calibre
are unlikely to be attracted except by high salaries which may not
be acceptable either to councillors or to local government unions.
Membership of a 'think tank' must by its nature be temporary
because a particular individual will only have a certain number of
ideas and a certain amount of knowledge to contribute. Having
made their contribution, they will be expected to return to a more
routine professional working existence. This problem may be
overcome by the secondment of suitable staff from departments to
the central policy units for a fixed term.

The existence of central policy units is now much more common
than it was in the 1970s, when Greenwood *et al.* (n.d.) found that
few local authorities had created such units, despite the Bains

Committee's recommendation that they should do so. However, half the metropolitan authorities had done so then. Also, it has become increasingly common practice for leading councillors to be allowed research assistants to assist them in developing policies, although they can only be employed on a temporary basis and at relatively low salaries as a result of the implementation of the Widdicombe Committee's recommendations to this effect in the 1989 Local Government and Housing Act.

Corporate management: doubts and problems

Many benefits have been claimed for corporate management. The Leeds Conservative Group argued that their scheme for streamlined committees and fewer meetings freed the council's committees and officers from the excessive political control which, they argued, had been imposed by their Labour predecessors. Also, the establishment of stronger central controls over committees and departments by the 'troika' and the enhanced Finance and Planning Committee led to considerable savings of money through the centralisation of such activities as the purchase, maintenance and repair of the council's fleet of vehicles. The Labour opposition, however, denounced the reorganisation of committees and the reduction of meetings as a sacrifice of democracy on the altar of business efficiency.

This highlights a dilemma facing those who demand that local authorities be reorganised in the interests of greater efficiency. Some critics of corporate management have warned that the intention behind its introduction is to reduce the amount of influence that the working class and its political representatives can bring to bear on local authority policy-making and administration. Thus Cynthia Cockburn argued that in the early 1970s, working-class members of the council were doubly excluded from influence. They were excluded in the first place because one of corporate management's effects is to widen the gap in power and influence between the authority's leading figures and their backbench followers and few councillors of working class origin achieved leading positions even where the Labour Party was in control. Second, working-class councillors are often unable to grasp the complexities and abstractions of corporate plans, sophisticated budgetary processes and the like (Cockburn, 1975). This view may be patronising and unduly pessimistic about the ability of working-class politicians to grasp complex issues or make their voices heard but corporate management does increase the complexity and the abstraction of the material with which councillors must deal (Barron, Crawley and Wood, 1991).

Cockburn's warnings were echoed by other writers in more general terms. John Bennington (1976) described corporate management as 'a seductive new ideology' which induces councillors and officers to continue to favour the interests of industry and commerce because corporate planning encourages strong links with them. However, it does not, he feels:

> illuminate problems as they are experienced by other communities of interest, whether these are residents, trades unions, councillors or other groups . . . corporate management helps to advance certain interests and values at the expense of others and at the same time to make it harder for those biases to be observed and challenged.
>
> (Bennington, 1976, p.26)

Certainly, statements of corporate objectives are often so bland and general as to be hard to challenge. Hence, John Dearlove (1979) argued that one of the effects of corporate management is to depoliticise issues in local government. It conceals the true state of affairs, which he alleges is that local authorities govern in the interests of some groups in society and against those of others. Apparently benign and uncontroversial statements of corporate objectives should therefore be approached with considerable suspicion, especially by left-wing politicians.

More generally, the prescriptions of the apostles of corporate management have been adopted to some extent by most local authorities but the extent of their adoption varies widely. Councillors are reluctant to accept policy-making roles and relinquish their case work because of its political and personal importance to them. Many of them also become so absorbed in the work of one or two committees that they become uninterested in more general policy matters. They are also suspicious of changes, including the delegation of functions, which may confer greater powers on officers and reduce councillors' control over them. Back-bench councillors may also be reluctant to cede influence to leading members through the establishment of policy committees and other leadership groups within the council.

Officers, for their part, may be reluctant to engage in meetings and activities, such as management teams and corporate planning groups, which they see as a distraction from their professional concerns and the provision of services to the public. Ambitious techniques such as PPBS are rarely successful and many in local government would share Aaron Wildavsky's scepticism:

> Programme budgeting is like the simultaneous equation of society in the sky. If every major programme were connected to every other with full knowledge of their consequences then all social problems would be solved simultaneously. Programme budgeting fails because its cognitive requirements – relating causes to consequences in all important aspects of policy – are beyond individual or collective human capacity.
>
> (Wildavsky, 1980, p. 32)

John Dearlove argued that such complexity would baffle officers and members alike so that corporate plans would be left to gather dust where they disturb no-one (Dearlove, 1979, p. 178). Such has commonly been the case. Above all, corporate management has commonly not changed the behaviour of most members and officers and if it does not do this, it cannot fully succeed. Robert Haynes wrote of Birmingham City Council that 'the behavioural norms and cultural characteristics associated with the traditional bureaucratic organisation remained firmly entrenched after the introduction of the new structural and procedural patterns'. This in turn produced 'serious operational inefficiency' which enabled the new system's opponents to attack and eventually destroy it (Haynes, 1980, p. 195). However, there is widespread recognition of the need for better co-ordination and as financial stringency has increased, the drive to secure increased efficiency and value for money have become more central in local government (Jordan, 1987; Midwinter and Monaghan, 1993). In any case, the role of corporate structures changed with that of local authorities them-selves in the new management climate which came into existence after 1979.

Getting closer to the public: the public service orientation

In Chapter 1, we noted that local authorities adopted a wide range of methods to develop their relations with the people who use their services. During the 1980s, the range of these approaches became bewilderingly wide. We can make sense of them by looking at Hoggett and Hambleton's (1987) division of them into market-based solutions on the one hand, or consumerist and collectivist solutions designed to increase public use of and support for the provision of services by local authorities themselves, on the other (see also Hague, 1989). Alternatively, we can classify them as John Gyford (1991) does into initiatives designed to create local shareholders, local consumers or local citizens. The range of initiatives taken by local authorities in their efforts to restore their lost legitimacy in the eyes of the public are very varied (Hague, 1989; Harrop and Fenwick, 1990). In consequence, the structures and processes by which local authorities conduct their business have become even more varied than they already were as a result of the development of corporate management.

In the mid- to late 1980s, these developments were increasingly brought together under new approaches to local authority management. A much abused phrase describing these new approaches is the 'enabling' local authority, but it has been used to convey two very different sets of approaches to local government management. On the one hand, it was used by the late Lord Ridley (when, as Nicholas Ridley, he served as Secretary of State for the Environment) to denote a local authority which let the provision of its services to successful tenderers for them; the ideal local authority, on this analysis, meets once a year to let its contracts for the next period. On the other hand, it was used by John Stewart (1986) to denote a local authority which had adopted a new approach to service provision, which might include contracting services out but which also involves consumer awareness by the local authority's staff, decentralisation schemes of one or more of the various kinds discussed in Chapter 1 and recognises a general need to adapt its activities to the changed national policy environment and the new demands from local citizens for participation and above all for good quality, sympathetic and accessible public services in the 1980s and 1990s.

John Stewart and a number of colleagues have proposed that local authorities need to develop what they describe as the 'public service orientation' (Stewart, 1986; Stewart and Clarke, 1987; Clarke and Stewart, 1988). Like corporate management, many of the issues involved in the 'public service orientation' were crystallised by the ever fertile brain of John Stewart (1986; Ranson and Stewart, 1989). The 'public service orientation' developed from a desire to find ways for local authorities to recover their lost legitimacy as providers of local services, coupled with the increasing influence of the management literature on 'excellence', especially the 'principles of excellence' enunciated by Peters and Waterman (1982). Stewart and Clarke summarise the values of the 'public service orientation' as being as follows:

A local authority's activities exist to provide services for the public.

A local authority will be judged by the quality of service provided within the resources available.

The service provided is only of real value if it is of value to those for whom it is provided.

Those for whom services are provided are customers demanding high quality service.

Quality of service demands closeness to the customer.
(Steward and Clarke, 1987, p. 161)

Some observers argue that such an approach confines the scope of local authority management too closely within the marketing sphere. The people who use the services are regarded as individual customers; a local authority is hence to be seen as an organisation providing services in a manner which is attractive to those customers rather than one whose responsibility is to protect and promote the individual and collective rights of local citizens (Connelly, 1993).

The impact of the 'Public Service Orientation' on the management structures and processes of the local authority itself are significant. On the one hand, to change a local authority's culture in the direction of greater awareness of consumers' demands and responsiveness to them requires strong central direction and hence an effective core executive whose members can transmit new directions through the authority's departmental hierarchies. Central training facilities will also be needed to help managers and front-line staff to adjust to the new expectations people will hold of them. Another requirement for improved performance is the more systematic evaluation of services and the setting of performance indicators for the improvement of services and the efficiency of resource use. In this activity, we have seen that local authority accountants, together with the Audit Commission, have played a major role.

On the other hand, consumer responsiveness requires the extensive devolution of functions and decentralisation of control, whether through systems of accountable management or through schemes of departmental, corporate or political decentralisation (see Chapter 1). Managers at all levels need to:

- Know the services wanted by the public;
- Be close to the customer;
- Seek out customer views, complaints and suggestions.

In consequence, attitudes need to change throughout the authority. Councillors should give directions leading to greater consumer awareness and responsiveness to their views and needs, as well as setting out the values they wish to see promoted by the staff. In this context, the old notion that councillors should withdraw from their involvement in the details of administration and case-work has been revived but we have seen that this is a forlorn hope given that many councillors both derive their main satisfaction from their case-work and regard it as an important means of ensuring their own political survival (see Barratt and Downs, 1988; Hague, 1989).

The services desired by the public and those provided by the authority must be analysed to ensure that the services provided are those the public wants. They must be provided in ways which encourage the public to accept and use them. Traditional bureaucratic rules and regulations, which were often introduced to secure the equitable provision and rationing of services, must be examined to see whether they can be removed. However, both their statutory obligations and their responsibilities for various forms of social control prevent local authorities from concentrating wholly on making their services attractive to consumers. Citizens' rights, including their right to participate, must be protected and promoted as well as ensuring that local authority staff are close to their customers. In this context, established professional orthodoxies will have to be challenged where they inhibit responsiveness to members of the public.

Within departments, traditional hierarchies need to be replaced by systems of accountable management, with the relatively junior staff with whom the customers mainly deal having the discretion they need to try and meet these customers' needs without having to make frequent reference to the higher levels of bureaucratic chains of command, as well as having or acquiring the will to be responsive. Middle managers must be prevented from, or persuaded against, exercising more than the minimum of supervision over the 'street-level bureaucrats' (Lipsky, 1980; Elcock, 1986). Hence, extensive retraining is required for both managers and the staff who deal with the public.

Increasingly too, Government policies and legislation have enforced pluralistic provision of services by local authorities, which are encouraged and often required to put their services out to competitive tender or in other ways to offer the task of providing them to private companies or voluntary organisations. To a greater or lesser extent, therefore, local authorities need to define the services they wish to provide and how they want them to be provided, to guide not only their own staff but also the other agencies whom they commission to provide services on their behalf.

CONCLUSION: THE MANAGEMENT OF CHANGE

The changing environment of local authorities, coupled with their own changing perceptions of their roles produce two apparently inconsistent consequences for their management. On the one hand, the need to co-ordinate not only their own departments but an increasing range of contractors and other service providers, entails the development of stronger core executives and central departments. Policy directions need to be developed by councillors who must be advised by 'topocrat' officers. Financial stringency necessitates the development of better financial control. Consistent policies for the provision of services need to be developed. Managers and staff need retraining to meet the demands of the 'public service orientation'.

On the other hand, the desire to provide services which are appropriate to citizens' needs and wishes demands greater devolution and decentralisation of powers and responsibilities. The staff providing the services must be given more discretion so that they can respond to people's needs and wishes. This at the very least requires local authorities to devolve greater powers on junior managers and front-line staff. If they wish to encourage public participation, political decentralisation in the form of neighbourhood committees is required. Decentralisation may also occur through the provision of services by a wide range of private and voluntary agencies. The conundrum of reconciling these sets of demands, for more central control on the one hand and greater decentralisation of action on the other, is the principal task for local authority managers to face in the 1990s.

Its urgency is increased by the increasingly pluralistic organisational environment in which local authorities are now required to operate. This is the subject of the next chapter. What is clear is that management as a local authority discipline will have to continue to challenge the established professional orthodoxies and working practices which have dominated local authorities' policy-making and service provision since the nineteenth century.

Its task in doing so is further complicated by the conflicting values which are likely to dominate local government managers' activities. Christopher Hood (1991) has identified the conflicting origins of the 'new public management', from which many of the innovations discussed in this chapter have come. On the one hand there are:

> a set of administrative reform doctrines built on ideas of contestability, user choice, transparency and close concentration on *incentive structures*. Such doctrines were very different from traditional military-bureaucratic ideas of 'good administration', with their emphasis on orderly hierarchies and elimination of duplication or overlap.
>
> (Hood, 1991, p. 5, author's italics)

These values, which are clearly reflected in the 'public service orientation' discussed in the last section, must be related to:

> a set of administrative reform doctrines based on the ideas of *'professional management' expertise as portable, . . . paramount* over technical expertise, requiring high *discretionary power* to achieve results ('free to manage') and *central* and indispensable to better organisational performance, through the development of appropriate cultures . . . and the active measurement and adjustment of organisational outputs.
>
> (Hood, 1991, p. 6, author's italics)

The dilemma is therefore between how far the management of public services can be improved through better management, in order to resist the demands of the 'new Right' that only market solutions will bring about real improvement in local authorities' efficiency and in the services they provide. In order to achieve this, local authorities' structures, cultures and working methods will require continuous re-evaluation. Fortunately, the variety of experience now available should enable local government to continue to reassess and improve its managerial performance.

Chapter 10

Local governance: local authorities and the other local governments

INTRODUCTION: THREE PHASES OF FRAGMENTATION

Local governance has become increasingly fragmented since the Second World War, with the reversal of the trend established in the nineteenth century towards replacing the single-purpose boards or commissions which were then responsible for the provision of many local services, with their administration by multi-purpose local authorities. These are controlled by elected councils, thus ensuring the democratic accountability of those responsible for providing the services. Some writers have seen the renewed trend towards the establishment of single-purpose authorities, whose accountability to the public is often at best tenuous, as constituting half a century of municipal decline (Loughlin, Gelfand and Young, 1985). Certainly, a great many functions have been removed from local authorities and transferred elsewhere since 1945. In consequence, systems of local governance are now so fragmented that the approach adopted in previous editions of this book, of discussing the individual regional and local agencies that existed alongside local authorities is no longer practicable; there are too many such bodies to permit us to do so in the space available. Furthermore, their structures and functions are so various as to exclude any such neat approach. Instead, we must explore the nature of modern local governance by examining the development of the fragmented system we now have, which has developed since the first signs of the reversal of the nineteenth century trend towards multi-functional local authorities appeared in 1945.

Three main periods of such removal of functions can be detected. The first, which took place after the Second World War, saw most of local authorities' public utility functions, such as the supply of gas and electricity, transferred to nationalised industries run by boards appointed by ministers. Only a few isolated instances remain of the local authority provision of such utilities and trading services, such as the Hull telephone system, which is still provided by Hull City Council for Hull and its surrounding area. During this period local authorities were transformed from being primarily organisations delivering public utilities to become organisations concerned chiefly with the provision of social welfare services (broadly defined), including education, welfare services and leisure amenities (Loughlin, Gelfand and Young, 1985).

A second major change occurred during the orgy of reorganisation which occurred in the early 1970s (Stacey, 1975). At this time, local authorities were deprived of their control over water supply, sewerage and related services, which were transferred to regional water authorities. The regional boundaries which were drawn up for this purpose in the early 1970s were based on England and Wales's principal watersheds. The object was to unify control of those parts of the county which supply water – mainly mountainous rural areas – with those who use most of it – the industrial conurbations – in order to reduce conflicts of interest between them, which frequently delayed such decisions as where to construct new reservoirs. Initially these regional water authorities were controlled by boards of councillors from the local authorities in each water authority area but most local authority representation on their boards was removed in 1988 and the regional water authorities were privatised in 1990. Hence, first local authority control was removed, then councillors' influence was virtually eliminated and finally the water industry was privatised (C. Chapman, 1990). At the same time that councillors' representation on regional water authorities was abolished, these authorities were exempted from the Public Bodies (Admission to Meetings) Act of 1985 on the ground that they needed to take their decisions shrouded by commercial secrecy. Hence, they were not expected to practise the open democratic accountability required of local authorities, especially since the passage of the Public Bodies: Admission to Meetings Act in 1985.

A similar trend can be detected in the case of the National Health Service. At the same time as they lost their water supply and related functions, local authorities lost most of their health-care functions to the regional and area health authorities which were established in 1974. These replaced the former tripartite management of the health-care system through hospital boards and management committees, local authorities (which were required to appoint a medical officer of health) and practitioner committees, with a unified system of health care management by regional and area health authorities, with district management teams reporting to them. However, the need for close collaboration with the local authorities which are responsible for the personal social services was recognised by the drawing of co-terminous boundaries between most area health authorities and the county or metropolitan district councils which became responsible for providing the personal social services and therefore had to establish social services committees and departments.

Furthermore, the members of the new health authorities were appointed from three groups, on the basis of three principles, one of which was the need to involve local authorities in the management of health-care. First, the NHS professionals had to be represented: each health authority had to include a hospital consultant, a general practitioner and a nurse among its members. The intention of this 'syndicalist' form of representation was to improve the influence of general practice and nursing within the service, relative to that of the hospital doctors who had traditionally dominated decision-making within it, by ensuring that the two former groups had representatives on each health authority (Brown, 1979). Second, some health authority members were appointed by the Secretary of State from among local business people, trade unionists and others. Often these members were activists in local health-care charities such as hospital leagues of friends. Finally, a group of councillors representing the local authorities responsible for the personal social services were appointed. Initially four councillors were appointed to each health authority but between 1976 and 1979, this local authority presence was increased to one-third of the members of each health authority, in order to increase at least an indirect form of accountability to the electorate. The result was that seven or eight councillors were appointed (Elcock, 1979). However, this trend towards enhanced local authority influence in the Health Service was reversed when first, the coterminosity between health authorities and local authorities was diluted or lost when the NHS was further reorganised in 1982. The ninety area health authorities were replaced by some 200 smaller district health authorities. Furthermore, councillor representation was again reduced to four per authority in 1979 and then abolished entirely in 1989. Hence again the trend of the Thatcher years was first to reduce and then to eliminate local government representation within the NHS.

The only area where some local authorities gained major functions in the 1970s was the absorption of the passenger transport authorities (PTAs) established in the largest English conurbations by the Transport Act of 1968, by the Greater London Council and the six metropolitan county councils created in 1972. They provided their services through passenger transport executives. The result was some major developments in public transport provision. One was the integrated transport system developed in Tyne and Wear focused on the Metro Light Railway system. Another was the decision of South Yorkshire County Council to freeze passenger transport fares within its area at their 1975 levels in order to encourage drivers to make a progressive switch from using their cars to using public transport. Within their own terms of reference, both these schemes were highly successful and other PTAs are now developing light railway systems, for example Greater Manchester and, more recently, South Yorkshire.

However, in the 1980s first the GLC was deprived of control over London Transport and then the PTAs lost their controlling authorities when the GLC and metropolitan county councils were abolished in 1986. However, they are still controlled by committees of metropolitan district councillors and administered by one of their number or through joint arrangements but their discretion to operate services on anything other than a financial profit basis has been largely withdrawn. In a particularly doctrinaire piece of legislation, passed in 1986, the then Secretary of State for the Environment effectively destroyed both Tyne and Wear's integrated transport system and stopped South Yorkshire's low fares experiment. Many local-authority-owned bus operators were then also privatised or forced into the control of separate operating companies, which were required to run them largely according to commercial criteria of profit. Local authorities' powers to subsidise bus services were heavily restricted. Hence, the freedom of local authorities, individually or collectively, to develop their own public transport policies was considerably reduced. Their annual transport policy and planning documents became little more than bids for central government spending on local roads.

The establishment of new authorities in the 1970s to control functions which had formerly been entrusted to local authorities, following their post-war loss of most of their public utility services, caused Peter Campbell (1973) to advise the Commission on the Constitution that

> in the last twenty-five years the prevailing tendency of the previous sixty years towards the elimination of *ad hoc* authorities has been reversed and a large number of *ad hoc* authorities have come into existence.
>
> (Campbell, 1973)

The boards which controlled these new authorities were mostly appointed by ministers, who therefore acquired the power of the appointment and dismissal of the boards' chairmen and members, as well as the possibility of the informal interference with their management which became the bugbear of the nationalised industries, for which ministers and civil servants could not be effectively called to account (Coombes, 1967; Fiennes, 1967).

In the early 1970s, D.C. Hague (1971) provided an illuminating analysis of the motives which lie behind the establishment of such *ad hoc* agencies, which offers valuable insights into the nature of these agencies then and since. He argued that ministers have six main reasons for creating such agencies. First, the 'buffer' theory applies where a service needs to be protected from political interference, as in the cases of public service broadcasting and university teaching. Here, funds were distributed by agencies which were kept at arms length from ministerial influence, but these 'buffers' have been eroded almost to vanishing point since 1979.

Second, the 'escape theory' suggests that public service organisations would be unduly hampered in their operations if they were required to observe the procedures of the traditional Government department, in particular its preoccupation with record-keeping and Parliamentary accountability. Thus Lord Morrison of Lambeth (1964) argued that the nationalised industries must be able to take commercial risks without the fear of incurring Parliamentary wrath if a particular decision proved to be mistaken. This argument has been carried to its logical conclusion through the Government's privatisation programme, which has been justified in part because it liberates the industries from Treasury control over their investment decisions and removes their financing from the public sector borrowing requirement. On this analysis, privatisation was presented as a means for enabling the industries to escape from the constraints of Treasury rules. The third and related argument is that an autonomous organisation may be able to utilise talent which would not be available to an ordinary government department or local authority. The membership of health authorities, for example, includes many people who would never contemplate seeking election to a local authority (Brown, 1979; Elcock, 1979; Elcock and Haywood, 1980).

In the light of recent concerns about the attenuation of democratic accountability by J.D. Stewart (1992) and others, Hague's fourth argument now looks somewhat old fashioned: it is that the creation of autonomous agencies reduces the risk of concentrating too much power in too few hands. However, the Thatcher administrations' evident determination to appoint 'people who think like us' to the membership of the boards of organisations within the Government's powers of patronage suggests that a concentration of power rather than its dispersal has been the result of the creation of autonomous agencies in the 1980s. Furthermore, the independence of local bodies from central control has been reduced, for example through the Buses Act of 1986 which severely restricts local authorities' and other public transport operators' ability to subsidise the provision of services which they deem to be desirable for social purposes. Annual review meetings in the National Health Service between the Secretary of State and the regional health authority chairmen, which are followed by similar meetings between RHA and district health authority chairmen, are concerned mainly with reviewing the extent to which the Secretary of State's policies are being carried out. There are well authenticated episodes of health authority chairmen being threatened with dismissal unless their authorities comply with Government policies. Thus, local and regional agencies have had their wings severely clipped since 1979, both through increased legislative constraint and by more informal pressures imposed by the Government.

The last two parts of Hague's analysis can be stated more briefly. The 'back-double theory', as W.J.M. McKenzie (1971) called it, proposes that autonomous agencies are created to carry out functions which the Government feels it cannot carry out itself for fear of appearing to intervene in a heavy-handed manner in local or regional concerns. The establishment of the Manpower

Service Commission (MSC) in 1970, for instance, enabled Governments to interfere in local labour markets without being seen directly to do so. However, when the MSC proved to be itself too independent of Government control it was replaced first by the Training Agency and then by the regional training and enterprise councils (TECs). Lastly, autonomous agencies enable the Government to employ people without having to count them in the total of civil service numbers, so that the Government can deny expanding the civil service or claim that it has reduced its size. In the 1980s this trend can be seen both in the privatisation of parts of the civil service and the creation of autonomous units such as the Property Services Agency. However, so far the staff of the executive agencies created since 1988 under the terms of *The Next Steps* report (Efficiency Unit, 1988), remain civil servants. At 1 April 1993 more than two-thirds of civil servants were employed in such agencies and parts of them are likely to be hived off to private companies under the Government's market testing programme, the civil service equivalent of the compulsory competitive tendering legislation in local government (Fenwick, Shaw and Foreman, 1993).

In the light of what has happened in the 1980s and 1990s, it is significant that most of this reasoning takes little account of the need for the democratic control of local service provision, which is nonetheless a central reason for the existence of local authorities. The first two of Hague's arguments support its reduction in the interests of freedom of speech, research and teaching, or of entrepreneurial decision-taking. The fourth, 'pluralist', theory, that there is safety in numbers from central domination, is often adduced by ministers in defence of their fragmentation of local governance, but it is rendered nugatory by the extent of the control from Whitehall which is now generally practised. The last two are concerned with escaping public criticism – which is an important aspect of holding public servants and services to account. Nonetheless, before the 1980s local democratic accountability figured largely in justifications for the creation of local or regional organisations on which local or regional interests could be represented (Stanyer and Smith, 1976).

The weaknesses of many of Hague's arguments have emerged in the third major period for the loss of control by local authorities, which occurred during the 1980s, through a series of Government initiatives which either reduced local authorities' controls over their functions or removed their functions to other organisations completely. Thus developers in the enterprise zones established in the early 1980s were exempted from most local authority planning controls. These controls were removed altogether from local authority control in the areas where urban development corporations were set up from 1982 onwards. The establishment of a General Development Corporation may further erode local authorities' powers in urban planning.

At much the same time, first the former polytechnics and then colleges of further education were removed from local authority control and placed under the control of Government-appointed funding councils. Again, schools have been encouraged to desert their local education authorities in favour of direct funding by the Department for Education, by holding a ballot of parents in favour of 'opting out'. One in eight secondary schools had thus 'opted out' by 1993. Tenants on council housing estates have been offered ballots on whether to leave local authority control in favour of an alternative landlord, although few such ballots have yet produced support for a change of landlord. Control over much training, especially for the sixteen to nineteen age group, has been removed from local education authorities and handed over to TECs whose members are mainly local business people. Local authority representation on police authorities is soon likely to be diluted by the appointment of business people to those authorities by the Home Secretary, as well as retaining some representation for magistrates, under proposals which have been developed by successive Home Secretaries during 1993.

The threat to democratic accountability

These developments have led John Stewart (1992) to warn of the development of a 'new magistracy' and a consequent dangerous decline in the democratic accountability of local public service providers. Stewart warned that the removal of functions from local authority control to that of organisations controlled by ministerial nominees meant that:

> There is no sense in which those appointed can be regarded as locally accountable. Indeed the membership of these bodies is largely unknown locally. Nor are they necessarily subject to the same requirements for open meetings, access to information

and external scrutiny that local authorities are subject to. Accountability such as it is rests upon the accountability of these bodies to central government, although even that appears uncertain in the case of the governing bodies of, for example, hospital trusts and grant maintained schools.

(Stewart, 1992, p. 7)

The system of local governance is thus not only fragmented; it is also less and less accountable to the public it serves, except through the market mechanism or surrogates for it, such as the 'internal market' in the National Health Service created in 1989. This has itself further eroded the public accountability of health-care providers through the establishment of autonomous trusts outside health authority control, together with the granting of autonomous control over their budgets to some larger general medical practices, whose members have become 'fund-holding' GPs.

All these reforms constitute a process of change which has raised crucial questions about the diminishing extent of local authorities' powers and functions. They also reduce the validity of some of the arguments in favour of autonomous agencies offered by Hague and others in the 1970s because their purpose is frequently to reduce the accountability of local service providers to local citizens. Rather, the users of these services are to be regarded as customers who can refuse to buy a service or choose another supplier if they are not satisfied with the product they are getting. However, many of these services must by their nature be provided by monopolies or at best, sometimes, oligopolies, in which customer choice is in the nature of the service being provided, of necessity limited or non-existent. This in turn raises the issue of the decline of democratic accountability. It has also presented major problems for local authority policy-makers who have increasingly to try and co-ordinate the activities of organisations other than their own, while increasingly being deprived of the means to control or influence them.

Regional government and regional governance

On the other hand, there have been indications that a regional tier of governance may be emerging which might ultimately lead to the acceptance of a need to create elected regional councils. First, many national services have long been provided on a local or regional basis, through decentralised structures of central government administration. These include the regional offices of such Government departments as the Department of the Environment, the Department of Employment and the Department of Trade and Industry. These offices may sometimes act as the implementers of national policies in their regions but their controllers and other senior officers may also 'go native', becoming their regions' advocates in Whitehall (Young, 1982; Elcock, Fenwick and Harrop, 1988; Fenwick, Harrop and Elcock, 1989). Second, the control of public services through regional authorities with boards appointed by ministers provides a further element of regional governance. For example, the National Health Service, although controlled and funded from the Department of Health, is operated by regional and district health authorities which demonstrably have a substantial degree of autonomy, including some discretion as to how far they implement ministers' policies (Elcock and Hayward, 1980; Haywood and Elcock, 1982). However, that area of discretion has been reduced by the annual review meetings instituted in 1982 and the strengthening of Government control over the appointment of the chairmen and members of health authorities. Wendy Ranade has suggested that health authority members may become either tribunes, representing local needs to the Secretary of State, or prefects responsible for the execution of central government policy in their areas (Ranade, 1985). Since 1989, local authority representation on health authorities has been removed.

Again, before privatisation, many of the nationalised industries and other public undertakings were organised on a regional basis; indeed some of their privatised successors are still organised regionally, including the electricity supply companies and the water companies.

In the 1970s and early 1980s, the existence of a wide range of regional administrative authorities, including also the regional economic planning councils and boards established in 1965 (but abolished in the 1980s), had led to the creation of a substantial tier of regional administration in England which indicated to some observers at least, a need for regional councils to establish greater democratic control over their activities. This development suggested that Scottish and Welsh devolution should be accompanied by the establishment of elected regional authorities in the English regions (Hogwood and Keating (eds), 1982; Caborn, 1992). However, the exit of devolution from the national political agenda which resulted from Margaret Thatcher's accession as Prime Minister in 1979 has also removed regional government from the political agenda, and her successor, John Major, seems to be almost as adamantly opposed to the constitutional changes required by devolution. Since Mrs Thatcher's election, some regional organisations, including the Economic Planning Councils, have been abolished and others have been privatised (Pliatzky, 1992).

On the other hand, the increasing pressure from the European Commission to develop a 'Europe of the regions' in which regional governments or administrations can negotiate for development funds directly with Brussels without needing to go through their national governments, is increasing the need at least for some form of regional administrative representation. This need is increasingly being met through the establishment of consortia which include local authorities, private companies and others, through which representations of regional needs and interests can be made to the Commission and other EC institutions. The North-east of England has an extensive network of such organisations, including the Northern Development Company and a committee of European Community Development Officers which co-ordinates bids for European funds by the region's local Authorities (Elcock, Fenwick and Harrop, 1988; Fenwick and Harrop, 1989). Other English regions, notably the North-west, are showing signs of following suit. The Scottish and Welsh demands for devolution also continue, especially in the former and sooner or later this issue will return to near the head of the national governmental and political agendas.

The management of fragments

In the meantime, however, the fragmentation of local governance gives rise to two sets of issues. The first is how the activities of these various agencies are to be co-ordinated in order to provide services and facilities when and where they are needed. The privatisation of the gas, water and electricity industries, for example, has not obviated the need to ensure that these services are provided to areas where industrial or residential development is going to take place. Someone therefore needs to co-ordinate their provision and this has been a major function of the structure and local plans prepared by county and district councils. It will also be provided by the metropolitan borough councils' unitary development plans when these have been prepared but this is proving to be a lengthy process.

The provision of health-care and social services must be co-ordinated among an increasing range of actors, especially now that the Community Care scheme is in operation, with the likelihood that individuals who are in need of care will repeatedly have to cross the organisational boundaries between social services departments, hospital trusts, health authorities and GP fund-holders – not to mention the many services or facilities provided by private or voluntary agencies. The proportion of services provided by the private and voluntary sectors is expected by ministers to rise to 85 per cent of the total, so that the need for co-ordination will increase considerably.

Again, children in need of care must be dealt with by the social services departments, schools which may or may not have 'opted out' of local authority control, the probation service and – again – the various health-care agencies. A final example is individuals who have their gas, electricity or even water supplies cut off for non-payment of bills by privatised utility companies. Not only may this threaten a collective interest, for instance, it is leading to the spread of infectious diseases in inner-city areas where a significant number of residents have been deprived of clean water, but also there must be co-ordinated and coherent support avail-able for citizens who need assistance because they cannot pay their bills after they have been made redundant or ejected from their family homes.

It is no accident that in the 1970s, the co-ordination of the policies and activities of autonomous agencies became an import-ant concern of those concerned with the management of local government. This problem became increasingly urgent after the orgy of reorganisation that took place in the early years of this decade, which, as we have seen considerably fragmented local governance (Stacey, 1975). The inter-corporate dimension (Friend, Power and Yewlett, 1977) became increasingly important both because local governance was becoming increasingly fragmented and because local authorities were increasingly accepting that they needed to develop a 'governmental' approach to their responsibilities, thus accepting a general responsibility for the prosperity and happiness of the people of their areas.

In consequence, John Friend and colleagues carried forward their analysis of the making of local strategic choices (Friend and

Jessop, 1969), to developing an analysis of how to manage inter-organisational co-ordination (Friend, Power and Yewlett, 1977). Local authorities need to co-ordinate the policies and activities of their own departments, as well as those of other local authorities and other agencies in order to secure the development and implementation of coherent and efficient local public policies. Hence, they need to develop inter-organisational policy planning as a network of communications in which certain individuals or organisations ensure that others whose activities overlap or conflict understand one another's actions and co-ordinate them one with another. Friend, Power and Yewlett (1977), call this the 'reticulist role'. Reticulists stand at the crossroads, as it were, of the inter-organisational communications network and are therefore well-placed to direct information or proposals to those quarters where they need to be taken into account, or from which information or pressure to modify policies may come. In local governance, it is still arguable that local authorities are uniquely fitted to play this role because of the wide range of their responsibilities, although the reduction of their powers and functions relative to those of other agencies may render their activities less immediately acceptable to those other organisations. In particular, the reduction in importance attached to structure planning in the 1980s has largely removed one avenue for reticulist activity, through the planning committees and departments of county councils, many of which have disappeared.

The arguments in favour of local authorities carrying out such a reticulist role emerge from the three types of local government activity discussed earlier: the provision of services for citizens, the management of their resources and planning as a means to reduce uncertainty. In the context of service provision there are a great many links between local authority services departments and other organisations. The local authorities responsible for the social services need to develop and maintain close links with the NHS and have been required to establish joint consultative committees with health authorities for this purpose. The importance of this link has been increased by joint funding schemes under which health authorities pay for the initial construction of facilities, after which the social services department progressively takes over running and paying for them (Brown, 1975, 1979; Haywood and Alaszewski, 1980). They also need links with the local and regional offices of the social security benefits, contributions, child support and other agencies, as well as with a vast range of voluntary organisations. The last are of great importance because they are intended to become service providers under contract to the social services department under the community care scheme – under this scheme the Secretary of State has directed that up to 85 per cent of community care services should be provided by private or voluntary agencies, rather than by local authorities directly. Within the same authority the social services need links with the education service, including schools as well as the education department itself; also with housing departments in their own or other local authorities. Thus, because of their many functions and their need for a wide range of links with other organisations, social services departments should be able to play the reticulist role of co-ordinating the provision of care for children, the disabled and the handicapped, the elderly and the many other individuals, families and groups who are in need of care and assistance. They are the better placed to do this because they have a statutory obligation to prepare community care plans for the development of these services in their areas.

Again, the departments of local authorities which are responsible for major capital or infrastructure developments, such as housing estates, schools and highways, will need extensive links with other organisations to ensure that houses or schools are not built where the necessary services cannot or will not be provided. Hence, a local authority in its role as a provider of a wide range of services will need to develop a multitude of links with other organisations, through which not only will these organisations be able to communicate with the local authority itself but also they will be able to communicate with one another through the medium of the local authority's members and staff – who will therefore function as reticulists. Despite the decline in the powers and functions of local authorities relative to the many other organisations which now play a role in the government of local communities, local authorities still have a wider range of responsibilities than any of these other organisations and are therefore still the natural choice to act as reticulist organisations.

In terms of resource allocation, some of the regional or local autonomous agencies depend for part of their income on local authority grants. An increasing number are also the recipients of contracts and therefore funds to provide services on behalf of local authorities. The giving or withholding of funds or contracts gives local authorities an opportunity to influence the policies and activities of other bodies. In terms of grants, regional arts associations and regional tourist boards are heavily dependent on local authorities and the latter are strongly represented on their governing boards. In terms of contracts, voluntary organisations are becoming increasingly important providers of services on behalf of local authorities but they need to negotiate and secure the contracts local authorities have on offer. Again, they frequently include councillors on their boards of governors, which provides a further communication link with the local authority and through it, with other agencies.

In other cases, however, there is little financial interdependence and hence less scope for local authority influence. Urban development corporations are funded entirely from central grants and the income they generate from their property developments. Local authority funding of the NHS is very limited, the only significant interdependence being the joint financing scheme for the construction of hostels and similar facilities, for which specific funds are earmarked by the Department of Health from the sums allocated to health authorities.

It is perhaps in the planning field that the greatest potential exists for local authorities to play the reticulist role, although the diminished influence and importance of the town and country planning system in the 1980s and 1990s has reduced planners' ability to play a reticulist role. Nonetheless, in the preparation of their structure and local plans local planning authorities have collected a great deal of information which is of use not only to themselves but also to other local and regional agencies. Thus, population projections prepared by county planning authorities for structure planning purposes can also assist health authorities to decide where new hospitals or specialist facilities should be located. Such projections indicate, for example, where concentrations of elderly people are likely to make special demands on health services. In the early 1970s, for example, Humberside County Council's planning department discovered from an analysis of the 1971 Census that the number of old people in the seaside resort of Bridlington was increasing far faster than anyone had realised previously. A new hospital had to be built, increased facilities for primary health-care had to be created, as well as more residential homes and domiciliary care services which had to be provided urgently. This had major implications for the development of services and the construction of facilities by both the County Council's own Social Services Department and the then Humberside Area Health Authority (Elcock, 1985). As providers of information, local authorities may be of considerable assistance to other organisations, reducing others' as well as their own uncertainty about their environments. At the very least the existence of local authority data may enable other organisations to avoid the expense of collecting their own. In the example just given, the database which revealed the Bridlington age explosion was prepared jointly for Humberside County Council and the Area Health Authority by the council's planning department but funded by both authorities.

Second, local planning authorities are required to engage in public consultation processes, both during the preparation of plans and in dealing with specific planning applications. Hence, they become aware of the opinions, interests and policies of other organisations which they cannot only take account of themselves but also convey to others who need to take account of them. Finally, we have seen that structure and local plans provide a framework of relative certainty within which other organisations can take their own decisions in the assurance that if they conform with the plans, their decisions and actions are unlikely to be opposed by the local planning authorities and that the necessary facilities are likely to be available to them because other actors, such as the gas and electricity undertakings, are also guided by the local authorities' plans. Thus, the designation in a plan of a particular village for growth, for example, indicates to the water company that improved water supply and sewerage may be needed, to the local education authority that a new or larger village school will become necessary and to the district health authority that a GP's surgery or health centre needs to be provided. The provision of such facilities takes time – in some cases a great deal of time – and if the need for them can be anticipated in advance through using structure and local plans, they are more likely to be available when the need for them arises rather than their having to be provided as emergency measures when an unmet need causes problems and protests.

Not every local authority plays such reticulist roles to the full, although to some extent they must all do so because of their statutory duties, especially in town and country planning and the co-ordination of transport through their transport policy and programme documents, albeit that the importance attached to these duties has declined. Some local authorities, especially those controlled by the Conservative Party, still fight shy of the 'governmental' approach to their functions because they regard it as involving unnecessary and undesirable extensions of governmental interference in the lives of local citizens. Nevertheless, the local authority is uniquely well-placed to act as the main co-ordinator of public sector activities in its area and may reduce duplication and waste if it plays this role actively. Its potential to influence private and voluntary sectors too is increased by the development of the 'enabling' role whereby it is the source of contracts, because at the very least the council decides what contracts it wishes to offer and, within the statutory limits imposed on it, on what terms.

Local authorities still have one other attribute which no other local or regional body possesses: their members are elected. Local authorities are therefore the only focus for direct public accountability in Britain other than Parliament itself. Increasing concern has been expressed in recent times about the lack of accountability of autonomous government agencies and this concern has increased with the creation of more and more such agencies at the local and regional level (Stewart, 1992). Many would argue that the proliferation of *ad hoc* authorities in British public administration has resulted in a dangerous attenuation of democratic accountability. Furthermore, there seems to be no sign that the pace of this attenuation of democratic accountability is slackening in the 1990s. Parliament and the central government are too over-occupied to cope with the vast amount of work that would be entailed in effectively holding all these bodies to account, the statements by some members of the 'new Right' that the House of Commons is a sufficient guarantor of such accountability notwithstanding.

Equally, however, the centre has been unwilling, for a variety of reasons, to vest additional functions in elected local authorities, especially as the parties in opposition at Westminster have increased their influence over local authorities during the long period of Conservative national domination since 1979. Thus, after the 1993 county council elections the Conservatives retained control of only one 'shire' county, Buckinghamshire. The central government also seems unwilling to concede the degree of independence from central control which local authorities enjoy by virtue of their large resources of finance, information, political legitimacy and statutory powers (Rhodes 1981, 1987). Furthermore, many local authority areas are still too small for the effective administration of several of the services presently controlled by *ad hoc* authorities, especially where large capital projects need to be undertaken. In any case, the central government, for whatever reason, chronically lacks confidence in the ability of local authorities to manage their affairs competently and efficiently.

For all these reasons, neither the central government system nor our present local authorities appear to offer practical solutions to the problems posed by the *ad hoc* administration of many public services, in particular for ensuring their effective public accountability and their coherent provision. The Citizen's Charter is an attempt to increase a form of accountability downwards to individual citizens in their roles as customers or consumers but it does not provide for the effective participation by citizens in decision-making (Connelly, 1993; Elcock, 1993). Some would argue that this problem can best be overcome by the establishment of elected regional assemblies in England, together with devolution to Scotland and Wales, as part of which the powers and functions which are at present entrusted to *ad hoc* agencies could be vested in elected regional authorities. Others see these proposals as being likely to create an undesirable further layer of bureaucracy in a small and, it is argued, relatively homogeneous country. However, local authorities which actively assert their roles as reticulist organisations in relation to these *ad hoc* authorities will be able to have some influence over their activities and councillors sitting on their governing bodies can bring at least an element of representation of local opinions and interests to their proceedings. The need to maintain democratic accountability is therefore a further argument for local authorities and their members taking an active interest in the activities in the other local governments in their areas. It is essential that they continue to play their reticulist role despite their decline in importance relative to that of other agencies. It is also a major reason for accepting the retention of an active local government system in the United Kingdom.

Chapter 11

Concluding speculations*

INTRODUCTION: IS DEATH NEAR?

At least since the Second World War, councillors and officers as well as academic students of local government have been warning of its imminent demise. Thus, for example, the Town Clerk of Stockport did so in 1948 (Glen, 1949) and Professor John Griffith did likewise in a lecture to the Association of Municipal Corporations in 1961 (Griffith, 1961). The Layfield Committee argued in 1976 that a clear choice needed to be made between accepting the creation of a centralised governmental system and enabling local authorities to govern their areas with a significant amount of local autonomy. John Stewart (1983) has likewise urged the recognition and acceptance by the central government and others, of local authorities' right and ability to make local choices. However, local government has so far survived all these warnings and it continues to survive, despite the onslaught on its powers, functions, structure and the financial freedom of manoeuvre of local authorities which was conducted by the Thatcher administrations. In the first edition of this book, the caution was administered that local government has cried wolf too often; that caution is still valid. Although local government is often seen as a patient passively undergoing a series of painful operations at the hands of ministers and their advisers (see Chandler, 1988, for example), it nonetheless has the potential to reassert its vigour and its independence, if those involved in it choose to do so rather than constantly issuing dire warnings about its imminent assassination by arrogant ministers and unsympathetic civil servants.

* An early draft of this chapter appeared under the title 'Turn the Town Hall Lights Back On' in *The Independent*, 10 May 1993.

The power–dependence analysis of central–local relations developed by R.A.W. Rhodes in the early 1980s (Rhodes 1981, 1987) is invaluable for explaining why local government continues to survive, as well as to support the argument that it has the means to defend and reassert its independence and its vitality. It recognises that local authorities will always retain significant financial, political, information and constitutional-legal resources, which they can deploy in order to resist or evade restrictions imposed by the central government. Equally the stewardship analogy developed by J.A. Chandler (1991) recognises that the steward always has an area of discretion, within the limits imposed by his master. These authors therefore enable one not only to take a more hopeful view of the future of local government than is offered by the pessimists but also to explain it in terms of the real powers that local authorities still possess and will continue to possess unless local government were to be abolished entirely.

What is needed is not further cries of wolf from those involved in local government, whether as practitioners or as academics, but a reassessment of the situation in which local government finds itself and the development of proposals for reform which will strengthen its position. Such reforms must in some cases involve their acceptance by the central government and the passage of legislation by Parliament. Several of them are susceptible to at least partial implementation by local authorities themselves, however. In any case, agreement within the local government policy community as to what needs to be done will enable effective lobbying in favour of change to be carried out and for the measures necessary to be put near the top of political agendas.

On the basis of the review of local government which has been presented here, there would appear to be five main areas in which the issue of reform needs to be addressed. However, fundamental to all of them is the issue of local government's weak legitimacy and its lack of an assured place in the British Constitution. The first of the five areas where reform is needed is the question of local authority areas: whether improving public interest in and support for local authorities can be achieved by devising local authority areas with which citizens are able to identify. Second, changing the electoral system used in local government in order to reduce the predictability of the results in many wards and councils will help to regenerate public interest in local politics. Third, the perennial issue of strengthening the core executives of local authorities needs to be addressed, possibly in radical terms, by the institution of directly elected political heads for local authorities, along the line of the 'strong mayor' system in the United States of America or the elected *Burgermeister* in Southern Germany. Clearly visible leadership, carried out by political heads directly chosen by the people, should increase the amount of public and media attention paid to local government and would be a logical development of the 'governmental' local authority. Fourth, the efforts which many local authorities have been making since the late 1970s to make their services more attractive to their users and to increase those users' participation in their administration and development must continue. Finally, the renewed assurance of significant financial autonomy for local authorities must be addressed. By discussing each of these reforms in turn, we can bring together and summarise the issues raised in the previous chapters.

Having considered an immediate agenda for reform, we can then review the wider question of whether British society and the British economy have changed so radically in the 'post-industrial' or 'post-Fordist' era that further change in local government is needed before its position is assured (Stoker, 1988). Other, wider influences, notably that of European integration; the principle of subsidiarity and the development of a 'Europe of the regions' in particular, must also be discussed, in the context of a debate about whether a Charter for Local government needs to be established (Jones and Stewart, 1984). This in turn implies that the United Kingdom may have to move a long way towards the adoption of a written constitution, especially if and when devolution and regional government return to the political agenda.

The reform agenda

Over the next few years, local government needs to gain or regain the support of three groups of people: the public, ministers and the civil service. Much will depend on the result of the General Elections to be held around the end of the twentieth century. The Labour Party is gradually moving towards accepting that radical constitutional reform must be high on its policy agenda, especially after the constitutional excesses of the Thatcher years. The Liberal-Democrats, on the other hand, clearly need no convincing. The animosity towards local government which was displayed by recent Conservative administrations has abated somewhat with the political demise of Margaret Thatcher; indeed her successor, John Major, has stated his wish to restore local government's position to some degree. That animosity survives among some of his colleagues, however, and is still reinforced by the civil service suspicion of local government which dates back to the days of Edwin Chadwick. That popular support can be won back by local authorities was demonstrated by the Greater London Council's campaign against its abolition, which in the end attracted the support of more than three-quarters of Londoners. Government and especially civil service hostility will be harder to alter, however. Nonetheless, the effort must be made and the following points are proposed as items for an agenda for change which should both revitalise local authorities themselves and win them a more secure place in the minds of politicians and the public.

Areas

Local government was reorganised in the 1970s largely with the intention of increasing its managerial efficiency and effectiveness, although the case that larger authorities are more efficient than small ones is not proven (Newton, 1978). In the process, its standing with the public was damaged in at least two ways.

First, the new local authorities created by the 1972 Local Government Act are very large, both by comparison with their predecessors and with local authorities in other European states. In consequence, they have often seemed to be remote from the concerns of the individuals who need to use their services and cope with the consequences of their decisions. Also, those services have often appeared to be inaccessible and unsympathetic to their users.

Second, violence was done in several parts of the country to traditional popular loyalties. The new county councils in particular often brought together people who saw themselves as having little in common with one another. Humberside combined the 'Tykes' of East Yorkshire with the 'Yellowbellies' of North Lincolnshire. It also combined under the same authority the fishing ports of Hull and Grimsby, whose rivalry was centuries old. The reasons for creating Humberside were and are still valid: the Humber Estuary needs to be developed on a coherent basis if its beauty is not to be lost and if the best use is to be made of its ports and deep-water berths. The Humber Bridge still provides development opportunities which need to be managed in a co-ordinated fashion on both banks of the Humber. However, although Humberside County Council was careful from the outset to respect such divided local loyalties, there has been a persistent campaign in favour of its abolition, which is now on the verge of success. In June 1993 the Local Government Commission recommended a reversion to the former Yorkshire Ridings and parts of Lindsey, albeit with revised boundaries and the latter being divided into two unitary authorities based on Scunthorpe and Grimsby.

Similar fates are likely to befall the other new county councils established in 1972. The Commission has recommended that Cleveland should be be divided into four districts, Avon is likewise set to disappear and be replaced by a Greater Bristol authority. As a result of the abolition of their county councils, the metropolitan counties are already like Italy in Prince Metternich's time, merely geographical expressions. However, the vigorous debate surrounding the recommendations of the Commission indicate that the new local authorities will themselves be the subject of considerable controversy and sometimes hostility. In consequence, like its predecessors, this reorganisation will generate the seeds for the next one. Incremental changes in the existing system would be safer and would be more likely to produce enduring results than a further attempt at radical reform in a short period.

The controversies surrounding the local government reorganisations of the early 1990s are all the more bitter because neither the county councils nor the district councils can claim victory so far in their bids to form the basis for the new local authority areas. In many areas, it is the counties which survive, albeit with some major areas removed from their control, as is the case with the recommendations for Derbyshire and Durham. In other areas, including Cleveland and South Humberside, the district pattern is set more extensively to prevail. The only fairly unambiguous gainers are likely to be the 'big nine', the largest cities and towns which lost their county borough status in 'shire' counties after 1972, together with other former county boroughs which seem likely to regain their lost services, albeit that they will have to absorb suburban areas which may affect the political balance of the council. This gift of extra territory mey therefore be unwelcome to their political leaders because it will threaten their majorities, as well as being resisted by the suburban areas concerned themselves, who will resist being amalgamated with a Labour-controlled city. However, the problem of the large size and therefore the remoteness of British local authorities is unlikely to be solved. Thus in Scotland sixty-five authorities are to be replaced by only twenty-eight successor authorities under the Secretary of State for Scotland's proposals announced in June 1993 (*The Guardian*, 9 July 1993). A similar reduction in numbers is planned for Wales.

The Local Government Commission has recognised this problem, however. In the first place, it is committed to carrying out extensive public consultations before the Secretary of State for the Environment asks Parliament to confirm the Commissioners' recommendations. The Secretaries of State for Scotland and Wales also claim to have consulted the public and in all cases ancient boundaries have been taken into account, at least to some extent.

Second, the Commission wishes to encourage the decentralised provision of services through 'one stop shops': local offices which provide access to all the council's services at points accessible to residents. This notion is similar to the corporate decentralisation to neighbourhood offices which many local authorities have developed in the 1980s, which was discussed in Chapter 1 (Hambleton, 1979; Elcock, 1988). A more radical approach would be to encourage the establishment of parish, town or community councils throughout the local authority's area, so creating elected bodies with some powers, especially to improve the local environment. These community councils would also be able to make representations on behalf of local communities to the unitary authorities, as well as to the many other organisations which are now responsible for the provision of local services and the governance of local areas. Such developments will be essential if the local authorities to be established as a result of the present reviews are to establish better links with their citizens that their predecessors, established by the 1972 Local Government Act, were able to achieve. Corporate decentralisation and community councils should enable citizens to feel greater ownership of and more confident of access to the services provided by our large local councils.

The new local authorities will still be fairly large and hence, like their predecessors, will tend to appear remote to most of the citizens in their areas. Significantly, it is likely that the English Local Government Commission will recommend the retention of two-tier structures in some of the more sparsely populated rural counties. The Commission has made such a recommendation for Lincolnshire and it seems likely that a similar approach will be adopted in Northumberland, although in North Yorkshire a few geographically rather large unitary authorities have been proposed to replace the present 'shire' county and district councils.

What is more ominous is that those councils which are threatened with abolition are already developing campaigns of opposition to the Commission's proposals. In the shorter term, this may result in ministers not endorsing the Commission's proposals because of opposition from the existing local authorities, as well as from the MPs in the area. We saw in Chapter 2 that this happened to the recommendations of the commissioners appointed to review local authority boundaries in 1958, with the result that their work gradually ground to a standstill.

In the longer term, the dissatisfactions that will inevitably be left by the present reorganisation will sow the seeds for a further reorganisation, especially if the Labour Party regards the new structures as having been gerrymandered by the recent Conservative Government so as to ensure Conservative control of at least some of the new authorities. Already the Scottish Labour Party has attacked the Secretary of State's proposals on this ground, specifically because Eastwood is to be split from Glasgow to form a new East Renfrewshire authority which would be likely to be safely under Conservative control. The Labour Party's Scottish local government spokesman has attacked the Secretary of State's proposals, arguing that 'These proposals are not about improving the delivery of services, not about cost, efficiency or local democracy. It is about Tory revenge on the Scottish people and on Scottish local government which clearly they utterly detest' (*The Guardian*, 9 July 1993). If senior Labour Party politicians hold such views they will be tempted to reorganise local government again in their own image when they gain office.

The only realistic approach to this problem is to eschew root and branch reorganisation altogether and proceed incrementally to correct the perceived faults of the established system, once they become apparent, one at a time. The French have a local government system, the foundations of which were laid in the time of Louis XIV and Napoleon. They make adjustments, such as merging small communes or adding a regional tier of government but they do not tear the whole system apart to rebuild it as the British did between 1972 and 1975 (Stacey, 1975). Peter Shore's aborted incremental approach of 'organic change' in the late 1970s, under which some of the more severe discontents engendered by the 1972 Local Government Act would have been progressively corrected, was inherently much more sensible than the further root and branch reorganisations that are currently taking place. However, if the new boundaries do indeed take account of local sentiments, as ministers and the Commission Chairman, Sir John Banham, have promised, then perhaps greater structural stability may ensue. The problem is that people either relate to very small areas like a street, a housing estate or a village, or to rather large and ill-defined regional areas like Yorkshire, Lancashire or 'Geordieland', so that relating those sentiments to realistic local authority boundaries will not be easy (Hampton, 1969). In late 1993 a major dispute between Sir John and the Secretary of State developed over this issue.

Local elections

Four problems combine to reduce the value of local elections as a means of building greater public support for local authorities. The first is a general apathy, indicated by the almost invariable failure of local election campaigns to generate a turn-out of more than 40 per cent. The second is the tendency for local elections to be decided mainly by the popularity or otherwise of the political parties nationally (Newton, 1976). Since the 1960s (although not before then) local elections have tended to produce a 'mid-term effect', with the party in government at Westminster suffering heavy losses of council seats wherever local elections take place. (L.J. Sharpe (ed.), 1967; Newton, 1976). The election campaigns tend to be fought largely on national issues, especially through the medium of television, which is too expensive and covers too wide an area for local candidates or local issues to find meaningful expression through it. Third, in many wards and councils, the results are in any case a foregone conclusion, which further depresses public interest in participating in the campaign or turning out on polling day. Lastly, the system produces councillors who, as we have seen, whatever their many virtues, are not very representative of the voters who elect them and must seek their assistance in time of need. There are still too many middle-class, middle-aged men sitting on local authorities.

Unless the Labour Party is disastrously unpopular when in government, it will never lose control of most councils in the North-east of England, South Wales or much of Scotland, for example. The same analysis applies *mutatis mutandis* to the Conservatives in Southern England and much of the Midlands, although they did suffer unusually heavy losses in these areas in the county council elections of 1993.

A further consequence of the local hegemony exercised by one party or the other may be that effective opposition is lacking on the councils themselves, both because there are insufficient numbers of members sitting on the opposition benches to challenge the ruling party and because perpetual opposition does not attract lively, ambitious politicians to serve in the ranks of a party which is condemned always to be in a minority. The result is at best lacklustre opposition which fails to mount challenges to the ruling party's policies and actions. At worst, it weakens the protection against corruption and abuses of power among majority coun-cillors which the oppositon should provide, both because the opposition never gain control and hence full access to the council's officers and books, as well as because they cannot scrutinise the ruling party's activities effectively (Doig, 1984). Such occasional examples of corruption in local authorities justify, in their own eyes at least, civil servants' suspicions about the honesty with which local authorities conduct their business, although an official inquiry in the mid-1980s made it clear that almost all councillors and officers are both honest and efficient (Widdicombe, 1986).

Be that as it may, these impediments when added together mean that local elections usually serve as a poor conduit of public opinion about local issues or of the popular judgement of local personalities. However, any reform of the local franchise which is likely to be accepted by local authorities, political parties and councillors themselves, must preserve the link between coun-cillors and their wards, especially since as we have seen, the majority of councillors derive their principal satisfaction from their ward case-work.

Local authorities should therefore consider adopting the single transferable vote in local elections and the central government should enable them to do this by passing a statute permitting variations in local electoral systems. This would in one sense appear to be a radical reform but in another sense it would not be so because variations in local electoral systems already exist between the various classes of local authority. Thus, all county councillors are elected every fourth year, while one-third of metropolitan borough councillors are elected each year. In 'shire' districts there is a choice between several possible systems. Hence, precedents exist to justify allowing variations in local electoral systems. Permitting authorities to adopt the single transferable vote and other forms of proportional representation would enable local authorities to experiment with ways of increasing public interest in local elections. It might also secure the election of a more representative section of the population to council seats (Bogdanor, 1980). We saw in Chapter 1 that one of the values of local government is that local authorities can experiment with different management structures: there is no *prima facie* reason why they should not be allowed to experiment with local electoral systems too, hence the function of social learning could be extended from service management and management structures, to the conducting of electoral politics as well.

If the link between the councillor and his or her ward were to be preserved, a change in the electoral system could be accepted without requiring radical changes to take place in the ways in which local politicians compete for the people's votes or in how local authorities conduct their business. Established party groups and their leaders might have to campaign harder to retain their majorities. Their policies and the council's approach to management would need to take greater cognisance of local citizens' needs and wishes but public interest and support for local authorities would become greater (Bogdanor, 1980). In turn, this would strengthen local authority leaders' hands in their negotiations with ministers. The claim that councillors as well as MPs have the legitimacy conferred by popular election, which is one of the principal political resources available to local authorities in their contest with ministers, (Rhodes, 1980; 1987) would carry greater conviction.

Leadership and management

We have seen that departmental isolationism and the resultant fragmentation of the local authority's staff and activities constitute a major problem for those 'topocrat' members and officers whose roles are concerned primarily with the overall management and policy direction of the local authority. Furthermore, although some local authority leaders have always become publicly identified figures, such as in their times Sir Richard Knowles in Birmingham, (*The Guardian*, 21 July 1993), Jack Braddock in Liverpool (Baxter, 1972), Sir Leo Schulz in Hull and Sir Ron Iremonger in Sheffield among others, most of the public is unaware of who leads their local authority and is not interested to find out.

There are therefore two issues to be addressed in terms of the leadership of local authorities. The first is the perennial one of how to co-ordinate fragmented departments whose policies and service provision still tend to be dominated by professional ideologies rather than by any perception of service to the community as a whole, or to implement such management values as efficient resource use. The attempt since 1972 to address this problem through the appointment of chief executive officers and the establishment of management teams, policy and resources committees and the rest have met with some success but they do not commonly provide a focus for popular perceptions of the local authority and its policies. The need for publicly visible co-ordination has been increased by the development of the 'governmental' local authority, which entails a need for publicly visible and effective leaders of local authorities who can co-ordinate services and initiatives, as well as focusing attention on major needs or crises.

The question therefore can at least be asked, as to whether a local authority needs a publicly identifiable head with whom both the council's staff and its citizens can identify. In Southern Germany and those cities of the United States which have "strong mayor" systems, this need is met through a directly elected political executive who assumes overall control over the local authority's policies and management (Clements, 1978; Lavery, 1992). A study of leadership structures in different states of the Federal Republic of Germany provides some interesting pointers to the value of such an elected executive. In Nordrhein-Westfalen, where the local government system now in use was established under the supervision of the British Occupation authorities after the Second World War, administrative leadership is clearly separated from political leadership. The leading political figure (the *Burgermeister* or *Oberburgermeister*) is elected by his or her fellow councillors and is nowadays a leading figure in whichever political party has the most members elected to the *Rat* (council), while management is the responsibility of an appointed officer, the *Stadtdirektor*, who is the equivalent of the British chief executive officer. The result is a degree of public confusion as to who is responsible for the decisions taken by the council and the services provided by it. In Southern Germany, by contrast, where post-war local government was established under American influence and the system therefore resembles the "strong mayor" form, the *Burgermeister* or *Oberburgermeister* is directly elected by the people and assumes overall responsibility for the policies adopted by the authority, as well as its management (Elcock and Schwegmann, 1991). The *Burgermeister* may be and sometimes is elected from a different party to that which controls the council but in such circumstances, a *modus vivendi* emerges (Clements, 1978). In any case, he or she provides a focus both for the co-ordinated management of the authority and for public lobbying for services or other forms of local provision. Similarly, Kevin Lavery found that 'strong Mayors' in the United States 'were highly visible and helped focus public attention on local issues. As a result, local accountability was enhanced' (Lavery 1992, p. 10). Although some mayors promoted cults of personality to the neglect of developing policies and ideas, they provided a focal point for public campaigns. Furthermore, both strong mayors and the council-manager form of local government (where control is vested in a city manager under the overall supervision of the council) produced more centralised and hence more coherent management of the authority (Ibid, pp. 11–12). The council-manager form of local government would appear to be closer to the model of general management advocated increasingly by the Local Government Management Board in recent years.

The adoption of a directly elected executive leader to head British local authorities would be a radical departure from the formal provisions of past local government legislation, although it would seem less radical when one looks at the power wielded in practice by local authority leaders in many major cities, who stood or stand at the head of party groups elected to control the council in part through their own prominence at election time. Such dominant leadership has declined among Labour-controlled local authorities (Baxter, 1972; Jones and Norton, 1979; Elcock, 1981) but is still to be found among Conservative councils (Dearlove, 1973; Saunders, 1979). Such a leader would be able to co-ordinate the council's policies, oversee its entire management and provide a figurehead with whom the people could identify, albeit probably with either approbation or detestation depending on the citizen's party allegiance. Furthermore, the election of such a leadership figure would be likely to provoke a lively campaign which would be attractive to the local and regional media because of the significance of personalities during the campaign. In consequence, public interest and hence electoral turn-outs would be likely to increase.

Management, the citizen and the consumer

Many local authorities, their members and their staff have well learnt the lessons of the increasing unpopularity, indeed unacceptability of 'bureaucratic paternalism' in the late 1970s. They have also had to reassure the public that their lives are not becoming dominated by 'disabling' professionals (Illich et al., 1977) who control public services and even citizens' lives in ways that reduce their control over their lives and even their personal dignity. In the context of social work, John McKnight offers a vivid illustration of the dangers inherent in the professional domination of public services:

> The service ideology will be consummated when citizens believe that they cannot know whether they have a need, cannot know what the remedy is, cannot understand the process that purports to meet the need or remedy and cannot even know whether the need is met unless professionals express satisfaction. The ultimate sign of a serviced society is a professional saying, 'I'm so pleased with what you've done.' The demise of citizenship is to respond, 'Thank you.'
>
> (McKnight, 1977, p. 89)

If he is correct, not only are social work clients becoming increasingly dependent on their professional helpers but also local councillors may be increasingly bamboozled, deliberately or otherwise, into putting resources into policies and procedures whose only real benefit is to secure the employment of increasing numbers of professional servicers. Such radical suspicions are also shared by many writers and politicians of the 'new Right' whose policies have dominated British government since 1979.

However, local authorities have developed a wide range of responses to these public fears and suspicions of professionalism. They have ranged from the cosmetic, including new logos, telephone jingles and enquiry bureaux, through creating neighbourhood offices, to the most radical reforms under which local citizens have been invited to participate to a greater or lesser degree in the management of local services.

The promulgation of the Citizen's Charter by the Major Government in 1991 provides to some degree a further spur towards being responsive to the needs and wishes of local people. However, the Charter limits the agenda of change in two ways because it is at once both less than it claims to be and also more than it claims to be, in that it provides a cloak for a hidden agenda. It is less than it claims to be because its concerns are confined entirely to the rights of customers and consumers, who should have a right to choose who provides the services they need and to complain when services are inadequate or worse. It does not, however, protect or renew for them their rights as citizens to participate in the taking of the decisions that affect them (Elcock, 1993; Connelly, 1993). Indeed, such rights have been reduced both by the reduction of local authorities' areas of discretion and by the removal of their powers and functions to non-elected local agencies – John Stewart's (1992) 'new magistracy'.

On the other hand, the Citizen's Charter does much to confirm the legitimacy of customer choice but only if it is exercised either through the market mechanism or through a surrogate for it. Again, other forms of choice, for instance through the ballot box, are excluded from consideration. Citizens will, on this argument, obtain high quality services if they are provided through competitive markets and, where possible, the consumer is given a choice as to who should provide the service. In consequence, the Charter can be seen as a device to legitimate the market-orientated reforms that have been imposed on local authorities, especially in the period since the 1987 General Election. This is the hidden agenda of the Charter: to legitimate exclusively market-led reforms of the management of public services.

Such market-orientated reforms clearly constitute an important aspect of local authority management in the late twentieth century. More and more of the staff directly employed by local authorities are employed in the preparation, letting and monitoring of contracts with other agencies to provide services; by the same token, fewer local authority employees are directly involved in providing those services directly for the council. However, this market-orientated view of the 'enabling' local authority has a major competitor in the form of the public service orientation and the various initiatives which it offers for the provision of public services directly by local authorities in ways which are more responsive, more accessible and therefore more acceptable to local citizens (Stewart, 1986). Increasingly, good management in local government is going to be defined in terms of movement towards one or other of these two poles. Above all, however, popular participation in decisions about the services local authorities provide needs to be encouraged afresh and for this purpose, people must be able to see that when they vote for their councillors, they are making significant choices about how much service will be provided, how and at what cost.

In developing the management of local authorities, then, awareness of citizens' demands and needs requires an approach to corporate management which is concerned not only with trying to co-ordinate service provision from the top down through policy and resources committees, chief executives and management teams but also from the bottom up through 'one stop shops' or neighbourhood offices. In the latter, staff from different departments and professional backgrounds will collaborate to meet a citizen's needs or respond to his or her demands.

A set of means to do this were proposed in the early 1970s by E.F. Schumacher, in his discussion of how to manage the large organisations which he recognised must inevitably form an essential part of government and management in developed industrial societies (Schumacher, 1973). He argued that such organisations could be broken down into 'quasi-firms' each of which should be given its own area of responsibility and its own resources, for the effective use of which it should be accountable to the leaders of the organisation – in this case the local authority – of which it forms part. He summarised his proposed organisational structure and the traditional bureaucracy which it should supplant, in a pair of analogies:

The structure of an organisation can . . . be symbolised by a man holding a large number of balloons in his hand. Each of the balloons has its own buoyancy and lift and the man himself does not lord it over the balloons but stands beneath them, yet holding all the strings firmly in his hand. Every balloon is not only an administrative but also an entrepreneurial unit. The monolithic organisation, by contrast, might be symbolised by a Christmas tree, with a star at the top and a lot of nuts and other useful things underneath. Everything derives from the top and depends on it. Real freedom and entrepreneurship can exist only at the top.

(Schumacher, 1973, p. 239)

The 'balloon' structure will not only give more scope for creativity and initiative, thus producing better motivated staff working in close contact with service users in neighbourhood offices. It will also enable them to respond more quickly and flexibly to the needs and demands presented to them by citizens. At the same time, it ensures general control over policy by councillors in the policy committee and the 'topocratic' officers and management teams who must set general policies for the local authority as a whole and allocate resources to its various committees, departments and neighbourhood offices. They will also have a responsibility for changing the management culture of the authority so as to ensure that the neighbourhood office staff are allowed discretion to develop their services in the light of their contacts with the service users. They must also be allowed to make mistakes and learn from them, rather than being criticised and penalised by managerial superiors (Elcock, 1986).

Such an agenda for change inspired many of the decentral-isation experiments which local authorities and departments within them developed in the 1970s and 1980s and which now need to be explored anew as part of an alternative to market-based solutions (Payne, 1979; Hoggett and Hambleton, 1987; Elcock, 1986; 1988). Democratic accountability can be increased both by involving local councillors as members of neighbourhood com-mittees or councils, as well as by involving other citizens through such committees or councils. In particular, such neighbourhood participation could be a vehicle to increase working-class and minority groups' influence on local authorities' service provision and policy-making.

Finance

To achieve this improvement in local democratic accountability, the nature and the extent of local authorities' financial autonomy needs to be redefined. The proportion of local authorities' revenue which is raised through sources over which councillors have direct control as the public's elected representatives has now been reduced to around 20 per cent of local authorities' total incomes. The Layfield Committee (1976), by contrast, argued that for local democracy to have substantial freedom of decision, the extent of central government funding should not exceed 40 per cent.

However, the Layfield Committee's concern was chiefly with the increasing proportion of local authority expenditure which was being financed through central government grants rather than through local taxation and other revenues. This proportion fell during the Thatcher years but was increased once more to its pre-1979 level in 1991, in order to try and reduce the impact of the universally hated poll tax. Now, the proportion of local authorities' income that can be determined by their members has been reduced in other ways too, above all through the introduction of the Uniform Business Rate, whose level is set nationally and which the Government allocates to local authorities on the basis of their populations.

If local authorities are to recover their autonomy and hence convince local electors that their votes will make a real effect to the provision of local services, there needs to be a defined area within which financial choices about spending and taxation levels are made by councillors and by councillors alone. It is, of course, entirely legitimate for the central government to restrict its contribution to local government through grants in order to ensure that the Treasury does not have to meet unexpected and excessive bills levied upon it by local authorities. On the other hand, if local voters elect councillors who choose to spend more on local services and finance these through higher levels of local taxation, that is their democratic right, which ought to be respected even if such policies are not to ministers' taste. To do this, the present system of standard spending assessments could be retained, although its accuracy needs to be improved, while the 'capping' regime should be abolished, because it limits unduly the extent of local financial choices. When the Community Charge was introduced, one argument adduced by ministers and others in its support was that because most local residents would pay it, an excessive poll tax levy would produce a reaction against the councillors who voted for it at the next local elections. However, the availability and use of the power to 'cap' individual councils' tax levels has weakened or even denied local citizens the opportunity to make real choices as to the mixture of service provision and taxation they wished to see their councils adopt. The central government ought therefore to determine the contribution it is prepared to make to local government expenditures and then leave the rest to local political choices.

Local government in post-industrial society

Some authors, notably Gerry Stoker (1988) have argued that local authorities must be prepared radically to adapt in order to meet the demands of a 'post-industrial' or 'post-Fordist' society. In brief, this analysis postulates that a series of fundamental economic and social changes have changed the nature both of the demands made on local authority services and in the pressures put upon politicians and officials in local government. The most fundamental change involved is that mass produced uniform goods are being increasingly replaced by technologically sophisticated products which can be manufactured to suit individual tastes. Production runs can be short because of the development of highly automated and flexible production systems, which can produce short runs of products tailored for the needs of small customer groups or even individual customers. In consequence, traditional industries have disappeared, many skills have become obsolete and unemployment has not only increased generally but has spread to the skilled manual workers and white-collar office workers who were formerly immune from it. The working class itself is now divided between a small, highly trained and highly paid elite who operate the new automated production processes and an underclass of unskilled workers who are employed only as and when they are needed. The worker elite will have had extensive education and training before entering work. Inevitably, the members of the underclass have had limited educational opportunities, are poor and suffer multiple forms of social deprivation. The underclass includes disproportionately large numbers of racial and ethnic minorities and women, as well as of unskilled or semi-skilled workers. The underclass is concentrated in decaying inner-city areas and housing estates with few amenities.

Such an analysis can be deployed to make sense of the changing role of local government described in this book. On the one hand, positive developments include the increased sensitivity of local authorities, their members and their staff to consumer demands. In the Fordist economy, the clients of local services had to accept the services offered to them by a bureaucratic paternalist local authority, rather as the original Ford motor car was offered in any colour, so long as it was black. However, in the post-Fordist state these clients can expect service providers to be attentive to their individual or community needs and wishes. Decentralisation schemes and the establishment of neighbourhood committees and councils have encouraged this increased sensitivity and responsiveness. On the other hand, because local authorities are extensively involved in the provision of services for the less well-off members of the community, they have become extensively responsible for trying to cope with the needs of the underclass, especially in the inner-city areas where underclass members tend to be concentrated. The spending cuts of recent times have reduced their ability to support the underclass, however, with the result that members of that class periodically express their frustration in riots. For example, reductions in the youth service provided by North Tyneside Borough Council were widely blamed for the outbreak of riots on the Meadowell Estate in North Shields in the summer of 1991 which were formented by jobless youths whose youth club's opening hours had been reduced. Such riots quickly spread to the West End of Newcastle upon Tyne, largely for similar reasons.

Other trends cannot so easily be explained in terms of post-Fordist analysis, however. The constant effort within local authorities to strengthen the core executive can more adequately be explained by demands for increased efficiency in the face of demands to provide more services with fewer resources than through any wider socio-economic analysis.

Financial stringency has also imposed the need for stronger central control over the budgetary process (Elcock, Jordan and Midwinter, 1989). On the other hand, the necessity for 'governmental' local authorities to try and develop policies to reduce the suffering and dislocation caused by the collapse of traditional industries can be related more closely to the post-Fordist analysis. Against this has to be set the tendency for such initiatives to become increasingly the prerogative of Government-appointed agencies such as the urban development corporations rather than being undertaken by local authorities.

CONCLUSION: THE NEED FOR A GUARANTEE FOR LOCAL GOVERNMENT

The trends of development in local government as the turn of the millenium approaches are therefore varied and bewildering. Even the phrase the 'enabling' local authority which is in common use, is susceptible to radically different interpretations. It can be taken to indicate the development of market-led solutions such as competitive tendering, or the adoption by a local authority of a public service orientation. At the heart of the debate, however, are the much contested concepts of local democracy and local accountability.

Local authorities themselves could do more to improve their accountability to their electorates. The press could be encouraged to report local authority meetings and activities more fairly and more extensively if local authorities appointed press officers and information units to supply information, as well as to organise interviews for reporters with leading members and officers. Some local authorities have long done this and have benefited thereby in terms of the coverage they receive but many councillors regard the establishment of public relations units as an unnecessary extravagence. Political parties themselves can and should organise regular press briefings but often fail to do so. The establishment of community councils, including perhaps the extension of the parish council throughout the country, would assist in bringing councillors and officers closer to their publics, as long as they are prepared to hear and to respond to the criticism that these councils will undoubtedly make of them.

Other forms of public participation need to be strengthened, especially because, whatever the outcomes of the local government reorganisations of the early 1990s, local authorities will continue to be large organisations which appear remote to many of the citizens they govern – a sense of remoteness which is being reinforced by the development of the 'new magistracy' (Stewart, 1992). Administrative juggernauts refuse a person planning permission for a potting shed in his garden, or deprive him or her of house and garden in order to build a new road or yet more public buildings. If he or she lives in a council house and a tile falls off the roof, the tenant may still too often have to contact a distant administrative headquarters and wait weeks for the repair men to arrive. The council announces that it intends to build a Gypsy site or a school for maladjusted children near his or her home and seems impervious to his or her expressed anxieties about the environment, the safety of the family and the value of the family home. Those responsible for such decisions as these must ignore objections based solely on a desire to push undesired developments elsewhere (the NIMBY syndrome) but they must listen to them and take account of the more soundly based objections. Many of these problems have been blamed, often wrongly, on local government reorganisation. They have been made worse by the development of the 'new magistracy' with its total lack of democratic local accountability.

Overcoming these problems entails addressing three basic issues. The first relates to local authorities themselves: how to make local political systems more attentive to people's opinions and increase public involvement in local politics. This problem needs to be addressed above all by the political parties, assisted by a change in the voting method used in local elections.

The second is the need to persuade the professionals who are entrenched in the local government service that they must not impose their professional orthodoxies and solutions on the people whose needs they are trying to meet, without having regard for their clients' views and problems. Dominant professions and a low level of political interest are a combination dangerous to the future of democratic local government.

The members and officers of local authorities need to pay closer attention to addressing these problems. They can do so partly through developing decentralisation schemes within local authorities, as well as by pressing for changes in local authorities' internal cultures through market-based solutions and the development of public service orientations.

The third issue does not fall within the purview of local authorities themselves to correct. However, other forces may be coming to their assistance and their own reforms, together with constructive and effective campaigns, may assist them to achieve it. The crucial issue that must be addressed soon is that local authorities must be guaranteed a significant area of discretion, both in terms of finance and in the services they provide. The opportunity to make local choices as to what services to provide, how much of them to provide and therefore how high a local tax to levy, must be protected from elimination or undue constriction by the central government (Stewart, 1983; Jones and

Stewart, 1983). The adoption of the principle of subsidiarity by the European Community as part of the Treaty of European Union may prove to be of assistance to local authorities in seeking to protect and extend their sphere of autonomy against the central government.

However, the attacks made on it since 1979 demonstrate beyond all reasonable doubt that a new constitutional settlement for local government is required, as part of which local authorities' area of discretion must be defined and protected in new constitutional statutes. The promulgation of a written constitution for the United Kingdom is probably now inevitable in time, in part because of renewed pressure for devolution and regional government, in part because of the impact of European Community legislation and the decisions of the European Court of Justice and the European Court of Human Rights (Elcock, 1991). In this new constitutional settlement, Jones and Stewart's (1983) 'Charter for Local Government' must be an important part. However, even if these hopes do not come to fruition for many years, local government will continue to survive, because unless they are abolished altogether, local authorities will continue to possess the resources which will establish for them a field of action within which they can exercise their own discretion and make their own decisions and which they can defend against Whitehall domination. Like the Vicar of Bray, local authorities and local government will survive whatever King or Queen occupies No. 10, Downing Street in the next decade.

References

Adams, B., Oakley, J., Morgan, D. and Smith, D., 1975a: 'Gypsies: Current Policies and Practices', *Journal of Social Policy,* Volume 54, pp. 129–150.
—— 1975b: *Gypsies and Government Policy,* Heinemann.
Aldous, T., 1972: *Battle for the Environment,* Fontana Books.
Alexander, A., 1982: *Local Government in Britain since Reorganisation,* G. Allen & Unwin.
Allison, L., 1973: *Environmental Planning,* G. Allen & Unwin.
Anderson, J., 1929: 'The Police' *Public Administration.*
Arts Council, 1988: *An Urban Renaissance: The Role of the Arts in Local Authorities.*
Atkinson, R. and Durden, P., 1990: 'Housing Policy in the Thatcher Years', in Savage and Robins (eds), 1990, pp. 117–130.
Audit Commission, 1984: *The Impact on Local Authorities' Economy, Efficiency and Effectiveness of the Block Grant Distribution System,* Her Majesty's Stationery Office.
Audit Commission, 1990: *Local Authority Support for Sport: A Management Handbook,* Her Majesty's Stationery Office.
Audit Commission, Local Government Training Board and Institute of Local Government Studies, 1985: *Good Management in Local Government: Successful Practice and Action,* Her Majesty's Stationery Office.
Bacon R. and Eltis, W., 1978: *Britain's Economic Problem: Too Few Producers,* Second Edition, Macmillan.
Bains Committee, 1972: *The New Local Authorities: Management and Structures,* Her Majesty's Stationery Office.
Baldwin, R. and Kinsey, R., 1982: *Police Powers and Politics,* Quartet Books.
Banfield, E.C. and Wilson, J.Q., 1966: *City Politics,* Harvard University Press.
Barberis, J. and Skelton, A., 1987: 'Oldham Metropolitan Borough Council', in Elcock and Jordan (eds), 1987.
Barclay Report, 1981: *Social Workers: Their Role and Tasks,* Report of a Working Party commissioned by the Secretary of State for Social Services, National Institute for Social Work and Bedford Press.
Barke, M. and Harrop, K.J., 1993: 'Selling the Industrial Town: Identity, Image and Illusion', in J.R. Gold and S.V. Ward (eds) *Promoting Places,* Belhaven Press, forthcoming.

Barlow, John, 1987: 'Lancashire County Council', in Elcock, H. and Jordan, A.G. (eds), 1987, pp. 37–49.

Barnes, M., Prior, D. and Thomas, N., 1990: 'Social Services' in Deakin, N. and Wright, A. (eds), 1990, pp. 105–153.

Barratt, J. and Downs, J., 1988: *Organising for Local Government: A Local Political Responsibility*, Longman.

Barron, J., Crawley, G. and Wood, T., 1991: *Councillors in Crisis: The Public and Private Worlds of Local Councillors*, Macmillan.

Batley, S., 1989: 'London Docklands: An Analysis of Power Relations between UDCs and Local Government', *Public Administration*, Volume 67, pp. 167–187.

Baxter, R.J., 1972: 'The Working Class and Labour Politics', *Political Studies*, Volume 20, pp. 97–107.

Bealey, F., Blondel, J. and McCann, W.P., 1965: *Constituency Politics: A Study of Newcastle under Lyme*. Faber and Faber

Bell, K., 1969: *Tribunals in the Social Services*, Routledge and Kegan Paul.

Beloff, M. and Peele, G., 1980: *The Government of the United Kingdom: Political Authority in a Changing Society*, Wiedenfeld and Nicolson.

Bennington, J., 1976: *Local Government becomes Big Business*, CDP Publications and Intelligence Unit.

Birch, A.H., 1958: *Small Town Politics: A Study of Political Life in Glossop*, Oxford University Press.

Blackstone, T. and Plowden, W., 1988: *Inside the Think Tank: Advising the Cabinet 1970–1983*, Heinemann

Blaydon, S., 1974: *Municipal Review*, Volume 45, p. 90.

Blondel, J. and Hall, R, 1967: 'Conflict, Decision-making and the Perceptions of Local Councillors', *Political Studies*, Volume 15, pp. 338–343.

Blowers, A., 1977: 'Checks and Balances: The Politics of Minority Government', *Public Administration*, Volume 55, pp. 305–316.

Boaden, N. and Alford, R., 1969: 'Sources of Diversity in English Local Authority Decisions, *Public Administration*, Volume 47, pp. 203–223.

Bochel, J., 1966: 'The Recruitment of Local Councillors: A Case Study', *Political Studies*, Volume 14, pp. 360–364.

Bogdanor, V, 1980: 'Is it Time to End Town Hall Caucus Rule?', *The Guardian*, 17 November.

Booth S. and Pitt, D., 1985: 'Continuity and Discontinuity: IT as a Force for Organisational Change', 1985, pp. 17–38. " in Smith, B.C. and Pitt, D. (eds) 1985.

Boyle, E., 1965: 'Who are the Policy-makers?', *Public Administration*, Volume 43, pp. 251–259.

Bradford, City of, n.d.: Economic Development Unit, *Developing Bradford's Tourism Industry*.

Briggs, A., 1959: *The Age of Improvement*, Longman.

Brooke, R., 1989: *Managing the Enabling Authority*, Longman.

Brown, R.G.S., 1975: *The Management of Welfare*, Fontana.

Brown, R.G.S., 1979: *Reorganising the National Health Service: a Case Study of Administrative Change*, Basil Blackwell and Martin Robertson.

Bryson, J., 1988: 'Strategic Planning: Big Wins and Small Wins', *Public Money and Management*, Volume 8, No. 3, autumn, pp. 11–15.

Buchanan Report, 1963: *Traffic in Towns*, Her Majesty's Stationery Office.

Bulpitt, J., 1967: *Party Politics in English Local Government*, Longman.

Bulpitt, J., 1983: *Territory and Power in the United Kingdom*, Manchester University Press.

Bunyon, T., 1976: *The Political Police in Britain*, Friedmann.

Butcher, H., Law, I.G., Leach, R. and Mullard, M., 1990: *Local Government and Thatcherism*, Routledge.

Butler, D.E., 1963: *The Electoral System in Britain Since 1918*, Second Edition, Oxford University Press.

Butler-Sloss, 1988: *Report of Inquiry into Cases of Child Abuse in Cleveland*, Her Majesty's Stationery Office.

Caborn, R., 1992: 'Plan for the Implementation of Regional Assemblies in England, ' prepared for the Labour Party by Richard Caborn, M.P.

Campbell, P., 1973: 'Some Aspects of Democracy in Modern Britain', in Commission on the Constitution *Research Papers* No. 6, *Aspects of Constitutional Reform*, Her Majesty's Stationery Office.

CIPFA, Annual: *Financial, General and Rating Statistics*, Chartered Institute of Public Finance and Accountancy, published annually.

Chandler, J.A., 1988: *Public Policy-Making for Local Government*, Croom Helm.

Chandler, J.A., 1991: *Local Government Today*, Manchester University Press.

Chandler, J.A. and Darwin, J. (eds), 1993: *The Waves of Change: Strategic Management in the Public Services*, Sheffield, Sheffield Business School.

Charlton, J. and Martlew, C., 1987, 'Stirling District Council', in Elcock and Jordan (eds), 1987, pp. 181–199.

Chapman, C., 1990: *Selling the Family Silver: Has Privatisation Worked?*, Hutchinson.

Chapman, R.A., 1988: *Ethics in the British Civil Service*, Routledge.

Chinkin, C.M. and Bailey, R.J., 1976: 'The Local Ombudsman', *Public Administration*, Volume 54, pp. 267–282.

Clarke, M. and Stewart, J.D., 1988: *Managing Tomorrow*, Local Government Training Board.

Clements, Roger, 1978: 'A chief executive Elected by the Citizens: The Oberburgermeister of Wuerzburg, West Germany, *Public Administration*, Volume 56, pp. 321–337.

Clements, Roger, 1987: 'Avon County Council', in Elcock, H. and Jordan, A.G., 1987, pp. 37–49.

Cochrane, A. and Clarke, A., 1990: 'Local Enterprise Boards: The Short History of a Radical Initiative', *Public Administration*, Volume 68, pp. 315–335

Cockburn, C., 1979: *The Local State*, Pluto Books.

Collins, C.A., 1977: 'The Social Background of Local Councillors', *Policy and Politics*, Volume 6, pp. 435–477.

Colwell Report, 1974: *Report of the Committee of Enquiry into the Care and Supervision provided in relation to Maria Colwell*, Her Majesty's Stationery Office.

Community Development Project, 1974: *The Inter-Project Report*, Community Project Information and Intelligence Unit.

Connelly, J., 1993: *Citizens, Charters and Consumers*, Southampton Institute of Higher Education.

Coombes, D., 1967: *The MP and the Administration: The Select Committee on the Nationalised Industries*, G. Allen and Unwin/University of Hull Press.

Corina, L., 1974: 'Elected Representatives in a Party System: A Typology', *Policy and Politics*, Volume 3, pp. 69–87.

Cousins, P., 1984: 'Local Prime Ministers', *Teaching Public Administration*, Volume 4, pp. 44–50.

Cox, C. and Dyson, A.E., 1971: *The Black Papers on Education*, Davis-Poynters.

Crewe, I., 1982: 'The Labour Party and the Electorate', in D. Kavanagh (ed) 1982, pp. 4–94.

Critchley, T.A., 1967: *A History of the Police in England and Wales*, Longman.

Crompton, P., 1983: 'The Lothian Affair', in D. McCrone (ed.), 1983.

Crossman, R.H.S., 1955: *The Diaries of a Cabinet Minister:* Volume 1, *Minister for Housing and Local Government*, Hamish Hamilton and Jonathan Cape.

Crossman, R.H.S., 1977: *The Diaries of a Cabinet Minister: Volume 3, Secretary of State for Social Services*, Hamish Hamilton and Jonathan Cape.

Cullingworth, J.B., 1967: *Town and Country Planning*, G. Allen & Unwin.

Deakin, N. and Wright, A. (eds), 1990: *Consuming Public Services*, Heinemann.

Dean, M., 1979: 'A Profession that has Lost its Way?' *The Guardian*, 3 October.

Dearlove, J., 1973: *The Politics of Policy in Local Government: The Making and Maintenance of Policy in the Royal Borough of Kensingtion and Chelsea*, Cambridge University Press.

Dearlove, J., 1979: *The Reorganisation of Local Government: Old Orthodoxies and a Political Perspective*, Cambridge University Press.

Dell, E., 1991: *A Hard Pounding: Politics and Economic Crisis 1974–1976*, Oxford University Press.

Department of Education and Science, 1987: *Grant Maintained Schools; A Consultative Paper*, Her Majesty's Stationery Office.

Department of the Environment, 1971: *Development Plans: A Manual on Form and Content*, Her Majesty's Stationery Office.

Department of the Environment, 1974: Circular 98/74: *Structure Plans*, Her Majesty's Stationery Office.

Department of the Environment, 1979: *Organic Change in Local Government*, White Paper, Cmnd. 7457, Her Majesty's Stationery Office.

Department of the Environment, 1983: *Streamlining the Cities*, Cmnd 9063, Her Majesty's Stationery Office.

Department of the Environment, 1985: *Lifting the Burden*, Cmnd 9571, Her Majesty's Stationary Office.

Department of the Environment, 1986: *The Future of Development Plans*, Her Majesty's Stationery Office.

Doig, A., 1984: *Corruption and Misconduct in Contemporary British Politics*, Penguin Books.

Donnison, D.V., 1962: *Health, Welfare and Democracy in Greater London*, Greater London Group, London School of Economics and Political Science.

Donoughue, B. and Jones, G.W., 1973: *Herbert Morrison: Portrait of a Politician*, Weidenfeld Nicolson.

Dror, Y., 1973: *Public Policy-Making Re-examined*, Leonard Hill.

Dror, Y., 1975: 'Policy Analysis for Local Government', *Local Government Studies*, New Series, Volume 1, pp. 33–46.

Eddison, T., 1973: *Local Government: Management and Corporate Planning*, Leonard Hill and INLOGOV.

Efficiency Unit, 1988: *Improving Management in Government: The Next Steps*, Prime Minister's Efficiency Unit.

Elcock, H., 1969: *Administrative Justice*, Longman.

Elcock, H., 1971: 'Opportunity for Ombudsman: The Northern Ireland Commissioner for Complaints', *Public Administration*, Volume 50, pp. 87–93.

Elcock, H., 1975: 'English Local Government Reformed: The Politics of Humberside', *Public Administration*, Volume 53, pp. 159–166.

Elcock, H., 1979: 'Politicians, Organisations and the Public: The Provision of Gypsy Sites', *Local Government Studies*, Volume 5, pp. 43–54.

Elcock, H., 1981: 'Tradition and Change in Labour politics: the Decline of the City Boss, ' *Political Studies*, Volume 29, pp. 439–447.

Elcock, H. (ed.), 1982: *What Sort of Society? Economic and Social Policy in Modern Britain*, Martin Robertson.

Elcock, H., 1983: 'Disabling Professionalism: The Real Threat to Local Democracy', *Public Money*, Volume 3, No. 1, June, pp. 23–27.

Elcock, H., 1985a: 'Writing the Humberside Structure Plan', in H. Elcock and M. Stephenson (eds), 1985, pp. 64–78.

Elcock, H., 1985b: 'Information Technology: Stopping Big Brother Watching Us', in D. Pitt and B.C. Smith (eds), 1985.

Elcock, H., 1986: 'Going Local in Humberside: Decentralisation as a Tool for Social Services Management', *Local Government Studies*, July/August, pp. 35–49.

Elcock, H., 1987: 'The Importance of Being Local', paper read to the Political Studies Association Annual Conference, University of Aberdeen, April.

Elcock, H., 1988, 'Alternatives to Representative Democracy: Going Local, *Public Policy and Administration*, Volume 3, No. 2, pp. 38–50

Elcock, H., 1991: *Change and Decay? Public Administration in the 1990s*, Longman Academic.

Elcock, H., 1993: 'What Price Citizenship?' in Chandler and Darwin, (eds), 1993, pp. 143–174.

Elcock, H., Fenwick, J. and Harrop, K. 1988: *Partnerships for Public Service*, Local Authority Management Unit Discussion Paper 88/2, Newcastle upon Tyne Polytechnic.

Elcock, H. and Haywood, S., 1980: *The Buck Stops Where? Accountability and Control in the National Health Service*, Institute of Health Studies, University of Hull.

Elcock H. and Jordan A.G., (eds), 1987 *Learning from Local Authority Budgeting*, Avebury Press.

Elcock H., Jordan A.G. and Midwinter A.F., 1989: *Budgeting in Local Government: Managing the Margins*, Longman.

Elcock, H. and Schwegmann, F., 1991: 'Some Problems of Political and Administrative Leadership in Local Government', paper read to the Joint Staff Colloquium, Department of Economics and Government, Newcastle upon Tyne Polytechnic with the Fachhochschule fuer Öffentliche Verwaltung Nordrhein-Westfalen, Münster, April.

Elcock, H. and Stephenson M. (eds), 1985: *Public Policy-Making and Management*, Polytechnhic Products, Newcastle upon Tyne.

Elliott, J., 1971: 'The Harris Experiment in Newcastle upon Tyne', Boaden, N. and Alford, R., 1969: 'Sources of Diversity in English Local Authority Decisions, *Public Administration*, Volume 47, pp. 203–223. *Public administration*, Volume 49, pp. 149–162.

Entzioni, A., 1968: *The Active Society*, Free PRess of Glencoe.

Evans, N., 1990: 'A Caring Community? Social Services in the 1980s' in Savage and Robins (eds) 1990.

Farnham, D., 1993: 'Human Resource Management and Employee Relations', in Farnham and Horton (eds), 1993, pp. 99–124.

Farnham, D. and Horton, H. (eds), 1993: *Managing the New Public Services*, Macmillan.

Fenn, E, 1983: 'Launching a local authority district into the tourism market', *Local Government Policy-making*, Volume 9, No. 3, pp. 33–37.

Fenwick J. and Harrop K., 1989: *Consumer Responses to Local Authority Services: Notes Towards an Operational Model*, Local Authority Management Unit Discussion Paper no. 88/1, Newcastle upon Tyne Polytechnic.

Fenwick, J., Shaw, K. and Foreman, A., 1993: *Compulsory Competitive Tendering in Local Government: A Study of the Response of Authorities in the North of England: Main Findings*, Department of Economics and Government, University of Northumbria at Newcastle.

Fiennes, G.F., 1967, *I Tried to Run a Railway*, Ian Allan.

Flynn, A., Gray, A., Jenkins, W. and Ruterford, B., 1988: 'Implementing The Next Steps', *Public Administration*, Volume 66, pp. 439–445.

Flynn, N., 1990: 'The Impact of Compulsory Competition on Public Sector Management: Competition Within the Field', *Public Policy and Administration*, Volume 5, No. 1, pp. 33–43.

Forrester, A., Lansley, S. and Pauley, R., 1985: *Beyond our Ken: A Guide to the Battle for London*, London Weekend Television.

Friend, J.K. and Jessop, N., 1969: *Local Government and Strategic Choice*, Tavistock Press.

Friend, J.K., Power J.M. and Yewlett C.J.L., 1977: *Public Planning: The Inter-Corporate Dimension*, Tavistock Press.

Friend, J.K. and Hickling, A., 1987: *Planning under Pressure*, Pergamon Press.

Fulton Committee, 1968: *The Civil Service*, Her Majesty's Stationery Office.

Game, C., 1987: 'Birmingham City Council', in Elcock, H. and Jordan, A.G. (eds), 1987, pp. 50–67.

Glen, J.H.W., 1949: 'Changes in the Structure of Local Government', Institute of Municipal treasurers and Accountants.

Gold, J.R. and Ward, S.V. (eds), *Promoting Places*, Belhaven Press, forthcoming.

Goldsmith, M., (ed.), 1986: *Essays on the Future of Local Government*, West Yorkshire Metropolitan County Council and University of Salford.

Gordon, I., 1979: 'The Recruitment of Local Politicians: An Integrated Approach with some Preliminary Findings from a study of Labour councillors', *Policy and Politics*, Volume 7, pp. 1–37.

Gower Davies, J., 1972: *The Evangelistic Bureaucrat*, Tavistock Press.

Gray, E. and Jenkins, W.I., 1985: *Administrative Politics in British Government*, Wheatsheaf Books.

Greenwood, R., 1983: 'Changing Patterns of Budgeting in English Local Government', *Public Administration*, Volume 61, pp. 149–168.

Greenwood, R., 1987: 'Managerial Strategies in Local Government', *Public Administration*, Volume 65, pp. 295–312.

Greenwood, R. and Stewart J.D. (eds), 1974: *Corporate Planning in English Local Government*, INLOGOV and Charles Knight.

Greenwood, R., Hinings, C.R., Ranson, S. and Walsh, K., n.d.: *In Pursuit of Corporate Rationality: Organisational Developments in the Post Reorganisation Period*, Institute of Local Government Studies, University of Birmingham.

Greenwood, R., Walsh, K., Hinings, C.R. and Ranson, S., 1978: *Patterns of Management in Local Government*, Martin Robertson.

Griffith, J.A.G., 1961: 'The Future of Local Government', *Municipal Review*, December, pp. 804–809 and 818.

Griffith, J.A.G., 1966: *Central Departments and Local Authorities*, G. Allen & Unwin.

Griffith, J.A.G., 1977: *The Politics of the Judiciary*, Fontana/Collins.

Griffiths, R., 1988: *Community Care: Agenda for Action*, Her Majesty's Stationery Office.

Gyford, J., 1984: *The Politics of Local Socialism*, G. Allen & Unwin

Gyford, J., 1991: *Citizens, Consumers and Councils: Local Government and the Public*, Macmillan.

Gyford, J., Leach, S. and Game, C., 1989: *The Changing Politics of Local Government*, Unwin Hyman.

Haigh, R. and Morris, D., 1987: 'Sheffield City Council', in Elcock and Jordan (eds), 1987, pp. 102–112

Hambleton, R., 1979: *Policy Planning in Local Government*, Hutchinson.

Hague, B. 1989: *Local Authorities and a Public Service Orientation: Ideas into Action*, Local Authority Management Unit Discussion Paper No. 89/3, Newcastle upon Tyne Polytechnic.

Hague, D.C., 1971: 'The Ditchley Conference: a British View', in Smith, B.L.R. and Hague, D.C. (eds), 1991.

Hambleton, R., 1992: 'Decentralisation and Democracy in UK Local Government', *Public Money and Management*, July-September 1992, pp. 10–20.

Hammerton, H.J., 1952: *The Turbulent Priest*, Lutterworth Press.

Hampton, W., 1969: 'Local Government and Community', *Political Quarterly*, Volume 40, pp. 151–162.

Harding, A., 1990: 'Local Autonomy and Urban Development Policies: The Recent UK Experience in Perspective', in King and Pierre (eds) 1990, pp. 79–100

Harrop, K., Mason, T, Vielba, C.A. and Webster, B., 1978: *The Implementation and Development of Area Management*, Institute of Local Government Studies, University of Birmingham.

Harrop, K., and Fenwick, J., 1988: *Consumer Responses to Local Authority Services: Notes Towards an Operational Model*, Discussion Paper DP88/1, Local Government Management Unit, Newcastle upon Tyne Polytechnic.

Harrop, K. and Fenwick, J., 1990, *Consumerism and the Public Services*, Discussion Paper DP90/1, Local Government Management Unit, Newcastle upon Tyne Polytechnic.

Harrop, K., Rose, A. and Cousins, A., 1993: 'Leaner and Fitter, or Starving to Death? The Case of Local Authority Budget Settlements in the North for 1993–1994', *Northern Economic Review*, forthcoming.

Haynes, R., 1980: *Organisation Theory and Local Government*, G. Allen & Unwin.

Hayward, J.E.S., 1974: 'The Politics of Planning in Britain and France', *Comparative Politics*, Volume 7.

Hayward, J.E.S., and Watson, M. (eds), *Planning, Politics and Public Policy*, Cambridge University Press.

Haywood, S., 1977: 'Decision-Making in Local Government: The Case of an Independent Council', *Local Government Studies*, New Series, Volume 3, pp. 41–55.

Haywood, S. and Alaszewski, A., 1980, *Crisis in the NHS: The Politics of Management*, Croom Helm.

Haywood, S. and Elcock, H., 1982: 'The Regional Health Authorities: Regional Governments or Central Agencies?', in Hogwood and Keating (eds), 1982, pp. 75–95.

Heclo, H. and Wildavsky, A.V., 1974: *The Private Government of Public Money*, Macmillan.

Hepworth, N.P., 1984: *The Finance of Local Government*, Seventh Edition, G. Allen & Unwin.

Hoggett, P. and Hambleton, R., 1987: *Decentralisation and Democracy*, School of Advanced Urban Studies, University of Bristol.

Hogwood, B. and Keating, M. (eds), 1982: *Regional Government in England*, Oxford University Press.

Holgate, E. and Keidan, O., 1975: 'The Personal Social Services', in Mays., J., Forder, A. and Keidan, O. (eds), 1975.

Holtby, Winifred, 1936: *South Riding*, Virago Press.

Holman, R., 1979: 'A Home for Social Work', *New Society*, Volume 49, p. 455.

Hood, C., 1991: 'A Public Management for All Seasons', *Public Administration*, Volume 69, pp. 3–19.

Humberside County Council, 1976: *The Humberside Structure Plan*, Humberside County Council.

Isaac-Henry, K., 1980: 'The English Local Government Associations, *Public Administration Bulletin*, Volume 33, August, 1980, pp. 21–39.

Illich, I., Zola, I.K., McKnight, J., Caplan, J. and Shaiken, H., 1977 *Disabling Professions*, Marion Boyars.

Islington, 1986: *Going Local: Decentralisation in Practice*, Islington London Borough Council.

Jennings, R.E., 1977: *Education and Politics: Policy-Making in Local Education Authorities*, Batsford.

Jones, G.W., 1973: *Borough Politics*, Macmillan.

Jones, G.W. and Norton, A., (eds) 1979: *Political Leadership in Local Authorities*, INLOGOV.

Jones, G.W. and Stewart, J.D., 1984: *The Case for Local Government*, G. Allen & Unwin.

Johnson, G. and Scholes, K. 1988: *Exploring Corporate Strategy*, Prentice Hall, second edition.

Jordan, A.G., 1982: 'Iron Triangles, Woolly Corporatism and Elastic Nets: Images of the Policy Process', *Journal of Public Policy*, Volume 1, pp. 95–123.

Jordan, A.G., 1987: 'Introduction – Budgeting: Changing Expectations' in Elcock, H. and Jordan, A.G. (eds), 1987, pp. 1–22.

Judge, K., 1979: *Rationing Social Services: A Study of Resource Allocation and the Personal Social Services*, Heinemann.

Kavanagh D. (ed), 1982: *The Politics of the Labour Party*, G. Allen & Unwin.

Keating, M., 1985: 'The Rise and Decline of Micro-Nationalism in France', *Political Studies*, Volume 33, Nol. 1, pp. 1–18.

King, D. and Pierre, J., 1990: *Challenges to Local Government*, Sage Press.

Kingdom, J., 1991: *Local Government and Politics in Britain*, Philip Allan.

Kogan, M. and van der Eycken, W., 1973: *County Hall: The Role of the Chief Education Officer*, Penguin Books.

Laffin, M., 1989: *Managing under Pressure*, Macmillan.

Lansley, S., Goss, S. and Wolmar, C., 1989: *Councils in Conflict: The Rise and Fall of the Municipal Left*, Macmillan.

Lavery, K., 1992: 'The Council Manager and Strong Mayor forms of government in the USA', *Public Money and Management*, Volume 12, No. 2, pp. 9–14.

Layfield, 1976: *Report of the Committee on Local Government Finance*, Cmnd 6453, Her Majesty's Stationery Office.

Leach, S., 1989: 'Widdicombe: The Research, the Report and the Bill', *Local Government Studies*, July/August, pp. 1–8.

Leach, S., 1993: *Challenge and Change: Characteristics of Good Management in Local Government*, Local Government Management Board.

Leach, S. and Game, C., 1991: 'English Metropolitan Government Since Abolition: An Evaluation of the Abolition of the English Metropolitan County Councils', *Public administration*, Volume 69, pp. 141–170.

Leach, S. and Stewart, J.D., 1988: 'The Politics and Management of Hung Authorities', *Public Administration*, Volume 66, pp. 35–56.

Lee, J.M., 1963: *Political Leaders and Public Persons*, Clarendon Press.

Levin, P.H., 1979, 'Highway Inquiries: A Study in Government Responsiveness', *Public Administration*, Volume 57, pp. 21–49.

Likierman, A., 1988: *Public Expenditure: Who Really Controls it and How?*, Pelican Books.

Lipsky, M., 1980: *Street Level Bureaucracy*, Russell Sage.

Local Commissioners for the Administration, *Annual Reports*, Commissioners for local Administration.

Local Government Training Board, 1987: *Getting Closer to the Customer*.

Lomer, M., 1977: 'The chief executive in Local Government', *Local Government Studies*, Volume 3, pp. 17–44.

Loughlin M., Gelfand, D. and Young, K. (eds), 1985:*Half a Century of Municipal Decline*, G. Allen & Unwin.

McCrone, D. (eds), 1983: *Scottish Political Yearbook*, Edinburgh University Press.

McKenzie, R.T., 1963: *British Political Parties*, Second Edition, Heinemann.

McKenzie, W.J.M., 1961: *Theories of Local Government*, London School of Economics and Political Science.

McVicar, M., 1990: 'Education Policy: Education as a Business', in S Savage and L Robins (eds), 1990, pp. 131–144.

Mallabar, N., 1991: *Local Government Administration in a Time of Change*, Business Education Publishers.

Mallaby Report, 1967: *The Staffing of Local Government*, Her Majesty's Stationery Office.

Marshall, G., 1965: *Police and Government*, Methuen.

Marshall, G., 1973: 'Maladministration?', *Public Law*, 1973, pp. 32–44.

Martin, B. and Mason, S., 1988: 'Current Trends in Leisure', *Leisure Studies*, Volume 7, pp. 75–80.

Maud 1967; Report of Committee, *The Management of Local Government*, Her Majesty's Stationery Office.

Mays, J., Forder, A. and Kiedan, O. (eds), 1975: *Penelope Hall's Social Services of England and Wales*, Nineth edition, Routledge and Kegan Paul.

Midwinter, A., 1992: ' *The Scotsman*, 13th October.

Midwinter, A. and Monaghan, C., 1993: *From Rates to the Poll Tax*, Edinburgh University Press.

Midwinter, A.F., Keating, M. and Mitchell, J., 1991: *Politics and Public Policy in Scotland*, Macmillan

Mill, J.S., 1862: *Representative Government*

Moore, C. and Richardson, J.J., 1989: *Local Partnerships and the Unemployment Crisis in Britain*, Unwin Hyman.

Morrison, H., 1964 (Lord Morrison of Lambeth): *Government and Parliament*, Oxford University Press.

Municipal Yearbook, 1992: *Municipal Yearbook*, Association of District Councils annually.

Newcastle upon Tyne, City of, 1992: *Budget 1992–1993*.

Newcastle upon Tyne, City of, 1993: *Medium Term Plan 1993/4–1995/6*.

Newton, K., 1976: *Second City Politics: Democratic Processes and Decision-Making in Birmingham*, Oxford University Press.

Newton, K., 1978: *Is Small Really so Beautiful? Is Big Really so Ugly?* Glasgow, Centre for the Study of Public Policy.

Norris, G.M., 1989: *The Organisation of the Central Policy Capability in Multi-Functional Public Authorities*, Local Authority Management Unit, Discussion Paper No. DP 89/1, Department of Economics and Government, Newcastle upon Tyne Polytechnic.

Northumbria Police, 1992: *Strategic Plan 1992*, Northumbria Police.

Norton, A., 1983: *The Government and Administration of Metropolitan Areas in Western Democracies*, University of Birmingham: Institute of Local Government Studies.

Norton, A., 1991: *The Role of the Chief Executive in British Local Government*,

Institute of Local Government Studies, University of Birmingham.

Oakeshott, M., 1962: *Rationalism in Politics and other Essays*, Methuen.

Ollive, M., 1990: 'CCT in Local Government', *Management Services*, September 1990, pp. 20–23.

Orwell, G., 1948: *Nineteen Eighty-Four.*

Page, E., 1982: *Central Government Instruments of Influence on Local Authorities*, PhD Thesis, University of Strathclyde.

Painter, Joe, 1991: 'Compulsory Competitive Tendering in Local Government: The First Round', *Public Administration*, Volume 69, pp. 191–210.

Parker, D. and Hartley, K., 1990: 'Competitive Tendering: Issues and Evidence', *Public Money and Management*, Autumn, 1990, pp. 9–15.

Parkinson, M., 1985: *Liverpool on the Brink*, Policy Journals.

Parkinson, M., 1986: 'Financial Ingenuity in Local Government: The Case of Liverpool', *Public Money'*

Parkinson, M., 1987: 'Liverpool City Council' in Elcock, H. and Jordan, A.G., (eds), 1987, pp. 66–77.

Payne, M., 1979: *Power, Authority and Responsibility in Social Services Departments*, Macmillan.

Peschek, D. and Brand, J., 1966: *Policies and Politics in Secondary Education: Case Studies in West Ham and Reading*, London School of Economics and Political Science.

Perkin, H.J., 1970: *The Age of the Railway*, Panther Books.

Peters and Waterman, 1982: *In Search of Excellence*, Warner Books.

Poole, K.R., 1978: *The Local Government Service*, G. Allen & Unwin.

Pliatzky, Sir Leo, 1992: 'Quangos and Agencies', *Public Administration*, Volume 70, pp. 555–563.

Proctor, S., 1976: 'Planning since Reorganisation', *Local Government Chronide*, pp. 99–100

Pitt, D. and Smith, B.C. (eds), 1985: *The Computer Revolution in Public Administration*, Wheatsheaf Books

Public Finance Foundation, annual: *Public Domain: The Public Services Yearbook*, Public Finance Foundation annually.

Public Management Foundation, 1992: *Who Defines the Public Interest? The Consumer Paradigm in Public Management*, Public Management Foundation.

Puffitt, R.G., 1979: 'The fire service', *Local Government Studies*, March-April, pp. 118–120.

Pyper, R., 1990: 'Compulsory Competitive Tendering', *Social Services Review*, May, pp. 7–10.

Ranade, M.W., 1985: 'Motives and Behaviour in District Health Authorities', *Public Administration*, Volume 63, pp. 183–200

Ranney, A., 1975: *Pathways to Parliament: Candidate Selection in Britain*, Macmillan.

Ranson, S., 1990: 'Education' in Deakin, N. and Wright, D., 1990, pp. 182–211.

Ranson S., and Stewart, J.D., 1989: 'Citizenship and Government: The Challenge for Management in the Public Domain', *Political Studies*, Volume 37, pp. 5–24.

Rapoport, R. and Dover, M., 1976: *Leisure Provision and Human Need*,

Report prepared for the Department of the Environment by the Institute of Family and Environmental Research and the Dartington Amenity Research Trust.

Redcliffe-Maud, 1969: Royal Commission on Local Government in England, *Report: Local Government in England*, Cmnd 4584, Her Majesty's Stationery Office.

Rees, A.M. and Smith, T.A., 1964: *Town Councillors: A Study of Barking*, Acton Society Trust.

Reiner, R., 1992: *The Politics of the Police*, Second Edition,

Rhodes, G. and Ruck, S.K., 1970: *The Government of Greater London*, G. Allen & Unwin.

Rhodes, R.A.W., 1981: *Control and Power in Central-Local Government Relations*, Gower Press/Social Science Research Council.

Rhodes, R.A.W., 1987: *The National World of Local Government*, G. Allen & Unwin.

Richards, P.G., 1966: 'Rural Boroughs', *Political Studies*, Volume 14, pp. 87–89.

Richards, P.G., 1979: 'Questions about Local Authorities and Emergency Planning, *Local Government Studies*, Volume 5, no. 3, pp. 37–42.

Richardson, J.J. and Jordan, A.G., 1979: *Governing under Pressure*, Martin Robertson.

Robb, B., 1967: *Sans Everything*, Nelson Books.

Roberts, G. and Scholes, K., 1993: 'Policy and Base Budget Reviews at Cheshire County Council', in Chandler and Darwin (eds), 1993, pp. 481–498.

Robinson Committee, 1977: *The Remuneration of Local Councillors*, Cmnd 7010, Her Majesty's Stationery Office.

Saunders, P., 1979: *Urban Politics*, Penguin Books.

Savage, S. and Robins, L., (eds), 1990: *Public Policy under Thatcher*, Macmillan.

Scarman, Lord, 1981: *The Scarman Report*, Her Majesty's Stationery Office.

Schattschneider, E.E., 1960: *The Semi-Sovereign People*, Holt Reinhart and Wilson.

Schumacher, E.F., 1973: *Small is Beautiful*, Abacus.

Schumacher, E.F., 1979: *Good Work*, Jonathan Cape.

Seabrook J., 1984: *The Idea of Neighbourhood: What Local Politics Should be About*, Pluto Press.

Seebohm Committee, 1968: *Report of the Committee on Local Authority and Allied Social Services*, Her Majesty's Stationery Office.

Senior, J., 1966: *The Regional City*, Longman.

Sewel, J. and Dyer, M., 1987: 'Banff and Buchanan District Council' in Elcock and Jordan (eds), 1987.

Sharpe, L.J. (ed.), 1967: *Voting in Cities*, Macmillan.

Sharpe, L.J., 1975: 'Innovation and Change in British Land-use Planning', in Hayward and Watson (eds), 1975, pp. 316–357.

Sheldrake, John, 1992: *Modern Local Government*, Dartmouth.

Sisson, C.H., 1959: *The Spirit of British Administration*, Faber and Faber.

Sisson, C.H., 1991: *English Perspectives: Essays on Liberty and Government*, Carcanet Press.

Skeffington Report, 1969: *People and Planning*, Her Majesty's Stationery Office.

Smith, B.C., 1976: *Policymaking in British Government*, Martin Robertson.

Smith, B.C. and Pitt, D. (eds), 1985: *The Computer Revolution in Public Administration*, Wheatsheaf Books.

Smith, E.L.R. and Hague, D.C. (eds), 1971: *The Dilemmas of Accountability in Modern Government*, Macmillan.

Smith, D. and Scholes, K., 1993: 'Bringing Planning to Life at Northumbria Police', in Chandler and Darwin (eds), 1993, pp. 499–518.

Smith, D.L., 1974: 'The Progress and Style of Structure Planning', in Hayward and Watson (eds), 1975, pp. 316–357.

Smith, T.A., 1966: *Town and County Hall*, Acton Society Trust.

Spiers, M., 1974: *Techniques in Public Administration*, Fontana.

Stacey, F., 1971: *The British Ombudsman*, Oxford University Press.

Stacey, F., 1975: *British Government 1966–1975: Years of Reform*, Oxford University Press.

Stacey, F., 1978: *Ombudsmen Compared*, Oxford University Press.

Stalker, J., 1988: *Stalker*, Penguin Books.

Stanyer, J., 1976: *Understanding Local Government*, Fontana.

Stanyer, J. and Smith, B.C., 1976: *Administering Britain*, Fontana.

Stewart, J.D., 1971: *Management in Local Government: A Viewpoint*, Charles Knight/INLOGOV.

Stewart, J.D., 1983: *The Conditions for Local Choice*, G. Allen & Unwin.

Stewart, J.D., 1986: *The New Management of Local Government*, G. Allen & Unwin.

Stewart, J.D., 1992: *Accountability to the Public*, European Policy Forum.

Stewart, J.D. and Clarke, M., 1987: 'The public service orientation: Issues and Dilemmas', *Public administration*, Volume 65, pp. 161–177.

Stewart, J.D. and Stoker, G. (eds), 1989: *The Future of Local Government*, Macmillan.

Stoker, G., 1988: *The Politics of Local Government*, Dartmouth.

Stoker, G. and Wolman, H., 1992: 'Drawing Lessons from US Experience: An Elected Mayor for British Local Governmment', *Public administration*, Volume 70, pp. 241–267.

Thompson, K., 1991: 'The Office of the Commissioner for Local administration in Scotland: A Socio-Legal Study of its Nature and Effectiveness,' PhD Thesis, Glasgow Polytechnic.

Thornley, A., 1990: *Urban Planning under Thatcherism: The Challenge of the Market*, Routledge.

Travis, A.J., 1983: 'Leisure Services in England and Wales', *Local Government Policy-making*, Volume 9, pp. 25–32.

Travis, A.J., Veal, A.J., Dvesbury, K. and White, J., 1991: *The Role of Central Government in Relaiton to the Provision of Leisure Services in England and Wales*, University of Birmingham, Centre for Urban and Regional Studies, Research Memorandum No. 86.

Weber, M., Gerth, H. and Wright Mills, C., 1975: *From Max Weber*, Routledge.

Wells, H.G., 1908 (original): *The War in the Air*, Penguin Books.

Widdicombe, D., 1986: Report of Committee: *The Conduct of Local Authority Business*, Cmnd 9797, Her Majesty's Stationery Office.

Wildavsky, A.V., 1969: 'Rescuing Policy Analysis from PPBS', *Public Administration Review*, Volume 29, March-April.

Wildavsky, A.V., 1973: 'If Planning is Everything, Maybe it's Nothing', *Policy Sciences*, Volume 4, pp. 127–153

Wildavsky, A.V., 1979:*The Politics of the Budgetary Process*, Little, Brown.

Wildavsky, A.V., 1980: *The Art and Craft of Policy Analysis*, Macmillan.

Willinck, 1962: *Report of the Royal Commission on the Police*, Cmnd 1728, Her Majesty's Stationery Office.

Wilson, Woodrow, 1887: 'The Study of Public Administration', *Political Science Quarterly*.

Wintour, P., 1983: 'Breaking the Chains', *New Statesman*, 14 January 1983, pp. 8–10.

Wiseman, H.V., 1963: 'The Working of Local Government in Leeds', *Public Administration*, Volume 41, pp. 51–69 and pp. 137–155.

Wistrich, E., 1984: 'The Public Service Stream of the Institute of Chartered Secretaries and Administrators: A Public Administration Qualification?', *Teaching Public administration*, Volume 4, pp. 51–65.

Wolman, H., 1984: 'Understanding Local Government Responses to Fiscal Pressure: A Cross-national Analysis', *Journal of Public Policy*, Volume 3, pp. 245–64

Young, S., 1982: 'The Regional Offices of the Department of the Environment: Their Role and Influence in the 1970s', in Hogwood and Keating (eds), 1982, pp. 75–95

Index